Bloom's Modern Critical Interpretations

Bloom's Modern Critical Interpretations

Arthur Miller's

The Crucible

New Edition

Edited and with an introduction by
Harold Bloom
Sterling Professor of the Humanities
Yale University

BLOOM'S
LITERARY CRITICISM
An imprint of Infobase Publishing

Bloom's Modern Critical Interpretations: The Crucible—New Edition

Copyright © 2008 Infobase Publishing

Introduction © 2008 by Harold Bloom

Bloom's Literary Criticism
An imprint of Infobase Publishing
132 West 31st Street
New York NY 10001

Library of Congress Cataloging-in-Publication Data
Arthur Miller's The crucible / [edited by] Harold Bloom. — New ed.
    p. cm.
  Includes bibliographical references and index.
  ISBN 978-0-7910-9828-8 (hardcover)
  1. Miller, Arthur, 1915–2005. Crucible. 2. Trials (Witchcraft) in literature. 3. Salem (Mass.)—In literature. 4. Witchcraft in literature. I. Bloom, Harold. II. Title: Crucible.
  PS3525.I5156C7378 2008
  812'.52—dc22

                                        2007044298

Contributing Editor: Janyce Marson
Cover designed by Takeshi Takahashi
Cover photo The Granger Collection, New York

Printed in the United States of America
IBT EJB 10 9 8 7 6 5 4 3

This book is printed on acid-free paper.

Contents

Editor's Note

My Introduction grants humane theatricality to *The Crucible* and continued political relevance, while agreeing with the great critic of modern drama, Eric Bentley, that Arthur Miller did not know quite how to fuse representations of politics and of sexual love.

Edward Murray judges *The Crucible* to be "complex, coherent, and convincing," a splendid alliteration but alas not so.

A very dignified case for *The Crucible* is made learnedly by E. Miller Budick, after which the distinguished American colonial historian Edmund S. Morgan corrects Miller on the nature of Puritanism.

A feminist illumination of Miller's witches is ventured by Wendy Schissel, while Thomas F. Adler bring together Miller's version of Ibsen's *An Enemy of the People* and *The Crucible*.

Arthur Miller himself sets his *Crucible* into the history of his own life and times, after which Terry Otten contextualizes the play in Miller's career.

Sources of *The Crucible* are documented by Stuart Marrow, while Stephen A. Marino finds more poetic language in the play than perhaps it can sustain.

In this volume's final and best essay, Christopher Bigsby explores the relation of *The Crucible*, its dramatist, and the film made of it.

HAROLD BLOOM

Introduction

Fifty years ago, in his introduction to his *Collected Plays*, Arthur Miller meditated upon *The Crucible*, staged four years before, in 1953. A year after that first production, Miller was refused a passport, and in 1956–57 he endured the active persecution of the American witch-hunt for suspected Communists. The terror created in some of his former friends and associates by the possibility of being branded as warlocks and witches "underlies every word in *The Crucible*," according to Miller. "Every word" necessarily is hyperbolical, since *The Crucible* attempts to be a personal tragedy as well as a social drama. Miller, Ibsen's disciple, nevertheless suffers an anxiety of influence in *The Crucible* not so much in regard to Ibsen's *An Enemy of the People* but in relation to George Bernard Shaw's *Saint Joan*. The frequent echoes of *Saint Joan* seem involuntary, and are distracting, and perhaps fatal to the aesthetic value of *The Crucible*. For all its moral earnestness, *Saint Joan* is enhanced by the Shavian ironic wit, a literary quality totally absent from Miller, here and elsewhere. Though a well-made play, *The Crucible* rarely escapes a certain dreariness in performance, and does not gain by rereading.

This is not to deny the humane purpose nor the theatrical effectiveness of *The Crucible*, but only to indicate a general limitation, here and elsewhere, in Miller's dramatic art. Eric Bentley has argued shrewdly that "one never knows what a Miller play is about: politics or sex." Is *The Crucible* a personal tragedy, founded upon Proctor's sexual infidelity, or is it a play of social protest and warning? There is no reason it should not be both, except for Miller's inability to fuse the genres. Here he falls short of his master, Ibsen, who concealed Shakespearean tragic purposes within frameworks of social issues, yet invariably unified the two modes. Still, one can be grateful that Miller has not revised *The Crucible* on the basis of his afterthoughts, which have emphasized the absolute evil of the Salem powers, Danforth and Hathorne. These worthies already are mere facades, opaque to Miller's understanding and our own. Whatever their religious sensibility may or may not have been, Miller has no imaginative understanding of it, and we therefore confront them only as puppets. Had Miller made them even more malevolent, our bafflement would have been even greater. I am aware that I tend to be an uncompromising aesthete, and I cannot dissent from the proven theatrical effectiveness of *The Crucible*. Its social benignity is also beyond my questioning; American society continues to benefit by this play. We would have to mature beyond our national tendency to moral and religious self-righteousness for *The Crucible* to dwindle into another period piece, and that maturation is nowhere in sight.

EDWARD MURRAY

The Crucible

In *The Crucible* (1953), a four-act play, Miller's scene is Salem, Massachusetts in the year 1692 and the action is based on the witchcraft trials of that time. In "A Note on the Historical Accuracy of This Play," Miller says: "This play is not history in the sense ... used by the academic historian," for "dramatic purposes" prompted certain changes in the record. Nevertheless, Miller believes the "reader will discover here the essential nature" of the Salem trials (p. 224).

In his "Introduction," Miller recalls his mood at the time of writing the play:

> If the reception of *All My Sons* and *Death of a Salesman* had made the world a friendly place for me, events of the early fifties quickly turned that warmth into an illusion. It was not only the rise of "McCarthyism" that moved me, but something which seemed much more weird and mysterious. It was the fact that a political, objective, knowledgeable campaign from the far Right was capable of creating not only a terror, but a new subjective reality, a veritable mystique which was gradually assuming even a holy resonance.... That so interior and subjective an emotion could have been so manifestly created from without was a marvel to me. It underlies every word in *The Crucible*. (pp. 39–40)

From *Arthur Miller, Dramatist*, pp. 52–75, 184–185. © 1967 by Frederick Ungar Publishing Co.

Yet, says Miller, he would not have written the play had he "not come upon a single fact," namely, that a young girl, Abigail Williams, "the prime mover of the Salem hysteria, so far as the hysterical children were concerned," who had worked for John and Elizabeth Proctor, had accused Elizabeth of witchcraft but refused "to include John ... in her accusations despite the urgings of the prosecutors" (p. 41). In short, Miller thought he detected a sexual motive in Abigail's "fastidiousness" toward John which "made the play conceivable for" him. (p.42)

In another passage, Miller relates how his interpretation of the trials affected the structure of *The Crucible*:

> As in any such mass phenomenon, the number of characters of vital, if not decisive, importance is so great as to make the dramatic problem excessively difficult. For a time it seemed best to approach the town impressionistically, and, by a mosaic of seemingly disconnected scenes, gradually to form a context of cause and effect. This I believe I might well have done had it not been that the central impulse for writing at all was not the social but the interior psychological question ... of that guilt residing in Salem which the hysteria merely unleashed, but did not create. Consequently, the structure reflects that understanding, and it centers in John, Elizabeth, and Abigail. ("Introduction," p. 42.)

Enough has been said about Miller's "intentions"; it is time, now, to discuss "achievement" in *The Crucible*. I wish to devote a detailed paragraph to each of Miller's four acts in an effort to trace the line of development, giving particular attention to the point of attack, complication, the turning point, and crisis, climax, and conclusion.

Act One, which Miller calls an "Overture," occurs in the spring of 1692. The scene is the "small upper bedroom" of the Reverend Samuel Parris. When the curtain rises, Parris is discovered kneeling beside the bed of his daughter, Betty, aged ten, who is suffering from a strange illness. Tituba, Parris's Negro slave is introduced, and her abrupt dismissal by Parris suggests that there is a tension in the household, perhaps even a suspicion that Tituba is related in some way to Betty's illness. On what is actually the first page of dialogue, Abigail enters and relates that, according to the doctor, Betty might be suffering from something "unnatural." Parris, realizing that an "unnatural" influence would reflect on his household, had anticipated the doctor's opinion and sent for an "expert" in demonology—the Reverend Hale—in order to prove that Betty is not possessed. Parris then confronts Abigail, who is his niece, with a serious charge: he claims to have seen Betty, Abigail, Tituba, and other girls dancing in the woods—and, worst of all, one of the girls was naked.

Abigail insists that it was a joke, and not a devilish conjuring. Parris reminds his niece that he has enemies, people who wish to drive him from his pulpit. At stake, then, is Parris's job, and perhaps Betty's life. A crucial element in the plot structure is introduced in the following exchange between Parris and Abigail:

> Parris . . . : Abigail, is there any other cause than you have told me, for your being discharged from Goody Proctor's service? I have heard it said . . . that she comes so rarely to the church this year for she will not sit so close to something soiled. . . .
> Abigail: She hates me, uncle . . . for I would not be her slave. It's a bitter woman, a lying, cold, sniveling woman, and I will not work for such a woman!
> Parris: She may be. And yet it has troubled me that you are now seven months out of their house, and in all this time no other family has ever called for your service.
> Abigail, *in a temper*: My name is good in the village! I will not have it said my name is soiled! . . . (p. 232)

The exchange is interrupted by the appearance of Mr. and Mrs. Putnam, both of whom are convinced that witchcraft is operating in Salem. Under repeated questioning, Abigail finally weakens and admits that Tituba was conjuring in the woods. After the adults exit, Mary Warren, the Proctors' eighteen-year-old servant, joins the other girls and accuses Abigail of drinking chicken blood in the woods as a charm to kill Elizabeth Proctor. Abigail threatens to kill the girls if they expose her. (This is the eighth page of dialogue.) John Proctor enters and, after having angrily driven Mary back to work, is alone with Abigail (save for the unconscious Betty) in an expository scene which reveals the couple's past sexual relations. It is clear that Abigail still desires John, and, in spite of John's protests to the contrary, she affirms that John continues to yearn for her. Thus confronted, John admits to thinking of her "softly from time to time. But," he insists, "I will cut off my hand before I ever reach for you again" (p. 241). Suddenly the words "going up to Jesus" are heard from below and Betty sits up, wailing. Parris, the Putnams, Rebecca Nurse, and Giles Corey quickly enter the room. Rebecca is presented as a saintly old woman; Giles is eighty-three, and "canny" (p. 242). An argument develops between John and Parris in which the latter accuses the preacher of too much love for money, hellfire sermons, and the rights of authority. In fact, Proctor explains that it is these faults of Parris that have kept many, including Proctor himself, from attending church recently. There is also an altercation between John and Mr. Putnam over the latter's land claims. Hale enters just as John is leaving. Questioned by Hale, Abigail confesses that

Tituba forced her to drink chicken blood. Tituba admits to conjuring, but also implicates others in Salem. Abigail joins with the slave in this strategy, as do the other frightened girls, and the act ends with the girls "crying out" against various people.

Act Two takes place eight days later in the "common room of Proctor's house." A strain is evident between John and Elizabeth Proctor. Elizabeth urges John to go to court and reveal that Abigail told him that there was no conjuring in the woods. When John says there were no witnesses to Abigail's statement, Elizabeth traps her husband in a lie, for he had previously denied being alone with the girl. Elizabeth suspects John of still lusting after Abigail, while John accuses his wife of being unforgiving. When Mary returns from Salem, she gives Elizabeth a doll she made that day at court. The girl reports that if a prisoner confesses to witchcraft he is in no danger of being hanged. John, unimpressed by the "leniency" of the court, hotly forbids Mary to return to Salem. Mary defends herself by asserting that she saved Eliazbeth's life when the latter was accused of sorcery. Elizabeth is convinced that Abigail wants her dead. Hale enters, then, and probes into the spiritual life of the Proctors. He has noticed, in going through the church records, that John does not often appear at services. When John attempts to shift the blame to Parris, Hale requests that John recite the Commandments. John obliges— but omits the sin of adultery. Hale grows increasingly disturbed about the Proctors. Suddenly Giles appears and informs the Proctors that Rebecca and Mrs. Corey have both been arrested. Court officers arrive on the scene and, in a search of the house, discover the doll. Since the doll has a needle in it, Elizabeth is arrested as a witch, for that evening Abigail was stabbed with a needle. There is a moment of hope when Mary admits to having made the doll herself and that Abigail saw her stick the needle in it when she was finished. Nevertheless, the officers insist on removing Elizabeth to jail. Hale exits affirming his faith in the trials, claiming that some secret sin "may have drawn from heaven such thundering wrath upon you all" (p. 283). Proctor, who "has been reached by Hale's words" (p. 283), informs Mary that she must tell the truth in court. When Mary reminds John that Abigail will accuse him of "lechery," he declares that his wife will not die for him:

> Now Hell and Heaven grapple on our backs, and all our old pretense is ripped away.... It is a providence, and no great change; we are only what we always were, but naked now. *He walks as though toward a great horror, facing the open sky.* Aye, naked! And the wind, God's icy wind, will blow! (p. 284)

Act Three, which unfolds in the "vestry room of the Salem meeting house," occurs at some point during the following summer. Deputy-

Governor Danforth, who has condemned seventy-two people to be hanged, receives a deposition from John signed by Mary Warren and testifying that she saw no evil spirits. In addition, John has secured a list of names of people in Salem who protest the trials. Although Danforth is shaken, he remains unconvinced, for he suspects John of seeking to undermine the court. The Deputy-Governor grows more suspicious when John, even after Danforth agrees to drop charges against the pregnant Elizabeth for a year, refuses to destroy the deposition. John, however, asserts that he is merely fighting for others, such as Giles, who has also been arrested. Danforth is again shaken in his resolve when the girls, under questioning, own to having danced in the woods. When Abigail refuses to admit anything more, though, John feels constrained to confess "lechery" with her. To test the validity of John's confession, Danforth sends for Elizabeth. The Deputy-Governor reasons that Mrs. Proctor, being a good woman, would not tell a lie, even to save her husband's life. Danforth is mistaken about Elizabeth, however, for she does lie to protect John. Danforth thus feels vindicated, but Hale, who is no longer certain about the rightness of the trials, defends John. To distract the court, Abigail suddenly starts screaming. Mary, caught up by her friend's fakery, accuses John of being "the Devil's man" (p. 310). John is immediately arrested, and Hale quits the court.

The concluding act takes place in the fall of 1692 in a "cell in Salem jail." It is reported that Abigail has stolen Parris's money and has disappeared. Although rebellion threatens Salem, Danforth is determined to continue the trials. Hale, horrified by the excesses of the trials, pleads with Elizabeth to get John to confess, declaring that it would be better for John to lie than to hang—a line of persuasion that Elizabeth brands the "Devil's argument" (p. 310). When Elizabeth is alone with John, she informs him that Giles is dead. John, feeling unsuited for the heroic role, is confused about what he should do. Elizabeth wants John alive, but she says that whatever he does, she believes him to be a good man now. Elizabeth even admits to having prompted his affair with Abigail by being a cold wife to him. John, however, refuses to believe in his goodness. "Nothing's spoiled," he says, "by giving them this lie that were not rotten long before" (p. 322). John, who wants his life too, finally decides to confess. When Danforth demands John's signature to his confession, however, something within John rebels: "How may I live without my name? I have given you my soul; leave me my name!" (p. 328). Furiously, John destroys the confession. As he is removed for execution, John declares:

> now I do think I see some shred of goodness in John Proctor. Not enough to weave a banner with, but white enough to keep it from such dogs.... Show honor now, show a stony heart and sink them with it! (p. 328)

After John's exit, Hale says: "Shall the dust praise him? Shall the worms declare his truth?" To which Elizabeth replies: "He have his goodness now. God forbid I take it from him!" (p. 329).

Reviewers were in disagreement whether the opening act, or Overture, was too slow or too fast. My summary of Act One should suggest an answer to this critical problem. Abigail, it was noted, enters on the first page of dialogue; by the next page, an atmosphere of witchcraft and perverted sexuality is suggested; and by the third page, it is related that Abigail was discharged by Elizabeth and that her name has been "soiled." This would seem to be economical and subtle foreshadowing and exposition. True, John, who is the protagonist, does not enter until the eighth page of dialogue; but once he does enter, the future development of the play begins to outline itself. Moreover, according to Lajos Egri, there are various ways of determining the point of attack. "A play might start at a point where at least one character has reached a turning point in his life"; if so, the first page of *The Crucible* qualifies because Parris has clearly "reached a turning point." "A play might start exactly at the point where a conflict will lead up to a crisis"; if this is true, the first page again qualifies, since the argument between Parris and Abigail prepares the reader for future complications. "A good point of attack is where something vital is at stake at the very beginning of the play"; on the first page, Betty's life is in danger, and on the second page, Parris's job is at stake. However, if the point of attack be reserved for the protagonist, for the moment when John is caught up in the conflict, then the attack occurs on the ninth page, in the scene between Abigail and John when their past and present relations are disclosed, and a question is raised concerning their future relations. But the major dramatic question, which I will discuss in its complexity below, is posed in the person of Parris from the very start of the play: How should a man act in the face of evil? (Parris's "I reply" seems to be that one should protect himself at any cost.) Since there are about twenty-five pages of dialogue in Act One, it is safe to say that the point of attack (however defined) occurs before one-third of the act is completed. Even if the attack arrives relatively late (ninth page), the situation is not comparable to the first act of *All My Sons*, for here Miller has provided sufficient conflict from the opening curtain. By the seventh page of dialogue, the situation of the frightened girls begins to assume shape. Nine characters (eight, if we omit Betty, who does not engage in dialogue) appear prior to John's entrance; however, they are introduced slowly, they are each, depending on their relative importance in the action, given time to establish themselves, and the dramatic line, as I have tried to show, is kept sufficiently clear and relevant. Much more is going on here, for Miller is skillfully creating a dense social context within which John Proctor will work out his fate. It would seem, then, that Act One is more than a mere introduction to the action; that the point of attack occurs immediately or, at the most, fairly early; that, from the standpoint of conflict, the act is moderately paced, and, finally, that the exposition is clear and direct.

In terms of sustained conflict, Acts Two and Three are the most dramatic. These middle acts focus on thrust and counter-thrust, and the tension is generally high. The outcome is never certain until John is arrested at the conclusion to Act Three, and even here there is a question raised—hence continuing suspense—because the reader is not certain whether John will confess or die. Gerald Weales has criticized the turning point, which he calls "romantic" and "sentimental," because it hinges on Elizabeth's lie to save her husband, and he compares the plot in this respect to the hidden-letter revelation in *All My Sons*, adding that this device is removed from the main line of motivation in the play represented by John's inner torment of conscience. There is, of course, no scientific test to prove that Miller's scene is not "romantic" or "sentimental"; but one might point out that the comparison to *All My Sons* is not in order. In the earlier play, the letter was a complete surprise, and, moreover, a character whom the audience had never seen untied the knot for Miller. In *The Crucible*, as will be shown in detail below, Elizabeth prepares the reader for her behavior at the turning point, and, what is perhaps more important, her action is not divorced from the main line of motivation in the play, for her response is part of the thematic thrust of the play, one "answer" to the question: How should a man—or woman—act in the face of evil?

In Act Four, the thematic question is very largely focused upon a single issue: Will John Proctor confess to save his neck—or will he die? Tension grows out of John's struggle with his conscience. Dialogue, it should be noted, is used effectively to augment tension through the constant references to the dawn, which spells execution, for there are five such references within thirteen pages. The crisis occurs about two and a half pages before the final curtain:

> Proctor has just finished signing when Danforth reaches for the paper. But Proctor snatches it up, and now a wild terror is rising in him, and a boundless anger. (p. 327)

At this point, we do not know whether Proctor will return the confession or die, but we sense that the decisive moment has at last arrived. The climax comes about a page and a half later when John "tears the paper and crumbles it" (p. 328). Kenneth Tynan has called the last scene "old melodrama." Admittedly, John's speeches are somewhat stagy at the end. As I have tried to suggest in the description of Act Four, however, the action develops to its crisis and climax through a series of smooth transitions. John's growth is consistent and credible. It is a gross misreading of the play to view it in terms of the "wholly right" and the "wholly wrong"—that is, in melodramatic terms—for an analysis of theme will make clear that *Crucible* is more complex than critics have generally allowed. Miller himself has distorted this feature of his play. In the "Introduction," he claims that the characters are black in *Crucible* because the "historical facts . . . were immutable," and he adds that if he were to write it again he would make them even more black (pp. 42–43).

It might be objected that John, being the protagonist, is absent from the scene too much of the time. In fact, John is absent on about twenty-eight pages out of the roughly ninety-three pages of dialogue—in short, John is not "there" during one-third of the play. Abigail, who is the antagonist, does not appear at all in the second and fourth acts. Perhaps adherence to his sources imposed certain restrictions on Miller's creative imagination. However, in view of the fact that *Crucible* has a multi-focused theme, John's absence from the scene for certain periods would not appear to be a serious matter. The mere report of Abigail's disappearance in Act Four, on the other hand, seems like a weak device. One would not wish to imply that Miller has missed an obligatory scene here; yet it is no doubt true that the reader misses a confrontation between John and Abigail in the last act. True, the struggle in Act Three is highly effective: John's confession of "lechery" is a strong thrust, and Abigail's ability to sway Mary against John is a powerful counter-thrust. Nevertheless, one feels a gap in Act Four. One looks for a scene to balance the one in the "Overture" a scene, for example, in which Abigail seemingly triumphs over John ("seemingly," because not "spiritually") and, since nobody would believe John anyway, informs him herself of her plans to disappear, for the concrete is preferable to the abstract report.

Perhaps it was some sense of a lack in the structure of the play that prompted Miller to add a new scene between John and Abigail in a later production of *Crucible*. The printed version of the new scene appeared in *Theatre Arts* in October 1953. Although the scene is said to have been added to Act Two, it appears in *Theatre Arts* in isolation after the first act curtain. It is a short scene and, in my opinion, it adds nothing vitally significant to the original version; it merely makes explicit what was fairly obvious from Abigail's actions in the original treatment. In addition, the new scene is marred by a too overt straining after irony. When Miller brought out the *Collected Plays* four years later, the new scene was not in evidence.

The main characters in *Crucible*, contrary to some critical reports, are far from flat. John Proctor is described as a "farmer in his middle thirties" (p. 238), "powerful of body" (p. 239). In his first scene, John reveals himself as a man with a strong personality: "Abigail has stood as though on tiptoe, absorbing his presence, wide-eyed," while the other girl is "strangely titillated" (p. 239). That Abigail is willing to murder in order to possess John invests this farmer with a sense of importance. That John lusted with the girl in the past—against the law of God and Salem—reveals a certain daring in the man.

That John has the will power to resist Abigail now, even while part of him still desires her, shows determination. Repeatedly, John displays his dislike of authoritarianism.

In Act Two, John makes a determined effort to please Elizabeth. He kisses her perfunctorily; he lies in saying that her cooking is well-seasoned (perhaps a kind of irony on the lack of spice in Elizabeth?). John seems motivated by guilt feelings in this scene. When Elizabeth urges him to go to court and expose Abigail, he is afraid that his relations with the girl will be brought to light. The question of whether the court will believe him (p. 262 and p. 275) would seem of secondary importance. The cardinal point is that John must struggle against his own fear. Miller attempts to integrate the "personal" and the "social" in a number of ways. "I cannot speak but I am doubted," says John, ". . . as though I come into a court when I come into this house!" (p. 265). Although John lies to Elizabeth about being alone with Abigail in Parris's house (p. 264), he persists in defending his honesty (p. 265).

John continues to struggle, throughout Act Three, against both his inner contradictions and his outer antagonists. He reveals his resourcefulness in securing a deposition. He shows his persistence in extracting a confession from Mary. When the charge against Elizabeth is suspended, John does not falter—he concentrates his attack on the court for the sake of others. And when Abigail seems to be winning the struggle, John makes public confession of his "lechery."

In Act Four, John "is another man, bearded, filthy, his eyes misty as though webs had overgrown them" (p. 320). The physical transformation signals an inner change in John. "I have been thinking," he tells Elizabeth, "I would confess to them" (p. 322). After a few months in jail contemplating his death a change of appearance and attitude on John's part is credible. John defends himself by saying: "Spite only keeps me silent" (p. 323); "I want my life" (p. 324). However, John has not overcome his inner conflict; he hesitates to implicate others (p. 326); he balks at signing the confession (p. 327). Gradually, John moves to a position of final defiance of the court: "I have three children—how may I teach them to walk like men . . . and I sold my friends?" (p. 327).

The foregoing shows clearly that John is rich in traits; that there is continuous development of his character; and that there is adequate preparation for his revelation in the last act.

No critic, as far as I know, has questioned John Proctor's status as a "tragic hero." The controversy over the "common man" versus the "traditional hero" (usually Aristotelian), occasioned by the fate of Willy Loman, is absent from discussions of *Crucible*. Miller would seem to have provided Proctor with all the heroic attributes dear to the heart of "traditionalists." Miller himself says: "In *The Crucible* ... the characters were special people who could give voice to the things that were inside them.... These people knew what was happening to them" (*Theatre Arts*, October 1953). Whether this increase in articulateness makes *Crucible* a more powerful dramatic piece than *Death of a Salesman* is arguable.

Dialogue, it should be noted, fails to illuminate John's past. Is this lack of background a serious failing in *Crucible*? In *All My Sons*, lack of adequate character exposition impaired credibility; in *Salesman*, the revelation of Willy's past had a direct bearing on the present line of development. In *Crucible*, however, the past would not seem to be pertinent. Each play should be approached on its own merits. *Crucible* focuses on a specific situation, and the reader possesses all the necessary facts for believing in that situation. Nor should one conclude that, since John's final speeches sound too theatrical, the language in the play is not adequate. The various summaries presented in this chapter should indicate that preparation, especially foreshadowing of character development, is expertly handled. Miller, in a very subtle manner, uses key words to knit together the texture of action and theme. Note, for example, the recurrent use of the word "soft." In Act One, John tells Abigail: "Abby, I may think of you *softly* from time to time...." (p. 241, italics mine); in Act Two, Hale tells John: "there is a *softness* in your record, sir, a *softness*" (p. 273, italics mine). Dialogue, moreover, suggests that behind John's denunciation of Parris lies a guilty conscience. Hale says that John has missed church services a good deal in the past seventeen months (p. 252); since Abigail has been removed from Proctor's house for the past seven months (p. 232), the inference is that the real reason for John's backsliding has not been expressed.

Miller is even more sparing than usual in his physical description of Elizabeth; that is, not one word is uttered about her appearance. Nor, as was the case with John, is anything conveyed about her background. Nevertheless, Elizabeth has many traits and she grows throughout the play. She is sensitive: "It hurt my heart to strip her, poor rabbit" (p. 262); here, of course, Elizabeth is a foil to the murderous Abigail. Elizabeth betrays a weakness in asserting herself against Mary Warren, a weakness which John brands a "fault" (p. 263). She is also proud (p. 273), slow to forgive (p. 265), and suspicious (p. 265). Frequently, Elizabeth—who is "cold" (p. 323)—fails in charity (p. 265). But she will lie for a loved one (p. 307), and, since she learns humility (p. 323), she is capable of change. Elizabeth's dominant motive is her yearning for John's undivided love. In Act Two, for instance, behind Elizabeth's self-righteous and intolerant posture, there is love for John. She proves this love in Act Three when she lies to save John's life. Elizabeth continues to grow in the last act. "Her wrists," says Miller, "are linked by heavy chain.... Her clothes are dirty; her face is pale and gaunt" (p. 319). The trials have worked their effect on Elizabeth, too. Danforth, uncomprehending, sees in her "dry eyes" the "proof of [her] unnatural life" (p. 320). Alone with her husband, however, Elizabeth says:

> I have read my heart this three month John. . . . I have sins of my own to count. It need a cold wife to prompt lechery. (p. 323)

> John, I counted myself so plain, so poorly made, no honest love could come to me! Suspicion kissed you when I did; I never knew how I should say my love. It were a cold house I kept. (p. 323)

Since Elizabeth remains in character, her development in Act Four, as was the case with John, is logical and believable.

Abigail is much less complex and interesting than either John or Elizabeth. She is described as "seventeen . . . a strikingly beautiful girl, an orphan, with an endless capacity for dissembling" (p. 230). Dialogue fails to disclose anything about Abigail's past. In the course of the play, however, she reveals several traits: she is supersensitive (p. 238), sexually passionate (p. 240), and mentally alert (p. 259); she is commanding (p. 238) and vain (p. 305); she is a thief (pp. 315–316); and throughout the play, she makes painfully evident that she is capable of murder. Abigail's dominant motive is to destroy Elizabeth and sleep with John. Abigail remains in character; but she does not grow.

The minor characters, with the exception of Hale, are flat and static. There is a question of Miller's economy here, and Miller himself was not unaware of the problem ("Introduction," p. 42). In *All My Sons*, Miller seemed to have employed more characters than he needed for the furtherance of either action or theme. In *The Crucible*, in spite of the fact that there are at least twenty-one characters, the problem does not seem acute, for as was pointed out in the discussion of structure, Miller managed to keep the developing action in thematic focus. If the numerous characters, such as, Marshall Herrick or Ezekiel Cheever, contribute very little, if anything, to action or theme, it is also true that they do nothing to impede or becloud action and theme. Some readers might find many of these secondary figures mere "scenery"; whether Miller might have profitably eliminated them entirely is an interesting, but hardly a burning, technical question.

Although the characters will be discussed again in the following section, it should be noted here that all the leading ones represent various shadings on a thematic spectrum. John wavers between principle and compromise, and chooses, finally, principle; Elizabeth opts for John's "goodness," no matter what he finally chooses; Abigail is completely self-seeking; so is Parris; Rebecca is a witness to principle above compromise or deceit; Danforth is similarly unyielding about the inviolability of principle; while Hale, who alone among the minor characters grows, would abandon principle for the sake of life. This schematic neatness suggests that *Crucible* is not to be evaluated by a narrow adherence to a realistic or naturalistic norm. In the *Theatre Arts* issue last cited, Miller says: "*The Crucible* is not more realistic but more theatrical than *Death of a Salesman.*" Yet it would be a serious error to leap to the other extreme and dismiss Miller's play as a mere oversimplified morality play. Miller himself, as I have suggested, invites the latter approach, but it is entirely possible that the playwright, no less than his hostile critics, has missed the very real thematic complexity that is in *The Crucible.*

Certainly Eric Bentley has missed this complexity, for—dubbing Miller "the playwright of American liberalism"—he finds in *Crucible* "a conflict between the wholly guilty and the wholly innocent." Bentley agrees that, "The guilty men are as black with guilt as Mr. Miller says," but adds, "What we must ask is whether the innocent are as innocent." (That, as Bentley says, the "guilty" are as "black" as Miller claims seems like a rather curious statement; presumably Bentley intends the "historically guilty"—though one never knows for certain in this article, since Bentley hops in and out of Salem, contemporary events, Miller's essays, and *The Crucible*, without leaving a discernible trail.) Robert Warshow (highly praised by Bentley—perhaps because Warshow finds Miller's plays "neat" but "empty") and David Levine, among others, are disturbed because Miller has falsified history—Levine adding that the "error" is also an "aesthetic" one.

Let us dispose of the historical argument, at least for the moment, by agreeing that Miller might have written an enjoyable and complex play had he given more attention to religious and philosophical factors that were important to Salem in 1692. In fact, however, Miller wrote this play—*The Crucible*—and regardless of his "intentions," his historical "errors," or his faulty contemporary parallel, the task for the critic is whether the play that is, is sufficiently complex and "aesthetic" on its own terms. One might read the play, as many critics have done, as an attack on enforced conformity; in my opinion, however, such a reading is narrow and superficial, and misses the deeper thrust of the play. Warshow asks: "But if Mr. Miller isn't saying anything about the Salem trials, and can't be caught saying anything about anything else [read McCarthy], what did the audience think he was saying?" What follows is an attempt to discover what Miller is "saying" in *The Crucible.*

As has been said, the thematic question projected by the action of the play would seem to be: How should a man act in the face of evil? It has also been suggested that the individual "replies" to the question are represented by the various significant actors in the drama. Abigail may be omitted from serious consideration here; although she is vital to the plot she contributes little or nothing to the theme. Similarly, the other girls may be placed to one side here, and the same stricture applies to Parris and the Putnams; no noble aims seem to motivate them. (I will return to these characters later, however, in discussing the motives for the trials.) All the significant responses to the action are conveyed by six principal characters.

Danforth, it is important to remember, is motivated by the fact that he is an orthodox Puritan who fully believes in the existence of evil spirits (p. 291). As the symbol of authority, Danforth assumes exact knowledge of "God's law" (p. 318), and, taking a rigid stance on the letter of that law, he pursues the logic of what he conceives the facts to be to their inevitable end (p. 297). Danforth's mind, the mind of a lawyer, makes sharp, rational distinctions (p. 293): for him, a principle is sacred, and he would not hesitate, since he sees his way clearly, to sacrifice all human life for a single principle (p. 318). Like many God-surrogates, Danforth seems to be a proud man; but behind his stiff posture there now and then lurks the fear, never wholly embraced or articulated, that he might be in serious error (p. 301). After Danforth has sentenced nearly one hundred men and women to be hanged, he has a *personal* stake in the justice of the trials; he is almost coerced into assuming an "either-or" view of good and evil (p. 293), for to admit the unknowable, the ambiguous, the irrational, into experience would be to expose "God" [read Danforth and Salem law] to the confusion and uncertainty of a world suddenly turned upside down by inexplicable events.

Hale might be considered as a foil to Danforth. He begins as fully confident of his moral position as the Deputy-Governor, for in his books, Hale has evil neatly "caught, defined, and calculated" (p. 253). Life, however, refutes the books; and Hale, more sensitive than Danforth, more comprehending, permits doubt to enter, like a corrosive chemical, into his soul (pp. 275, 292). As a result, Hale no longer is convinced that he is privy to the decrees of the most high; on the contrary, asserting that God's will is often in darkness, he assumes the radical ambiguity of moral questions (p. 320). Where Danforth declares that he would "hang ten thousand that dared to rise against the law" (p. 318), Hale avers: "life is God's most precious gift; no principle ... may justify the taking of it" (p. 320).

Rebecca Nurse resembles the very man who condemns her to be hanged. Like Danforth, she would not sacrifice a principle even if it should cost her her life (p. 325). Like Danforth, she appears to have no sense of guilt; she tells John: "Let you fear nothing! Another judgment waits us all!" (p. 328). Like Danforth, Rebecca sees little of life's complexity (are there no "real life" counterparts to Danforth and Rebecca?); she is merely "astonished" at John's lie to save his life (p. 325).

Giles Corey's position on the thematic spectrum suggests a stance somewhere between the extremes of "nobility" (represented by those who take morals seriously) and "ignobility" (Parris, say, or the Putnams). Although Giles fights against the evil of the trials, he dies—not for the sake of an abstract principle of right—but in such a way as to insure that his property will go to his sons (p. 322).

Elizabeth Proctor is more complex than Danforth, Hale, Giles, and Rebecca. Elizabeth, like Hale, is willing to sacrifice an abstraction when it seems, to her, expedient to do so; but, unlike Hale, she does not "rationalize" her argument; "subjective," not "objective" arguments dictate her actions. In Act Two, Elizabeth sacrifices logic to her pride; she tells Hale that she believes in the Gospels (and the Gospels affirm the existence of witches); but she adds that if Hale thinks that she could "do only good work in the world, and yet be secretly bound to Satan, then I must tell you, sir, I do not believe it" (p. 276). In Act Three, Elizabeth sacrifices a principle to save her husband's life; her motive here is not pride, as it was above, but love. In Act Four, she refuses to answer John's question whether she would lie to save her own life; John believes that she would not lie (p. 324). On the basis of her record, how can John—or the reader—be certain? Elizabeth says she wants John alive (p. 322)—which scarcely allows John much choice in the matter. No longer self-righteous, Elizabeth stresses her own frailty (p. 323); repeatedly she says: "I cannot judge you, John" (p. 322, p. 323, and twice on p. 324); and she adds: "Whatever you will do, it is a good man does it" (p. 323). This is important. Elizabeth seems to be saying that a man may lie and be "good"—or, equally, a man may refuse to lie and be "good." How can this be "true"? It would seem idle to argue the matter philosophically or semantically; for instance, one might say that "good" is a vague term, or that Elizabeth means that John has not confessed until now, and regardless of what he does later, that (as Elizabeth tells John): "speak goodness in you" (p. 323). However, it would seem more rewarding, for the critic if not the philosopher, to ask: What has Elizabeth revealed about herself that permits her to hold such a belief? Early in Act Four, when Hale suggests that Elizabeth persuade John to lie in order to save himself, she says: "I think that be the Devil's argument" (p. 320); but when faced by John, she says, in effect, that a man might use the "Devil's argument" and still be a "good" man. Elizabeth is not inconsistent here; we have seen that she has previously sacrificed principle for personal ends; we have also seen that she has reached a stage in her growth toward humility when she is, at least for the moment, more concerned with the "beam in her own eye."

John Proctor's response to events is, of course, the most complicated one in the play; moreover, his role as protagonist would appear to lend his position more validity than that of the other characters. Since John's development has been traced above, little need be added here. It is worth stressing, however, that John thought he was "good" in Act Two (p. 265); but as it developed, John was self-deceived—in his heart, he still lusted after Abigail (p. 241). At the end of the play, John again believes in his "goodness"

(p. 328); but Hale, in effect, says that John is once again self-deceived: "It is pride, it is vanity" (p. 329).

Who is right? I repeat: *The Crucible* would not seem to be the simple, didactic, polemical play that most critics, including Miller himself perhaps, would have us believe. Although the characters, with the exception of John, Elizabeth, and possibly Hale, are constructed along relatively simple lines, the multiple points of view are complex and well-orchestrated. John's role in the play, then, would seem to be limited, and the position he takes qualified, by the stance of the other characters. *The Crucible* cannot be reduced to a single statement, or thesis, without doing violence to the total impression conveyed by the play. In *All My Sons*, it was otherwise; but John's death "proves" nothing—Hale is not made to "see the light" (as, say, Chris Keller was illuminated), Danforth does not kill himself (as Joe Keller was made to do). At the end of the drama, the "meaning" of the play is focused from four different angles: Danforth considers John's death a just punishment: "Who weeps for these, weeps for corruption!" (p. 328); Hale views John's death as meaningless: "What profit him to bleed?" (p. 329); John's view has already been quoted (p. 328)—in the last analysis John belongs with those who refuse to sacrifice a principle; while Elizabeth says: "He have his goodness now. God forbid I take it from him!" (p. 329). Since Elizabeth's line is the final one of the play, the critic may not automatically assume that it is the only "right" one; after all, *had John lied Elizabeth would have said the same thing.* The play is complex because John is a "good" man; so is Hale; so is Giles; Elizabeth and Rebecca are "good" too—for only "good" people do battle with evil. Even Danforth is not black—given his cast of mind and the times, one can, at least, understand his position (those who call him "wholly guilty" would seem to be doing the play an injustice through oversimplification). "In my play," says Miller, "Danforth seems about to conceive of the truth, and surely there is a disposition in him at least to listen to arguments that go counter to the line of the prosecution. There is no such swerving in the record" ("Introduction," p. 43). The text supports Miller's statement. At the end of Act Three, however, when John accuses Danforth of knowing that the trials are a fraud, there is no evidence in the text to prove John right. Similarly, in the last act, when Danforth asserts that he "will not deal in lies" (p. 328), there is no data in the play itself which will refute him. In regard to the ending of the third act, one suspects (which was the case in the Requiem of *Salesman*) that Miller has sacrificed a fine regard for the facts in his play for the sake of an effective curtain. The sharpest conflict in the play, ideologically, might very well be between Hale's counsel of compromise and John's inflexibility. And who is wise enough to dogmatize upon the matter once and for all?

Granting, it might be objected, that *Crucible* contains more variety than is usually allowed for it, is it not true that it remains a bit too simple? For some readers, the neatness of the thematic spectrum is perhaps an argument against the play's complexity, and for those who demand shading, not among multiple points of view but in each individual character, Miller's play is unsatisfactory. The same readers may also feel that Proctor's infidelity is not enough of a complication, that it is too flimsy a foundation on which to erect the structure of *Crucible*. The crucial question, however, is: Does Miller succeed in fusing the "personal" and the "social"? A close reading of the play would suggest that he does. A flaw in Proctor's marriage allows the trials to materialize; no act—even the most intimate of sexual relations—would seem isolated from the "social." Elizabeth admits to being "cold"; but it is not due to being "puritanical," as some critics would have it, or to "lack of love"; she says (as I have quoted previously): "John, I counted myself so plain, so poorly made, no honest love could come to me! ... I never knew how I should say my love" (p. 323). John asks: "Is the accuser always holy now?" (p. 281). This has both a "personal" and a "social" reference; "personal" because Elizabeth accuses John of evil and she is not "holy" (although she admits her faults later), while John himself learns that he is not as "holy" as he had thought; "social" because, to take but one instance, Abigail and the girls are not "holy" but they accuse others. This much is fairly obvious. As was also quoted above, Miller *intended* to focus on "that guilt residing in Salem which the hysteria merely unleashed" ("Introduction," p. 42). Is it necessary that the guilt be of a single kind? Is it not possible—indeed probable—that various kinds of guilt may come to focus upon a single "social" situation? Of course, Elizabeth admits to keeping a "cold house" (p. 323); and Salem is a "cold" community; and the activity of the girls in the woods suggests sexual repression—but this is far from being the entire explanation of events. And, as Miller *dramatizes* his material, guilt is not the sole motive for the trials. Nor would it seem either necessary or desirable that it should be in order to link the "personal" to the "social." Some critics want a single explanation for the "enemy"; but certainly the interest of the play, for a mature reader, is that the "enemy" assumes many shapes and refuses to be reduced to a single motivation. Mrs. Putnam is filled with hate because she lost seven babies at birth; Mr. Putnam wants land; Parris wants to protect his job; Tituba wants to save her neck; Abigail wants John—and so it goes. If it be objected that few of these characters seem genuinely convinced of witchcraft, that would seem to be more of an historical than an aesthetic question. Miller, it must be owned, exposed himself to such criticism by identifying his play with a specific period. It is certainly arguable whether we get, as Miller says we do, the "essential nature" of the Salem trials; but no matter—what we do get is an extremely effective drama. Yet, even from the merely "historical" standpoint, Miller has complicated his action; for example, and this is to the modern taste, Betty appears to be suffering from some kind of self-damaging guilt complex brought about from the previous night's outing in the woods;

but there is a nice question how much Abigail and the girls really believe in witchcraft. Although Abigail tells Parris (p. 231) and John (p. 240) that it was just a "sport," she *did* drink chicken blood as a charm to kill Elizabeth (p. 238), which suggests that Miller has mixed various kinds of motives to propel his action.

Intrinsically, *The Crucible* is complex, coherent, and convincing; that is, it succeeds as a play on its own premises and merits. Although one might hesitate to agree that *The Crucible* is superior to *Death of a Salesman*—it seems to lack the sensuousness, the imaginative and technical brilliance, even the warm humanity, of the earlier play—still it remains one of Miller's best plays and one of the most impressive achievements of the American theater.

Works Cited

Eric Bentley, "Miller's Innocence," *New Republic*, CXXVIII (February 16, 1953), 22–23; John Mason Brown, "Seeing Things," *Saturday Review of Literature*, XXXVI (February 14, 1953), 41–42; Alan S. Downer, *Recent American Drama* (Minneapolis, 1961); Lajos Egri, *The Art of Dramatic Writing* (New York, 1946); Gascoigne; Gassner, *Theater at the Crossroads*; Walter Kerr, How *Not to Write a Play* (New York, 1955); Freda Kirchwey, "*The Crucible*," *Nation*, CLXXVI (February 7, 1953), 131–132; Lawson; David Levine, "Salem Witchcraft in Recent Fiction and Drama," *New England Quarterly*, XXVIII (December 1955), 537–546 Olson; Henry Popkin, "Arthur Miller's *The Crucible*," *College English*, XXVI (November 1964), 139–146; D. D. Raphael, *The Paradox of Tragedy* (Bloomington, 1960); Sharpe; Kenneth Tynan, *Curtains* (New York, 1961); Robert Warshow, "The Liberal Conscience in *The Crucible*," *Commentary*, XV (March 1953), 265–271; Richard Watts, Jr., "Introduction" to *The Crucible* (New York, 1959); Weales; Welland.

E. MILLER BUDICK

History and Other Spectres
in Arthur Miller's The Crucible

In his *Defense of Historical Literature*, David Levin has argued that Arthur
Miller's *The Crucible* fails to achieve artistic profundity because of Miller's
inability to project seventeenth-century sensibilities and thus to sympathize
with them. The play, in Levin's view, and in the views of many other critics as
well, is not seriously historical and, therefore, not seriously literary or political.
"Mr. Miller's pedagogical intention," writes Levin, "leads him into historical
and, I believe, aesthetic error. . . . Since Mr. Miller calls the play an attack on
black-or-white thinking, it is unfortunate that the play itself aligns a group
of heroes against a group of villains." Levin concludes his discussion with
the observation that "stupid or vicious men's errors can be appalling; but the
lesson would be even more appalling if one realized that intelligent men, who
tried to be fair and saw the dangers in some of their methods, reached the
same conclusions and enforced the same penalties" (90–92).[1] Miller's *Crucible*,
it would seem, fails to reach the social, historical, and (therefore) moral depth
of a great work of art, because it cannot imaginatively conjure the world that
it pretends to describe.

And yet, as Cushing Strout has pointed out, "Miller has argued for [the]
historical truth [of the play], pointed to its contemporary parallels, and defined
its transhistorical subject as a social process that includes, but also transcends,
the Salem witchcraft trials and the anticommunist investigations of the

From *Modern Drama 28* (December 1985): pp. 535–552. Reprinted in *The Critical Response to
Arthur Miller*, pp. 244–261. © 2006 by Steven R. Centola and Michelle Cirulli.

1950s" (139). Furthermore, Miller has declared that the Salem witchcraft trials, which form the central action of the drama, were of interest to him long before he confronted McCarthyism and decided to write a play implicating the country's contemporary hysteria.[2] How historically accurate, then, is Miller's play? And what are we to make of its use of historical materials, both past and present?

Though *The Crucible* is, to be sure, unrelenting in its opposition to the authoritarian systems represented by Puritanism and McCarthyism, its use of historical materials and the position on moral tyranny which it thus projects seem to me far more complex than criticism on the play would suggest. For Miller's play is not interested only in proclaiming a moral verdict, either on historical or on contemporary events. It does not want simply to inculcate a moral by analogizing between past experiences, on which we have already reached a consensus, and contemporary problems, from which we may not have the distance to judge. Indeed, as Miller himself has stated, while "life does provide some sound analogies now and again, . . . I don't think they are any good on the stage. Before a play can be 'about' something else, it has to be about itself" ("It Could Happen" 295). Analogizing, then, is not, I think, either the major subject of the play or its major structural device. Rather, *The Crucible* is concerned, as Miller has claimed it is, with clarifying the "tragic process underlying the political manifestation," and, equally important, with describing the role of historical consciousness and memory in understanding and affecting such a process.[3]

History is not simply a device which Miller employs in order to escape the unmediated closeness of contemporary events. Rather, it is a fully developed subject within the play itself. For history is for Miller precisely what enables us to resist the demon of moral absolutism. As Miller himself puts it:

> It was not only the rise of "McCarthyism" that moved me, but something which seemed much more weird and mysterious. It was the fact that a political, objective, knowledgeable campaign from the far Right was capable of creating not only a terror, but a new subjective reality, a veritable mystique which was gradually assuming even a holy resonance. . . . It was as though the whole country had been born anew, without a memory even of certain elemental decencies which a year or two earlier no one would have imagined could be altered, let alone forgotten. (Introduction 39)[4]

It is this "subjective reality," and the problem of "memory," that are, I believe, at the heart of Miller's play. And for this reason Miller turns to the Puritan Americans for his subject. For the Salem witch trials raised supremely well the same terror of a "subjective reality" metamorphosing into a "holy resonance" and assuming an objective truth. Indeed, in one sense, this is what the controversy of spectre evidence was all about. Furthermore, the re-creating of this "subjective reality" in the equally "subjective reality" of a drama representing both history and literature—themselves two versions of reality created by the human imagination—directly confronts the relationship of the subjective and the objective, and provides a model for mediating between the two, a model which has at its centre the very issue of memory which is also of paramount importance to Miller. Whether by intuition or by intention, "the playwriting part" ("It Could Happen" 295) of Miller digs down to the essential historical issues of the period as the historians themselves have defined them—issues such as spectral evidence, innate depravity, and its paradoxical corollary, visible sanctity—and relates these issues to the problem of human imagination and will.

Like so much historical fiction and drama, *The Crucible* forces a revolution in our perception and definition of reality. It causes what appears to us to be immediate and real—the present—to become dreamlike and subjective, while it enables what we assume to be the less stable aspects of our knowledge—the ghosts of the past—to assume a solidity they do not normally possess. As Miller says of his own relationship to the Salem of his play, "Rebecca, John Proctor, George Jacobs—[these] people [were] more real to me than the living can ever be"; the "only Salem there ever was for me [was] the 1692 Salem." The past for Miller is "real." Conversely, the subject of his play, the guilt which characterizes both Proctor and, by implication, many of the victims of McCarthyism, is an "illusion" which people only mistake for "real." What could be closer to the spirit of the Salem witch trials, in which people mistook illusions of guilt and sinfulness for "real" witches; in which they assumed a necessary correlation between inner goodness and outward manifestations of that grace? Guilt, writes Miller, is the "betrayer, as possibly the most real of our illusions." "Nevertheless," he continues, it is "a quality of mind capable of being overthrown" ("Journey" 29; and Introduction 41). If Miller's play intends to be revolutionary, it is in terms of this psychological revolution that it expresses itself.

Miller's play, we would all agree, is an argument in favour of moral flexibility. The fundamental flaw in the natures of the Puritan elders and by extension of the McCarthyites, as Miller sees it, is precisely their extreme tendency toward moral absolutism. "You must understand," says Danforth, "that a person is either with this court or he must be counted against it, there be no road between" (293). But Miller is interested, not only in establishing the fact of such absolutism and condemning it, but also in isolating the factors which cause the rigidity which he finds so dangerous. And he is anxious to propose avenues of escape from the power of an overactive, absolutizing moral conscience. As we have seen, critics have objected to Miller's apparently one-sided moralizing in the play. But this moralizing, we must note, is concentrated almost exclusively in the prologue introductions to characters and scenes, and these narrative intrusions into the action of the play may no more represent Miller, the playwright, than Gulliver represents Jonathan Swift or Huck Finn, Mark Twain. Indeed, as other critics have pointed out, the play proper portrays a remarkably well-balanced community of saints and sinners which deserves our full attention and sympathy.[5] Despite the annoying persistence of such unmitigated villainy as that represented by judges Danforth and Hathorne, there is moral education in the course of the drama (in Hale and Parris), while throughout the play such characters as Goody Nurse and Giles Corey represent unabated moral sanity and good will. Furthermore, John Proctor, the opponent of all that seems evil in the play, is not an uncomplicated hero. If we put aside for a moment Proctor's indiscretion with Abigail Williams, which itself has serious social, not to mention ethical, implications, Proctor, who has not taken his sons to be baptized, who does not appear regularly in church (all because of a personal dislike for the appointed representative of the church), and who does not respect Puritan authority even before the abhorrent abuse of power during the trials, does represent, if not an enemy, then at least a potential threat to a community which, Miller is quick to acknowledge, is involved in a life–death struggle to survive (see "Overture to Act I," 225–229).

In fact, it is in the ambiguous nature of the play's hero and his relationship to the rest of the community that Miller begins to confront the complexity of the work's major issue. For if the Salem judges suffer from an unabidable moral arrogance, so does John Proctor, and so, for that matter, do many other of the play's characters. *The Crucible* is a play seething with moral judgements on all sides, on the parts of its goodmen (and goodwomen) as well as of its leaders. The courts condemn the "witches," to be sure, and this act is the most flagrant example of over-zealous righteousness in the play. But the Proctors and their friends are also very free in their moral pronouncements (note the otherwise exemplary Rebecca's much resented *"note of moral superiority"* in Act One [253]), as is Miller's own narrator, who, as we have already observed, is totally unselfconscious in his analyses of his Puritan forbears' ethical deficiencies. The point, I think, is that moral arrogance, the tendency to render unyielding judgments, is not confined within the American power structure. It is at the very heart of the American temperament, and therefore it is at the heart of Miller's play as well. For *The Crucible* attempts to isolate the sources of moral arrogance, to determine the psychological and perceptual distortions which it represents, and thus to point the direction to correcting our moral optics.

Obviously John Proctor does not represent the same threat to freedom posed by Danforth and Hathorne. But this may be the point exactly, that

Proctor does not possess the power, the authority, which converts stubbornness, arrogance, guilt, and pride into social dangers. We must remember, however, that neither did the Puritans wield such dangerous authority until after they had ascended to power in the new world. The story of Proctor, therefore, may be in part the story of American Puritanism itself, Puritanism which wrestled with its own sense of original sin and damnation, which overcame enemies like the Anglican Church which would judge and persecute it, and which finally fought to establish the pure church, the church of the individual saints, in America. Proctor fails in his struggle against persecution of conscience. The Puritan church succeeded—but only for a time. Indeed, this apparent difference between Proctor and the Puritans serves only to stress how corrupting power can become in the hands of a certain kind of person, the Puritan American who is obsessed by his own guilt and driven by the desire to determine sanctity in himself and in others, and to make it conform to the visible human being.

As Miller himself states, guilt is a major force behind and throughout his drama (Introduction 41–42). The major action of the play revolves, therefore, not around the courts and their oppression of the community (the natural analogue to the McCarthy trials), but rather around the figure of Miller's goodman, John Proctor. Miller's real interest resides neither in the sin of tyranny (the courts) nor in the crime of subversion (Proctor's rebellion from authority), but in the sources of tyranny and rebellion both, and in the metaphysical (or religious) assumptions and psychological pressures which cause individuals to persecute and be persecuted for arbitrarily defined crimes of conscience. The personal history of Proctor is the very best kind of history of the Puritan theocracy, just as the story of the Puritans is the very best kind of history of America itself, for both stories probe to the roots, not only of a community, but of the very mentality which determined that community. It is a most powerful irony of the play that Proctor is victimized and destroyed by the very forces which, despite his apparent opposition, he himself embodies. The witch trials do, as Miller says in his "Echoes Down the Corridor," break "the power of theocracy in Massachusetts" (330). But the seeds of this destruction were less within the chimerical crime of witchcraft than within the rigours of the Puritan definition of sainthood which identified moral goodness with outward manifestations of salvation, a belief which, as we shall see momentarily, characterized "witches" and judges alike. For, as the Puritans themselves came to recognize, the implications of spectre evidence, the realization that the devil could assume the person of a child of light, essentially undermined the Puritans' conviction in visible sanctity and hence in the possibility of a federal community predicated upon such sanctity. If devils could parade as saints, how could one determine who in fact was saved, who damned?[6] The danger which Miller sees for his contemporary American public is not that it will fail to recognize totalitarianism in the Puritans, or even in McCarthy. Totalitarianism is too easy an enemy, as the McCarthy phenomenon itself demonstrates in its hysterical reaction to Communism. The danger is that the Americans will not be able to acknowledge the extent to which tyranny is an almost inevitable consequence of moral pride, and that moral pride is part and parcel of an American way of seeing the world, an aspect of the tendency to externalize spiritual phenomena and claim them as absolute and objective marks of personal or political grace.

The major historical fabrication of the play is, of course, the adulterous relationship between Proctor and Abigail Williams. Many explanations have been offered for this alteration of the historical facts (Miller himself comments on it),[7] but the chief necessity for inventing this adultery is, I think, that it provides precisely that inclination to perceive oneself as sinful, as innately depraved, which characterizes both Proctor and the Puritans, and which therefore delineates that field of ambiguous moral constitution in which both the individual and his community must define and measure moral "goodness." Proctor's adultery with Abigail establishes the hero a fallen man, fallen even before the action of the play begins. This may not be original sin as the Puritans defined it, but it is a sin which is prior and unrelated to the specific sin which the play explores, the covenanting of oneself to the devil, or, to put the problem in the more secular terminology that Miller would probably prefer, to the pursuing of a course of consummate, antisocial evil.

The question being raised in Miller's play is this: on what basis can an individual exonerate himself of evil, knowing that he is indeed sinful and that according to his own beliefs he is damned? To put the question somewhat differently: how can John Proctor or any man believe in his own possible redemption, knowing what he does about the nature of his sexual, sinful soul? Our distance from Proctor's dilemma may enable us to understand levels of complexity which Proctor cannot begin to acknowledge. But this does not alter in the least the conflict which he must resolve. Nor does it protect us from analogous complexities in our own situations which we do not have the distance to recognize. Indeed, as Miller himself argues, "guilt" of the vague variety associated with Proctor, was directly responsible for the "social compliance" which resulted in McCarthy's reign of terror in the 1950s: "Social compliance . . . is the result of the sense of guilt which individuals strive to conceal by complying. . . . It was a guilt, in this historic sense, resulting from their awareness that they were not as Rightist as people were supposed to be." Substituting "righteous" for Rightist, one has a comment equally valid for the Puritans.

Puritan theology, to be sure, had its own sophisticated answers to the question of the sinner's redemption. According to the Puritan church, the crucifixion of Christ represented the final act of reconciliation between man and God after man's disobedience in the garden of Eden had rent their relationship asunder. God in His infinite mercy chose to bestow upon certain individuals his covenant of grace, and thus to bring them, sinful as they might be, back into the congregation of the elect. God's will, in the process of election, was total, free, and inscrutable. Human beings were passive recipients of a gift substantially better than anything they deserved. This theological position is hinted at in the play when Hale pleads with Elizabeth Proctor to extract a confession from her husband:

> It is a mistaken law that leads you to sacrifice. Life, woman, life is God's most precious gift; no principle, however glorious, may justify the taking of it.... Quail not before God's judgment in this, for it may well be God damns a liar less than he that throws his life away for pride. (320)

Miller has secularized and diluted Puritan theology in Hale's speech, but the references to "sacrifice," "judgment," and "pride" suggest the outlines of Christian history from the Puritan perspective, and they point to the central fact that divine charity has made human sacrifice unnecessary, even presumptuous, in the light of the divine sacrifice which has already redeemed humankind.[8]

But, as we shall see in a moment, factors other than the covenant of grace had entered into the Puritans' religious views, forcing a conflict already evident in the first generation of New Englanders, and threatening to tear the community apart by 1660, between a strict Calvinism on the one hand and a federal theology on the other. This conflict was essentially a competition between the covenant of grace, which emphasized the charity implicit in Christ's crucifixion, and the covenants of church and state, which were essential to the Puritans' political objectives and which manifested themselves as legal contracts designed to forge an identity between inner grace and outer saintliness. In other words, in demanding outward obedience to the federal form of government which they had conceived for their "city upon a hill," the organizers of the new community of saints had hedged on their Calvinism; they had muted the doctrine of the absoluteness of the covenant of grace, the ineffectiveness of signs to evidence justification, in order to assert the importance of social conformity, of "preparation," and of an external obedience to the covenant, not of grace, but of church and state.[9]

From one point of view, the tragedy of John Proctor, which culminates in his execution for witchcraft, can be seen as stemming from his and his wife's inability to relent in their own moral verdicts, both of themselves and of each other, and to forgive themselves for being human. It originates, in other words, in their failure to understand the concept of divine charity which has effected their salvation and saved them from damnation. "I am a covenanted Christian woman," Elizabeth says of herself (273), but neither she nor John seems to understand what this covenant of grace means. Like the Puritan community of which they are a part, they seem to feel compelled personally to exact from themselves justice and to punish themselves for the sinfulness for which Christ's crucifixion has already atoned.

Not understanding the model of divine charity which determines their sanctity, they and their fellow Puritans are incapable of understanding the concept of charity at all. True, they plead charity. "We must all love each other now," exclaims Mary Warren in Act II (266). "Excellency," pleads Hale, "if you postpone a week and publish to the town that you are striving for their confessions, that speak mercy on your part, not faltering" (318). "You cannot break charity with your minister," Rebecca cautions John (246); "Learn charity, woman," Proctor begs Elizabeth (265); "Charity Proctor, charity" asks Hale (282); "I have broke charity with the woman, I have broke charity with her," says Giles Corey (287). But even as they beg for mercy and sympathy, charity in the largest, most theologically meaningful sense of the word, they act in accordance, not with charity, but with that other component of the divine will—justice—which God has specifically chosen not to express by substituting the covenant of grace for His justifiable wrath. Thus, in the name of justice, Parris forces a confession from Abigail, Hale from Tituba; Abigail threatens Betty and the other girls; Proctor (significantly) does not ask Mary Warren to tell the truth but demands it of her, and so on. We know we are in terrible trouble when Hale, upon hearing of Rebecca's arrest, pleads with her husband to "rest upon the justice of the court" (277). Justice alone simply will not do. Indeed, when justice forgets charity, it subverts the whole divine scheme of salvation, as the Puritans' theology had itself defined it.

Miller uses the issues of charity and justice both in order to locate the historical controversy which destroyed Salem, Massachusetts, and to develop an argument concerning the relationship between charity and justice as theological concepts, and charity and justice as the major features of human relationships—public and private. These issues, therefore, not only frame the play, but specifically define the relationship between John and Elizabeth Proctor, and they largely determine the course of their tragedy. In John and Elizabeth's first extended conversation, set in the "court" which is the Proctors' home, a play in miniature is enacted, a dramatic confrontation which explores the same issues of charity and justice portrayed in the play as a whole:

PROCTOR: Woman ... I'll not have your suspicion any
more.
ELIZABETH: ... *I* have no—
PROCTOR: I'll not have it!

ELIZABETH: Then let you not earn it.

PROCTOR, *with a violent undertone*: You doubt me yet?

ELIZABETH, *with a smile, to keep her dignity*: John, if it were not Abigail that you must go to hurt, would you falter now? I think not. . . .

PROCTOR, *with solemn warning*: You will not judge me more, Elizabeth. I have good reason to think before I charge fraud on Abigail, and I will think on it. Let you look to your own improvement before you go to judge your husband any more. . . . Spare me! You forget nothin' and forgive nothin'. Learn charity, woman. I have gone tiptoe in this house all seven month since she is gone. I have not moved from there to there without I think to please you, and still an everlasting funeral marches round your heart. I cannot speak but I am doubted, every moment judged for lies, as though I come into a court when I come into this house! . . . I'll plead my honesty no more. . . . No more! I should have roared you down when first you told me your suspicion. But I wilted, and, like a Christian, I confessed. Confessed! Some dream I had must have mistaken you for God that day. But you're not, you're not, and let you remember it! Let you look sometimes for the goodness in me, and judge me not.

ELIZABETH: I do not judge you. The magistrate sits in your heart that judges you. I never thought you but a good man, John—*with a smile*—only somewhat bewildered.

PROCTOR, *laughing bitterly*: Oh, Elizabeth, your justice would freeze beer! *He turns suddenly toward a sound outside. He starts for the door as Mary Warren enters. As soon as he sees her, he goes directly to her and grabs her by her cloak, furious.* How do you go to Salem when I forbid it? do you mock me? *Shaking her.* I'll whip you if you dare leave this house again! (264–65)

What is important in this scene is not just that Elizabeth's lack of charity toward John leads directly to Proctor's lack of charity both toward Elizabeth and toward Mary Warren as she enters the house; or that this cycle of anger and recrimination causes further hostility on the parts of the two women who hold each other's and John's fate in their hands. (An analogous kind of reading could be made for John's confrontation with Abigail earlier in the play, when John not only fails to respond to Abigail's very real and understandable hurt ["Pity me, pity me!", she pleads], but absolutely refuses even to acknowledge that the affair ever occurred: "PROCTOR: Wipe it out of mind. We never touched, Abby. ABIGAIL: Aye, but we did. PROCTOR: Aye, but we did not" [241].) The point is not simply that anger begets anger, nor that the characters do not trust each other. Rather, the problem is that the characters have not admitted humankind's very paltry powers of moral judgment. They have not accepted in their hearts that God alone can render judgment on humankind. The characters of the play—*all* the characters, and not just Danforth and Hathorne—have mistaken themselves for God, to paraphrase Proctor, and this misunderstanding is precisely the problem. Elizabeth cannot see the "goodness" in John just as she cannot see the "goodness" in herself (and John, later, cannot see the "goodness" in himself), because what both John and Elizabeth have forgotten is that, according to their own beliefs, the goodness within them is not a natural goodness but the goodness implanted there by God's grace, despite the fact that they are, to apply Elizabeth's own words about herself, "so plain" and "so poorly made" (323). We can expand the argument by pointing out John and Elizabeth's unwillingness to recognize that goodness is not contingent upon a single action or even upon a series of actions. Goodness does not depend upon what the Puritans would call "works." Rather, goodness is an indwelling potentiality—whether innate, for the secularists, or implanted there by God—which must be nurtured and allowed to express itself. On a larger theological scale, the fundamental problem for both John and Elizabeth is a lack of faith in a true sense, a failure to recall their religion telling them that God has saved them *despite* the fact that they are sinners, and that the means of their salvation was divine charity itself.

This playing out of the drama's theological issues as a conflict between a guilty adulterer and his suspicious wife serves supremely well Miller's ultimate object of "examining . . . the conflict between a man's raw deeds and his conception of himself; the question of whether conscience is in fact an organic part of the human being, and what happens when it is handed over not merely to the state or the mores of the time but to one's friend or wife" ("Brewed in *The Crucible*" 173). The Puritan Proctor could not have provided a fitter subject for the study of the organicism of conscience, because for the Puritans inner grace and outer obedience to the "state" and to the "mores of the time" had become hopelessly confused. Goodness had lost its theological meaning and degenerated into a merely human concept. Hence, to the end of the play neither Elizabeth nor John fully understands the meaning of the word "goodness," although Hale, again in an abbreviated and somewhat debased form, gives a basis for the theological definition when he tells us in the fourth act that "before the laws of God we are as swine" (320). The point is valid, despite the somewhat crude and objectionable formulation. Yet, even though in the final act of the play Elizabeth knows that she "cannot judge" Proctor (322), especially not his goodness, and even though Proctor has again and again reiterated that he and his goodness cannot be judged either by Elizabeth or by the courts, Elizabeth does continue to judge him and, more seriously, he accepts those judgements. Furthermore, John judges himself, and both John and Elizabeth pronounce these judgments about John's goodness, not in terms of divine grace or inherent humanness, but in terms of the kinds of superficial, worldly actions (in this case, silence and martyrdom) which have caused Elizabeth to misjudge John in the past. "Yet you've not confessed till now. That speak goodness in you," Elizabeth says to John as he is deciding whether or not to give a false confession; while John imagines that he himself is capable of estimating his place within the kingdom of God: "It is a pretense, Elizabeth," he says of his decision to hang for a crime which he has not committed:

> I cannot mount the gibbet like a saint. It is a fraud. I am not that man.... My honesty is broke ... I am no good man. Nothing's spoiled by giving them this lie that were not rotten long before.... Let them that never lied die now to keep their souls. It is a pretense for me, a vanity that will not blind God nor keep my children out of the wind. (322–323)

Elizabeth immediately confirms John in his belief that he is his own judge: "There be no higher judge under Heaven than Proctor is," she exclaims (323); and she recurs to her martyristic definition of goodness: "I never knew such goodness in the world" (323).

What is wrong with John's decision to confess, as it is presented in the play, is not only that it is a lie, though this of course is crucial, but more subtly that it is based on a definition of "saint"-hood which is a heretical offence against Proctor's own faith, a definition which depends upon setting oneself up as one's own judge, judging one's works and outer manifestations as evidences of sanctification or damnation. John confesses, not to his true sin, but to a sin he did not commit; not to his God, but to a community of men. In a sense, however, he does commit the sin of demonry when he thus falsely confesses, for he veritably signs a pact with the devil the moment he chooses both to lie and to inaugurate himself as his own judge, his own God as it were. We might even say that he has already begun the process of "devil worship" earlier in the play when he cries out in court that "God is dead" (311), or when he damns the Deputy Governor; and he extends that position later when he damns the village (327).

But the crisis of faith is further compounded when John refuses to sign the confession and thus assumes a stance of total silence. For Proctor covenants himself with the devil a second time when he refuses to sign, not because he ought to have signed what is a damning and false document, but because his refusal to sign it has more to do with protecting his "good name" than it does with the more noble virtues which the deed pretends to express

(326 ff.). It has more to do, in other words, with precisely that same mistaken sense of his own authority and his own ability to project outwardly as a name the inner components of spirit.

The matter of the "good name" is a tricky issue in the play.[10] On the one hand, the "good name" is as important to the playwright as it is to the protagonist. On the other, as again "the playwriting part" of Miller seems eminently aware, attention to one's good name represents an inability to separate inner goodness from outer goodness. In a phrase, the Puritan Proctor has confused "goodness" with a "good name," and this is a confusion, Miller suggests, which we must avoid at all costs. After all, it is also to protect John's good name that Elizabeth perjures herself in court and, in not confessing her real reasons for firing Abigail Williams, effectively ensures John's death ("She only thought to save my name," says John [307]). And we cannot forget Reverend Parris's and Abigail Williams's concern for their good names in Act I (231 ff.; see also Parris: "[Proctor] is blackening my name" [300]). Goodness for John and Elizabeth, and for their community, is identical with one's worldly deeds, with one's good name. "Now I do think I see some shred of goodness in John Proctor," says John of his final refusal to confess to witchcraft to which he has no reason to confess (328). He cannot see that his goodness pre-dates this decision, that it was implanted by his God despite his sinfulness.

Proctor's silence, Miller is suggesting, like his desire to confess, does not represent spiritual valour. Indeed, silence itself, rather than representing a virtue, is associated throughout the play with a lack of human feeling and warmth, with a lack of charity, we might say. It is silence, for example, that causes Elizabeth to indict John of continued unfaithfulness in Act II. It is silence which is directly responsible for Abby's not being seen for the whore that she is; silence which finally seals John's doom when Elizabeth refuses to confess the adultery in court; silence which encourages Proctor on his path to martyrdom: "PROCTOR: I cannot mount the gibbet like a saint. . . . [ELIZABETH] *is silent.*" Furthermore, silence is connected, throughout the play, by both John and Danforth, with a stony coldness. "[Y]our justice would freeze beer!" John says to Elizabeth in the scene I have already quoted (265); "Are you a stone?" Danforth asks her; and John's last rebellious advice to Elizabeth is to "show a stony heart and sink them with it . . ." (328). Giles Corey is pressed to death between stones because of his silence. Coldness and silence, furthermore, are very likely what prompted John's adultery in the first place. "It needs a cold wife to prompt lechery," Elizabeth confesses; "suspicion kissed you when I did. . . . It were a cold house I kept!" (323; Abigail: "she is a cold, sniveling woman" [241]). And coldness, of course, is also associated with the presence of the devil. (See Act III, 303 ff.). What Miller seems to be getting at is that silence itself may be a kind of presumption, a kind of pride. It may be a way of asserting one's control over events and their meanings by refusing to respond to the humanness of a human situation (note Elizabeth's silent smiles in Act II which are associated with her preserving her dignity). Hence, silence is associated with the condition of a stone, because it denies the importance of human communication. Silence, ultimately, divorces the individual from true repentance and true charity, either to other human beings or, more seriously, to their God.

Miller has created a true dilemma for Proctor, a literally damned-if-you-do, damned-if-you-don't situation. Both Proctor's confession and his silence represent a misunderstanding of the terms of divine grace, a mistaken worldly pride, and a commitment to external signs and symbols. Hence, Proctor's fate is sealed, not by his deeds, but by a mind-set which does not allow him to view himself or his actions charitably and thus truly. But this dilemma exists only because the Puritans, Proctor included, had identified saintedness with external goodness, a good name. Goodness, Miller implies, is a purely spiritual, inward state. It is not subject to the laws and dictates of men. In Miller's view, Senator McCarthy and judges Danforth and Hathorne were not the major enemies of American liberty. Moral absolutism, pride, contempt, and a marked tendency to see outward signs as evidence of inner being—these McCarthy-like, Puritan-like qualities—were the opponents of liberty, and they characterized victim as well as victimizer. The reason that McCarthy and the Puritan judges were able to hold court in America was that the Americans judged themselves as their dictators would judge them. The dilemma of John Proctor, then, was the dilemma of America itself. As Miller put it in his introduction to Proctor: "These people had no ritual for the washing away of sins. It is another trait we inherited from them, and it has helped to discipline us as well as to breed hypocrisy among us" (239). John and Elizabeth Proctor, like many other Puritans, perhaps like many other Americans, assumed a priori that they were sinful and thus worthless. Therefore they misread and misjudged their lives' experiences. They judged themselves guilty and were willing to accept the verdict of guilty by others. Most frightening for the nation, this self-destructive attitude of guilt had become institutionalized in the American theocracy, and when it was given power, these qualities which defined the victim became the instruments which supported and strengthened the oppressor. Neither the Proctors nor the Puritan elders, neither the American public nor the McCarthyites, were willing to recognize that only the moral authority of God or of some code larger than man (a secular equivalent of God) was absolute and binding. They had allowed a concept of visible sanctity to outweigh their commitment to inner grace; they had preferred their federal theology to their Calvinist religion. Miller points to this problem very precisely when he has Proctor naively demand that he be able to "speak" his "heart." Parris retorts *"in a fury What, are we Quakers? We are not Quakers here yet, Mr. Proctor. And you* may tell that to your followers!" (246). Miller here recalls the antinomian crisis in Puritan New England which, like the witchcraft trials, brought to the surface an inherent tension between the Puritans' strict Calvinist faith and their federal theology; the tension between an invisible covenant between man and God, eternal and unbreakable, and a visible covenant, highly perishable, between God and the people's religious and political institutions. Outward forms, names, and institutions had come to be more cherished than the sanctity of an individual soul, even to the Proctors, who perish as a consequence of what must be viewed not only as apostasy but as human hubris.

How are human beings, in Miller's view, to arrive at moral truth? Tom Driver has argued that:

> Miller's strident moralism is a good example of what happens when ideals must be maintained in an atmosphere of humanistic relativism. There being no objective good or evil, and no imperative other than conscience, man himself must be made to bear the full burden of creating his values and living up to them. The immensity of this task is beyond human capacity. (65–66)

"Strident moralism," however, is just what Miller is attacking in the play; and he does not leave us in an amorphous chaos of "humanistic relativism" with "no imperative other than conscience." For what he discovers in his investigations of history is a moral order larger and more adaptive than any formulation at which a single individual could arrive, an order which is analogous to the Puritan perception of God, and which is defined first and foremost by a recognition of one's own defective moral faculties and therefore of one's utter dependence upon the charity and good will which issue from God (if one is a Puritan) and/or from a similar recognition about themselves on the parts of others (whether one is a Puritan or a twentieth-century American). Morality, Miller suggests, is dependent upon recognizing and accepting our humanness—an acknowledgement which neither Proctor nor Parris nor any of the Puritans is willing to make. After all, the whole hysteria starts because Parris is incapable of dismissing his daughter's and his niece's juvenile midnight escapade for the child's play that it really is. Proctor's crime mirrors the crime of the children; his relentless accusations of himself are a version of Parris's inhuman persecution of the innocents.

According to Miller, our knowledge of morality, our ability to accommodate the imperfect humanness which defines us all, is to a large extent synonymous with our knowledge of history itself. History for Miller is not a judgemental catalogue of instances of human sinfulness. Rather, it is an exploration of the core reasons for human sinfulness—reasons such as guilt, pride, and the desire to render judgment, to see oneself as one of the elect—which allows sympathy for the human dilemma none the less. Miller searches deep into American history, not to discover a convenient analogy to a contemporary problem, but to indicate the importance of registering the relativity and subjectivity of moral justice within the *absolute* moral principles of charity and humility and forgiveness. "It is as impossible," Miller claims:

> for most men to conceive of a morality without sin as of an earth without "sky." Since 1692 a great but superficial change has wiped out God's beard and the Devil's horns, but the world is still gripped between two diametrically opposed absolutes. The concept of unity, in which positive and negative are attributes of the same force, in which good and evil are relative, ever-changing, and always joined to the same phenomenon—such a concept is still reserved to the physical sciences and to the few who have grasped *the history of ideas*. (243, emphasis added)

History, Miller is claiming, can provide both a sense of moral relativity and a set of values which enable us to behave morally within that relativity. This is what "the history of ideas" gives us, historical consciousness and historical knowledge thus becoming necessary prerequisites for moral behaviour. It is not that Miller does not believe in the devil: "Like Reverend Hale and the others on this stage, we conceive the Devil as a necessary part of a respectable cosmology" (248). As he argues in his introduction: "I believe ... that, from whatever cause, a dedication to evil, not mistaking it for good, but knowing it as evil and loving it as evil, is possible in human beings who appear agreeable and normal. I think now that one of the hidden weaknesses of our whole approach to dramatic psychology is our inability to face this fact—to conceive, in effect, of Iago" (Introduction 44). But this is the point exactly: that for Miller, evil is more primary than the devil who incorporates it. Satan indeed exists, but as an Iago of the self who is self-created. Thus, Miller puts the emphasis of his play on the importance of self-awareness, the recognition of evil within oneself, and the acknowledgement that this evil may be projected onto others through no fault of theirs.

When Proctor instructs Abby to "wipe it out of mind," and when he falsifies history by claiming that "[w]e never touched," he is already making himself ready prey to the devil's wiles, because he is denying, on a conscious level, the original sin and human fallenness—the evil—which are in fact a part of his nature, and for which, subconsciously, he is already punishing himself. He is, in other words, being dishonest with himself, and with Abby, and with Elizabeth as well, as Elizabeth makes clear for us in their long conversation in Act II. When Proctor thus tries to wipe clean the slate of history and thereby denies to his own consciousness the necessary lessons of his own experience, of his own history, he excludes the possibility for integrated consciousness of his goodness as coexistent with his sinfulness, of his salvation despite his evil.

The situation could not be more dangerous. As a consequence of his black-and-white morality, Proctor does not see that the Puritans' crimes against humanity, against himself, constitute versions of his own crimes against himself. He misunderstands his guilt and therefore misadministers his punishment. Proctor suffers from a misconceived sense of self in which he is either wholly saved or wholly damned. Because he fails to read the historical record, either about himself or about his community, he does not understand that humankind has been defined from the beginning of human history, in the Bible itself, by a curious admixture of good and evil, and that humankind misjudges morality when it ignores the morally vague context of human experience. Since Adam's fall, our relationship with the devil has been much closer than any of us would like to admit, and there are none among us who might not be charged, with a certain degree of truthfulness, with covenanting himself to the devil. This state of affairs is indeed why God has bestowed His grace upon mankind, why He has sacrificed His son.

By writing a historical drama, Miller is asking us to turn to the historical record in order to understand the ambiguous and changing nature of morality. He is evoking our sympathies for characters whose world-view and beliefs are totally different from our own, thus enabling us to do precisely what the Puritans themselves were unable to do—to accept the diversity of opinions, the variety of perceptions, the mixture of bad and good which characterize the human community.

Above all, however, Miller is making a statement about the relationship between objective fact and subjective fiction, or rather, about the existence of subjective fiction within objective fact and vice versa. *The Crucible* not only emphasizes the importance of sympathy in human relationships, but explores why sympathy must be a component of those relationships, not only if we are to see morally, but if we are to see at all. For historical fiction has the unique advantage of insisting upon the realness of the world with which it deals fictively, while simultaneously acknowledging that the world which it is now representing is a consequence as much of the readers' or viewers' subjective perceptions as of any objective fact or reality. In historical drama, the paradoxical relationship between fancy and fact is even more vivid than in written fiction, for the realness of actors enacting a history which has been fictionalized and put on the stage has, from Shakespeare on, inevitably raised its own theoretical arguments about the world and the play. "No one can really know what their lives were like," Miller begins the play (226). And yet he proceeds to convince us of exactly what their lives were like, as they themselves confronted what was knowable and unknowable, what was fact and fiction, in life itself.

In the case of a historical drama on the Salem witchcraft trials, the historical and literary interest found a coincidence of purpose and meaning that was startling in the extreme. For the issue of the witchcraft trials is precisely the question of the proportion of fiction to fact in our perceptions of the world; and the lesson is what can happen when individuals forget the limits of their own optical and moral senses, and fail to sympathize with fellow citizens suffering from the same impossibility of separating the imaginary from the real. Furthermore, by casting upon his contemporary audience the spectre of Salem, and pretending that Salem is contemporary America, Miller is asking us to recognize the elements of self within our projections of the devil, the subjectivity which ever colours our knowledge of the objective world.

The Crucible, then, by the very procedures which define its dramatic art, enforces upon us a recognition of the difficulty of distinguishing between the subjective and the objective, between the spectre and the witch. Hence, the play invokes our sympathy for the actors of a tragedy[11] who viewed their lives from much the same complicated perspective by which an audience views a play. The play, in other words, imitates the situation of the Puritans, who witnessed their world as the unfolding of a drama in which external events represented internal realities. But whereas the Puritans failed to recognize the fictionality of that dramatic performance in which their lives consisted, Miller's play, as a play, enforces our awareness of the fiction. It insists that life (i.e., history) and literature are both spectres of consciousness, ours or someone else's, projections of the imagination. The Puritans' principal failing, as it emerges in the play, was their inability to accord to each other, even to themselves, the privacy and individuality which are not simply human rights but inherent features of perception itself. By extending our imaginations over centuries of difference, by identifying with the ghosts which are the past and the ghosts in which the past itself believed, we attain to the sympathetic imaginations, the spiritual charity, which the Puritans could not achieve.

NOTES

1. Eric Bentley states the case fully when he argues that *The Crucible* "is a play in which Mr. Miller complains that the accuser is always considered holy, the accused guilty. . . . What is unusual about Mr. Miller's treatment of McCarthyism [is] that he sets up as the offense . . . an offense which it is impossible to commit: the practice of magic. If to the McCarthyites (of both periods) an accused man is almost automatically guilty, to Mr. Miller he is almost automatically innocent. . . . Mr. Miller has missed the essence of our political situation. . . . The punch [against America] is threatened; and then pulled. We are made to feel the boldness of the threat; then we are spared the violence of the blow." The play, concludes Bentley, represents a "dangerous" "liberalism" (*The American Drama* 197–99).

See also Robert Warshow, "The Liberal Conscience in *The Crucible*," who charges that in the final analysis what the play presents is "the astonishing phenomenon of Communist innocence" (200–201). Miller, argues Warshow, "reveals . . . his almost contemptuous lack of interest in the particularities—which is to say, the reality—of the Salem trials" (192); "Miller has nothing to say about the Salem trials and makes only the flimsiest pretense that he has" (196). See also Herbert Blau, "No Play is Deeper than its Witches," 61–66.

Miller takes the critics' point when he comments in his prologue to Hale that: "the analogy . . . seems to falter when one considers that, while there were not witches then, there were Communists and capitalists now, and in each camp here is certain proof that spies of each side were at work undermining the other . . . [Similarly] I have no doubt that people *were* communing with, and even worshiping the Devil in Salem" (250). See "It Could Happen Here—and Did" 294. As we shall see in a moment, analogy is not, I think, Miller's major purpose in the play.

2. See Miller's "Note on Historical Accuracy," which prefaces the play, and his statement in his "Introduction" to the *Collected Plays* that the "moral awareness of the play and its characters . . . are historically correct" (44). For Miller's statement on his interest in Salem, see the "Introduction" to the *Collected Plays*, 41. Miller also remarks that he "was drawn to write *The Crucible* not merely as a response to McCarthyism" ("Brewed" 172).

3. On Miller's analogizing art, see Strout, "Analogical History" 138–56, and Henry Popkin, "Arthur Miller's *The Crucible*" 139–46.

4. Note Miller's other statements on the matter of subjective reality: for example, "to write a realistic play of that world was already to write in a style beyond contemporary realism" (quoted in Blau 62). Miller also comments that: "A few years after its original production, *The Crucible* opened again . . . and the script was now judged by many of the same critics as an impassioned play rather than a cold tract. . . . In 1958 nobody was afraid any more. . . . And this forgetfulness is part of the tragedy" ("It Could Happen Here 297).

5. See Martin 279–92. Henry Popkin argues that: "Over against the bad individual, the vengeful adults, and the lying children, Miller sets the basically sound community . . . The underlying presence of the good community . . . reminds us that Miller, even in the face of his own evidence, professes to believe in the basic strength and justice of the social organism, in the possibility of good neighbors. If he criticizes society, he does so from within, as a participant and believer in it" ("Arthur Miller's *The Crucible*" 146).

6. Among the best discussions of the Puritans' doctrine of visible sanctity and their federal theology are: Edmund Morgan, *Visible Saints: The History of a Puritan Idea* (New York, 1963); Sacvan Bercovitch, *Puritan Origins of the American Self* (New Haven, 1975); and Michael Colacurcio, "Visible Sanctity and Specter Evidence: The Moral World of Hawthorne's 'Young Goodman Brown,'" *Essex Institute Historical Collections*, 110 (1974), 259–99.

7. Miller's comments are in his Introduction, 41–42. In "Arthur Miller's *The Crucible*," Robert A. Martin writes that, "in spite of an apparent abundance of historical materials, the play did not become dramatically conceivable for Miller until he came upon a 'single fact' concerning Abigail Williams" (281). Henry Popkin explains the necessity for the adultery as follows: "We can see why Proctor's adultery had to be invented; surely it came into existence because Miller found himself compelled to acknowledge the Aristotelian idea that the blameless, unspotted hero is an inadequate protagonist for a serious play" (144–45). I would argue that it is not the adultery that represents Proctor's fatal flaw, but his tremendous pride—a much more Aristotelian category than sexual indiscretion. Thus I would disagree with Popkin's conclusion that the play "falls short as a play of ideas, which is what it was originally intended to be . . . because the parallels do not fit and because Miller has had to

adulterate … Proctor's all too obvious innocence to create a specious kind of guilt for him; he is easily exonerated of both crimes (146).

    8. On the problem of self-sacrifice as a motif is American literature, see my essay "American Israelites: Literalism and Typology in the American Imagination," *Hebrew University Studies in Literature* 10 (1982): 69–107.

    9. See Perry Miller, *The New England Mind From Colony to Province* (Boston, 1953), 191–225. The phrase "a city upon a hill" is John Winthrop's in "A Model of Christian Charity."

    10. On the matter of the good name, see Popkin, 140 ff.; and Mottram: "Miller's point is that, since Proctor is a good man, it is vanity on his part not to recognize he is like all men whose wicked souls God sees and it is wicked not to leave his family provided for. So he may as well confess. But he switches the action here to focus on John's integrity. In a corrupt time, that alone is valuable" (140). I would not agree with the latter part of Mottram's statement.

    11. The controversy about whether or not Miller's play constitutes a tragedy in the classical sense might benefit from considering that the Puritans' doctrine of predestination superbly suits the tragic model. Proctor believes that his fate is determined, his adultery evidences to him that he is damned. Therefore, what remains for him to choose is how he will act, given that his sentence is already cast.

Works Cited

Bentley, Eric. "The American Drama 1944–1954." *American Drama and Its Critics*. Ed. Alan S. Downer. Chicago, 1965.

Blau, Herbert. "No Play is Deeper than its Witches." *Twentieth-Century Interpretations of The Crucible: A Collection of Critical Essays*. Ed. John Ferres. Englewood Cliffs, New Jersey, 1974.

Driver, Tom. "Strength and Weakness in Arthur Miller." *Arthur Miller: A Collection of Critical Essays*. Ed. Robert Corrigan. Englewood Cliffs, NJ, 1969.

Levin, David. *In Defense of Historical Literature: Essays on American History, Autobiography, Drama, and Fiction*. New York, 1967.

Martin, Robert A. "Arthur Miller's *The Crucible*: Background and Sources." *Modern Drama* 20 (1977).

Miller, Arthur. "Brewed in *The Crucible*." *The Theater Essays of Arthur Miller*. Ed. Robert A. Martin. New York, 1978.

———. "Introduction to *The Crucible*." *Collected Plays*. London, 1958.

———. "It Could Happen Here—and Did." *The Theater Essays of Arthur Miller*. Ed. Robert A. Martin. New York, 1978.

———. "Journey to *The Crucible*." *The Theatre Essays of Arthur Miller*. Ed. Robert A. Martin. New York, 1978.

Mottram, Eric. "Arthur Miller: The Development of a Political Dramatist." *American Theater*. Ed. John R. Brown and Bernard Russell. London, 1967.

Popkin, Henry. "Arthur Miller's *The Crucible*." *College English* 26 (1965).

Strout, Cushing. "Analogical History: *The Crucible*." *The Veracious Imagination: Essays on American History, Literature, and Biography*. Ed. Cushing Strout. Middletown, Conn., 1981.

Warshaw, Robert. "The Liberal Conscience in *The Crucible*." *The Immediate Experience: Movies, Comics, Theater and Other Aspects of Popular Culture*. New York, 1975.

EDMUND S. MORGAN

Arthur Miller's The Crucible *and the Salem Witch Trials: A Historian's View*

The historian who plays the critic runs the risk of being irrelevant as well as incompetent. A work of art must stand or fall by itself, and the author of *The Crucible* has warned off historians with the statement that his play is "not history in the sense in which the word is used by the academic historian." But when a play evokes a widely known historical event, art leans on history. No one who reads *The Crucible* can see it wholly fresh. The world into which it carries us is constructed from building blocks that are labeled Puritanism, Salem Village, witch-hunt, clergyman. Part of the verisimilitude of the play and part of its dramatic tension depend on our knowledge that men and women were hanged at Salem Village in 1692 for crimes they could not have committed.

Under these circumstances it may be permissible for a historian to examine the play's depiction of history and to ask how the author's assumptions about history have affected his understanding of his characters.

I do not expect an artist who deals with history to conform to every fact known to historians about the events he is concerned with. It does not bother me, for example, that Arthur Miller has simplified the legal transactions involved in the trials and assigned to some individuals judicial powers they did not have. Nor does it bother me that he has transformed Abigail Williams from a child into a woman and given her a love affair with his principal character,

From *The Golden & The Brazen World: Papers in Literature and History, 1650–1800*, pp. 171–186. © 1985 by the Regents of the University of California.

John Proctor, a love affair that is nowhere suggested by the records. Miller's Abigail is not so much a transformation as a creation. So, for that matter, is his John Proctor. It might have been better not to have given either of them the name of an actual person who figures in the historical record. But the artist's relation to the historical record has to be different from the historian's.

If the artist binds himself too closely to known factual details, the result may be an aesthetic disaster. The artist must bring to his work a creative imagination that transcends historical detail in order to recreate living people and situations. He must persuade his audience that they have been transported back to the time and place in question, or at least persuade them to suspend their disbelief that they have taken such a voyage. And the historical record is almost never sufficiently full to equip the artist with the details he needs for persuading them, details of things said and seen and heard, without which his enterprise is doomed. Even where the record is especially full, aesthetic considerations may require violating or ignoring the details it furnishes and substituting imaginary ones in order to achieve, within the limits of the particular work, the development of characters and situations through which the artist makes his statement.

In order to make use of the building blocks that the audience will recognize, the artist must have his characters say things and do things that conform in a general way to known fact. But his characters inevitably assume a life of their own. They may say and do things that actual historical people are known to have said and done, but they do a lot of other things on their own, as it were, things dictated by the author's vision of them and what they were up to. That vision may be the product of careful study of the historical record or it may not, but it can never be as closely tied to the historical record as the historian's vision must always be. In other words, the artist's reconstruction of people and events must take place on a level that is denied to historians and that most historians would not have the imaginative power to reach anyhow. Nevertheless, historians do engage, in their own less imaginative way, in the same sort of activity as novelists and playwrights and perhaps poets, namely, in the provision of vicarious experience. Granted, there are many pieces of historical writing that only faintly answer this description, the analytical and didactic and often unreadable monographs that historians direct at one another and which sometimes seem calculated to mystify outsiders. But it is surely at least one function, in my opinion the highest function, of the historian to recreate the past, however analytically and didactically, in order to release us from the temporal provincialism imposed on us by the time in which we happen to have been born, giving us experience of other times to expand our understanding of what it is to be a human being.

This function the historian shares with the novelist and playwright. The novelist and playwright, of course, are not confined to recreating experience out of the distant past. Indeed, they generally deal with experience available in their own time. And when they resort to history, they turn it into the present in a way that the historian does not pretend to do. But the artist and the historian do share some problems and responsibilities.

The artist by definition is governed by aesthetic considerations; the historian is less constrained by them but by no means exempt. He is not simply a compiler of annals or a transcriber of documents. He cannot attempt to tell everything that happened. He has to pick and choose. He has to leave things out. And though his choice of what to put in may depend on many considerations other than aesthetic, he has to construct something out of the details the record does furnish, something with a shape, a structure, a book or article that will have a theme and a beginning, middle, and end. Otherwise no one will read him, not even other historians.

In building a work around any theme, the historian and the artist who deals in history confront a problem that is particularly acute in *The Crucible*, as well as in the various historical treatments of the New England Puritans, the people whom Arthur Miller tries to bring to life for us. It is the problem of separating the universal from the unique, the timeless from the temporary. History does not repeat itself. No two persons are alike. Every event is in some way unique. And yet the only reason we are capable of vicarious experience is because history does in some sense repeat itself, because all persons are alike. In seeking to broaden our experience through art or through history we have to identify with people who think differently, talk differently, act differently; and we want to know precisely what was different about them. At the same time, we have to be able to recognize their humanity, we have to be able to put ourselves in their situation, identify with them, see in them some of the same weaknesses and strengths we find in ourselves. Otherwise they become too different to be believable and so can tell us nothing about ourselves.

It is easy to err in either direction, to exaggerate similarities to the past or to exaggerate differences. And it is all too tempting to do so in such a way as to flatter ourselves and avoid some of the hard lessons the past may have to teach us. If, on the one hand, we exaggerate differences, we may fall into the trap of viewing the past with condescension, bestowing a patronizing admiration on those quaint old folk who struggled along without benefit of the sophistication and superior knowledge we have arrived at. The past will then become a kind of Disneyland, an escape from the present, a never-never land of spinning wheels and thatched roofs and people dressed in funny old costumes. Or it may become simply a horror from which we can congratulate ourselves on having escaped, a land filled with superstition, poverty, and endless toil, a world of darkness from which we have emerged into the light.

If, on the other hand, we exaggerate the similarities of the past to the present, we may indulge in a comparable complacency, finding justification for everything we do or want to do in the fact that it has been done before: the founding fathers did it; what was good enough for them ought to be good enough for us, and so on. Or we may manufacture spurious arguments for some present policy or proposal on the grounds that it worked in the past, thus equating the past with the present, a very dangerous equation, as we know from those earnest military men who are always fighting the war preceding the one they are engaged in.

Historians and novelists and playwrights who take history seriously have to recognize both similarities to the past and differences. To overemphasize one or the other is not only to distort history but to diminish the impact of the experience it offers, indeed to escape that experience and nourish a temporal provincialism.

With regard to the Salem witchcraft of the 1690s, the temptation has always been to exaggerate the differences between that time and ours. The temptation was much more in evidence fifty or a hundred years ago than it is today. In the nineteenth century, when mankind, and especially Anglo-Saxon mankind, was progressing rapidly toward perfection, taking up the white man's burden, glorying in the survival of the fittest, and fulfilling manifest destiny, the Salem witch trials were obviously something long since left behind. Although it was a little embarrassing that the witch trials were not even farther behind, the embarrassment was compensated for by thinking how rapidly we had all progressed from that dreadful era of superstition and old night.

In the twentieth century, as perfection has eluded us and we have manufactured our own horrors to dwarf those at Salem, we have grown a little less smug. We even find something uncomfortably familiar in the Salem trials, with their phony confessions, inquisitorial procedures, and admission of inadmissible evidence. And yet there remains a temptation to flatter ourselves.

The temptation showed itself recently in the extraordinary publicity given to an article about the possibility of ergot poisoning as a cause of the symptoms displayed by the allegedly bewitched girls at Salem. Ergot poisoning comes from eating bread or flour made from diseased rye grain and produces seizures and sensations comparable to those that the Salem girls experienced or said they experienced. Although the evidence for ergot poisoning at Salem is extremely tenuous, and although if true it would in no way diminish the horror of what happened there, the article in a professional scientific journal was seized upon by the press as though modern science had now explained the whole episode. I can account for the attention given this article only by the flattering implication it seemed to carry (though probably not intended by the author) of the superiority of our own enlightened understanding of what happened in those benighted days. Yet what would be explained by ergot poisoning was only the odd behavior of a few teenage girls, not the hysteria of their elders, in which lay the shame of what happened at Salem.

Evidently the Salem trials are still something we feel uncomfortable about. We want to think that we would not behave the way people behaved then, we would behave better, we would not be fooled by a batch of bad bread. And that brings me back to *The Crucible*. Arthur Miller has probably done more than anyone else to remind us we are not so much better. *The Crucible*, as we all know, was written in the midst of the McCarthy era, and it was intended, I think, to suggest that we were behaving, or allowing our authorized representatives to behave, as badly as the authorities at Salem. There are no overt comparisons. The play is about Salem. But its success depends in part on the shock of recognition.

Let us look, then, at the design of *The Crucible*. How has the author dealt with the problem of similarity and difference? In spite of the apparent parallel with our own times, has he not flattered us a little, allowed us an escape from the hard lessons of Salem and thus denied us the full range of experience he might have given us?

The protagonist of *The Crucible* is John Proctor, a simple man in the best sense of the word, a strong man who does not suffer fools gladly. He has little of formal piety and even less of superstition. His wife is more devout but less attractive. She lacks his human warmth, or at any rate she has wrapped it in a shroud of piety and righteousness. Her husband has consequently found it the more difficult to resist the charms of an unscrupulously available serving girl, Abigail Williams. We cannot blame John Proctor. He is, after all, human, like you and me. But his wife does blame him, and he blames himself.

The antagonist of the play wears a mask, not literally but figuratively. And the mask is never fully stripped away because the author himself has never quite gotten behind it. The mask is Puritanism, and it is worn by many characters, to each of whom it imparts an inhuman and ugly zeal. Elizabeth Proctor wears it when she reproaches her husband for his weakness. Thomas and Ann Putnam wear it when they grasp at witchcraft as the source of their misfortunes. But mostly it is worn by the ministers, Samuel Parris and John Hale, and by the judges, Danforth and Hathorne. They are never explicitly labeled as Puritan; the author sees them so well as men that he has furnished them with adequate human motives for everything they do. Arthur Miller is too serious an artist to give us only a mask with no flesh and blood behind it. His object, indeed, is to show us human weakness. Nevertheless, the mask is there.

The men who kill John Proctor are easily recognized as Puritans. Miller has provided them with all the unlovely traits most of us associate with that name: they are bigoted, egotistical, bent on suppressing every joy that makes life agreeable. The worst of the lot, the most loathsome man in the play, is a

Puritan clergyman. Samuel Parris, we are told, never conceived that "children were anything but thankful for being permitted to walk straight, eyes slightly lowered, arms at the sides, and mouths shut until bidden to speak." We are also told that in this horrid conception Parris was not unusual. He was "like the rest of Salem."

Puritanism sometimes seems more than a mask. Sometimes it becomes the evil force against which man must pit himself. Puritanism, repressing the natural, healthy impulses of children, breeds in the girls of Salem village an unnatural hysteria that proves the undoing of good men like John Proctor. Proctor seems the most un-Puritan man in the play, and Proctor triumphs in death, triumphs as a human being true to himself, triumphs over the hypocrisy and meanness that Puritanism has evoked.

The Crucible is a powerful play. Arthur Miller says he tried to convey in it "the essential nature of one of the strangest and most awful chapters in human history." He has succeeded—almost. The Salem episode was both strange and awful. If the author had known more about the history of New England, however, it is possible that he might have found what happened at Salem less strange and more awful. To explain why, let me draw a picture of seventeenth-century Puritanism somewhat different from the one to be found in *The Crucible*. I speak not exactly as the devil's advocate but as what in this context may amount to the same thing, the Puritans' advocate.

Puritanism has been more often the object of invective than of investigation, and it is easier to say what it was not than what it was. It was not prudishness. The Puritans were much franker in discussing sex than most of us are outside the pages of the modern novel. The sober historical works of Governor Bradford and Governor Winthrop were expurgated when published in the present century. Puritanism was not prohibitionism. The Puritans did not condone excessive drinking, any more than we do, but they seldom drank water if they could avoid it. Puritanism was not drabness in clothing or furniture or houses. The Puritans painted things red and blue and wore brightly colored clothes, trimmed with lace when they could afford it. They forbade a number of things not forbidden today, such as the theater and card playing. They looked askance at mixed dancing and punished breaches of the sabbath. Otherwise their moral code was about the same as ours.

What distinguished the Puritans from us and, to a lesser degree, from their contemporaries was a profound vision of divine transcendence on the one hand and of human corruption on the other. The Puritan could never allow himself to forget God. Although he enjoyed the good things of life, he had always to do so with an awareness of the infinite perfection of the Being who created them. He had always to be comparing earthly pleasures with eternal ones in order to keep the earthly ones in proper perspective. This meant that he could never let himself go in sweet abandon; or rather, it meant that he must always blame himself afterwards when he did. To immerse oneself wholly, even for a short time, in the joys of the flesh was to put things above the Creator of things.

Other people have been overwhelmed with divinity in this way, but other people have found a refuge in asceticism: they have withdrawn from the world, turned their backs on the temptations that constantly invite man's attention away from God. For the Puritan, asceticism was no way out. God, he believed, had placed him in the world and created its good things for his use. He was meant to enjoy them. To turn his back on them was to insult their Maker. He had, therefore, to be in the world but not of it, to love God's creatures but not love them very much.

As he made his way through this too delightful world, the Puritan was inevitably a troubled person. His conduct might look exemplary to you and me, but not to him, because the errors he mourned lay more often in attitude than in act. A person might behave perfectly as far as the outward eye could detect—it was right to eat, to drink, and to be merry at it; it was right to love your wife or husband, play with your children, and work hard at your job. But it was wrong to forget God while you did so. And people were always forgetting, always enjoying food and wine and sex too much, and always condemning themselves for it. Sometimes the lapses were great and gross, sometimes trivial, but great or small they reminded Puritans constantly of their sinful nature. Every day of his life the Puritan reenacted the fall of Adam and felt the awful weight of God's condemnation for it.

The Puritan was as hard on his neighbors as he was on himself. When they visibly violated God's commands, he did not hesitate to condemn them. But his awareness of his own guilt and his conviction that all men are guilty made him somewhat less uncharitable than he may seem to us. He was a disenchanted judge who expected the worst of his fellow men and could not blame them more than he blamed himself. One of the first bands of Puritans to depart from England for the Massachusetts Bay Colony expressed the Puritan attitude well. In an address issued before their departure they implored their countrymen to consider them still as brethren, "standing in very great need of ...helpe,... for wee are not," they said, "of those that dreame of perfection in this world."

The Puritan knew that God demanded perfection but knew also that no one could attain it. And because God could forgive the sinner who repented, the Puritan felt that he too must do so. Anyone who reads the records of New England churches and New England law courts will see how ready the Puritans were to forgive. A convicted drunkard who showed repentance after sobering up would generally receive the lightest of fines from the civil judge or perhaps no fine at all, but merely an admonition. The churches were even more charitable. According to Puritan practice only a small part of a congregation was admitted to church membership, only those who could demonstrate that they were probable saints headed for eternal glory. When a saint was found in open sin, say breaking the sabbath or drinking too much or becoming too friendly with another man's spouse, the church might by a formal vote admonish him or even excommunicate him. But if he repented and expressed sorrow for his conduct, they would almost invariably restore him to membership even if his repentance came years later. The churches exercised an almost foolish patience toward repeating offenders. A person might get drunk pretty regularly. Each time he would be admonished or excommunicated and each time, when he repented, restored.

This combination of severity and forgiveness affected the Puritans' upbringing of their children. The Puritans never supposed that children enjoyed more innocence than their elders. Men did not learn evil as they grew; it was in them from the beginning. A parent's job was to repress it in his children; just as a ruler's job was to repress it in his subjects. But the methods of repression need not be cruel or unbending. A wise parent was supposed to know his children as individuals and fit his discipline to the child's capacities and temperament. As Anne Bradstreet put it:

> Diverse children have their different natures; some are like flesh which nothing but salt will keep from putrefaction; some again like tender fruits that are best preserved with sugar: those parents are wise that can fit their nurture according to their Nature.

Although Puritan parents following this precept might still find the rod the most useful instrument in correcting some children, there is no evidence that they used it any more regularly than parents do today. Samuel Sewall, one of the judges who tried the witches, records in his diary an instance when he was driven to it. His son Joseph, future minister of the Old South Church, had thrown "a knop of Brass and hit his sister Betty on the forehead so as to make it bleed and swell: upon which," says Sewall, "and for his playing at Prayer-time, and eating when Return Thanks [saying grace], I whipd him pretty smartly." In practice Puritan children seem to have been as spoiled as children in other times and ages. Parents expected them to err and corrected them without expecting perfection.

The role of the Puritan clergyman in suppressing evil was a minor one. His function was educational rather than authoritative. It was proper for the authorities in the state to ask his advice when they were having difficulties in interpreting the will of God. But it was wrong for him to proffer advice unasked, and there was no obligation on the part of the authorities to accept it after they got it. Even within his own church he had no authority. Every action of the church in admonishing or excommunicating members was the result of a vote, and in most churches unanimity was required. The minister's job was to instruct his flock, to justify the ways of God to man, to help men detect the evil in their hearts, and also to help them detect the first stirrings of divine grace. He could only hope that through his preaching God might summon some of his listeners to eternal glory.

During the eighteenth century New England preaching became increasingly hortatory and relied more and more on moving appeals to the emotions. Particularly after the Great Awakening of 1741 had set the example, preachers found it advantageous to depict the torments of hellfire vividly to their listeners, in order to frighten them into awareness of their sins. But during the seventeenth century hellfire was conspicuously missing. Seventeenth-century sermons were more didactic than admonitory; the preacher devoted most of his time to the exposition of theological doctrine and applied the doctrine to his listeners only briefly at the end of his sermon.

By the same token the seventeenth-century preacher found little occasion for discussing the devil or his demons. The evil that Puritans feared and fought lay in their own hearts, not in the machinations of the devil. This is not to say that they denied the existence of supernatural evil. They would have been an extraordinary people indeed had they done so, because scarcely anyone in the seventeenth century did. But Puritan ideas on the subject were conventional, the same ideas that seventeenth-century Europeans and Englishmen held. And Puritans were rather less interested in supernatural evil than their contemporaries. Puritans were too preoccupied with natural evil to pay much attention to supernatural.

Why, then, the hysteria at Salem in 1692? If Puritans gave less attention than their contemporaries did to the devil, why did the devil give more attention to them? Why were there not much greater epidemics of witchcraft and witch-hunting in England and Europe than in Massachusetts? The answer is that there were. During the sixteenth and seventeenth centuries some thousands of witches were executed in the British Isles, an estimated 75,000 in France, 100,000 in Germany, and corresponding numbers in other European countries.

The European trials have mostly been forgotten and the Salem ones remembered because the European ones were too widespread and too common to attract special attention. The human imagination boggles at evil in the large. It can encompass the death of Anne Frank but not of several million anonymous Jews. It can comprehend twenty men and women of Salem Village more readily than 75,000 in France. The Salem episode is the more horrible simply because we can take it in.

But even though we take it in, we can never quite understand it. In the effort to do so, we have tried to fasten the blame where it will not hurt any of us. Historians who should have known better once blamed it on the clergy. New ideas, we were told, had penetrated New England, ideas that were dissolving the enslavement of the people to Puritanism, ideas that threatened the dominant position of the clergy. In order to save their overweening influence, they blamed the devil and worked up the witch scare. All nonsense.

The witch scare was no heresy hunt; prosecutors and defendants alike were Puritans, and both believed in witchcraft. The role of the clergy was a deterring one. They recognized at an early stage that the trials were being conducted without regard to proper procedures. The court, on which of course no clergyman sat, was convicting on the basis of spectral evidence alone, evidence offered by a supposed victim of witchcraft to the effect that the devil tormenting him appeared in the shape of the accused. The assumption behind such testimony was that the devil could assume the shape only of a person who had confederated with him. The clergy knew that spectral evidence was considered acceptable in witch trials but that it was not generally considered sufficient in itself to warrant a conviction. The supposition that the devil could not assume the shape of an innocent person was questioned by many authorities, and courts generally demanded supporting evidence of a more objective nature. This might consist in the possession of dolls or wax images and the other paraphernalia of witchcraft. It might consist in the existence of so-called witch marks on a person's body. These were simply red or blue marks or excrescences, such as we would call birthmarks, at which the devil was supposed to suck, as on a teat. God help anyone who had both a birthmark and an old doll retained from childhood. And yet most previous trials of witches, where this kind of evidence was required, resulted in acquittals. The Salem court waived the necessity of such evidence and accepted the spectral evidence offered by a small group of hysterical teenage girls as sufficient in itself to justify conviction.

The clergy, knowing that this was dubious procedure, protested. They did not do so as soon or as loudly as they should have. And anyone occupying a position of influence and leadership who objected soon and loudly to the methods of the late Senator McCarthy is entitled to cast the first stone at the New England clergy of 1692. Some clergymen may have been caught up in the general hysteria; nevertheless, it was the belated protest of the clergy that finally brought the trials to a halt.

If the clergy did not promote the witchcraft scare, how did it happen? No one can give a complete answer. There was no leader who engineered it, no demagogue or dictator who profited from it or hoped to profit from it. It came when the times were out of joint, when the people of Massachusetts had suffered a cruel disillusionment.

Massachusetts had been founded as a city on a hill, to be an example to the world of how a community could be organized in subjection to God's commands. In the course of half a century the people of Massachusetts had seen the world ignore their example and go off after evil ways. Within Massachusetts itself, the piety of the founding fathers had waned in the second generation, or so at least the members of that generation told themselves. In 1685 the world moved in on Massachusetts. England revoked the charter that had heretofore enabled the colony to govern itself and installed a royal governor with absolute powers in place of the one elected by the people. New Englanders hardly knew at first whether to regard the change as a just punishment by God for past sins or as a challenge to a degenerate people to recover the piety and strength of their fathers. But in 1688, when England threw off its king, the people of Massachusetts gladly rose up and threw off the governor that he had imposed on them. There was great rejoicing throughout the colony, and everyone hoped and believed that God would restore the independence that might enable Massachusetts to serve him as only the Israelites had served him before. But the hope proved false. In 1691 the people of Massachusetts heard that they must serve England before God; the new king was sending a new royal governor.

A gloom settled over the colony far deeper than the depression that greeted the coming of the first royal governor. Men who had been rescued from despair only to be plunged back again were in a mood to suspect some hidden evil that might be responsible for their woes. They blamed themselves for not finding it; and when the girls of Salem Village produced visible and audible evidence of something vile and unsuspected, it was all too easy to believe them.

Although Puritanism was connected only indirectly with the witch scare, it did affect the conduct of the trials and the behavior of the defendants. Puritans believed that the state existed to enforce the will of God among men. If evil went unrebuked, they believed, God would punish the whole community for condoning it. It was the solemn duty of the government to search out every crime and demonstrate the community's disapproval of it by punishment or admonition. Once the witch trials began, the officers of government felt an obligation to follow every hint and accusation in order to ferret out the crimes that might be responsible for bringing the wrath of God on the colony. They were, of course, egged on by the people. Witch-hunts, whether in Massachusetts or Europe, generally proceeded from the bottom up, from popular demand. Even the Spanish Inquisition was much less assiduous in pursuit of suspected witches than were the people of the villages where the suspects lived. But popular pressure is not an adequate excuse for irregular judicial procedures. In their eagerness to stamp out witchcraft, the Massachusetts authorities forgot that they had a duty to protect the innocent as well as punish the guilty.

At the same time, they were trapped by their very insistence on mercy for the repentant. By releasing defendants who confessed and repented, they placed a terrible pressure on the accused to confess to crimes they had not committed. It is possible that some of the confessions at Salem were genuine. Some of the accused may actually have practiced witchcraft as they understood it. But undoubtedly a large percentage of the confessions were made simply to obtain mercy. Men and women who lied were thus released, whereas those whose bravery and honesty forbade them to lie were hanged. These brave men and women were Puritans too, better Puritans than those who confessed; their very Puritanism strengthened them in the refusal to purchase their lives at the cost of their souls.

Puritanism also affected the attitude of Massachusetts to the trials after they were over. No Puritan could do wrong and think lightly of it afterward. God was merciful to the repentant but not to those who failed to acknowledge their errors. And within five years of the witch trials, the people of Massachusetts knew that they had done wrong. They did not cease to believe in witchcraft, nor did they suppose that the devil had lost his powers or was less dangerous than before. But they did recognize that the trials had been unfair, that men and women had been convicted on insufficient evidence, that the devil had deluded the prosecutors more than the defendants. It was possible that Massachusetts had judicially murdered innocent men and women. The people therefore set aside a day, January 15, 1697, as a day of fasting, in which the whole colony might repent. On that day, Samuel Sewall, one of the judges, stood up in church while the minister, at his request, read his confession of guilt and his desire to take "the blame and shame" of the trials on himself. The jurors who had sat in the trials published their own confession. "We ourselves," they wrote, "were not capable to understand nor able to withstand the mysterious delusion of the power of darkness and prince of the air, whereby we fear we have been instrumental with others, though ignorantly and unwillingly, to bring upon ourselves the guilt of innocent blood."

These confessions brought no one back to life, but who will deny that it was good and right to make them? In 1927 the state of Massachusetts executed two men named Sacco and Vanzetti. They may have been guilty, just as some of the Salem witches may have been guilty, but experts agree that they did not receive a fair trial. A few years ago when the governor of Massachusetts acknowledged that fact officially, the people of Massachusetts, through their elected representatives, rebuked him. But today the people of Massachusetts are no longer Puritans and feel no need for contrition.

A knowledge of Puritanism can help us to penetrate behind the mask that disguises some of the characters in *The Crucible* and obscures the forces at work in the Salem tragedy. Arthur Miller knew his characters well enough as human beings so that they are never concealed from him by his faulty image of Puritanism. But he does not know them as Puritans. Too often their humanity is revealed as something at odds with Puritanism. We need to understand that their Puritanism was not really at issue in the tragedy. Insofar as it entered, it affected protagonist and antagonist alike. It conceals the issue to make Samuel Parris wear the mask of Puritanism and John Proctor stand like some nineteenth-century Yankee populist thrust back into Cotton Mather's court. Parris and Proctor were both Puritans and both men. We should not look on Proctor's refusal to confess as a triumph of man over Puritan. It was a triumph of man over man and of Puritan over Puritan. Elizabeth Proctor was a Puritan and a woman; we should not see her as a Puritan when she is cold to her husband and a woman when she is warm.

In other words, the profounder implications of the action in the play are darkened by a partial identification of the antagonist as Puritanism. The identification is never complete. If it were, the play would be merely a piece of flattery. But Miller has offered his audience an escape they do not deserve. He has allowed them a chance to think that John Proctor asserted the dignity of man against a benighted and outworn creed. Proctor did nothing of the kind. Proctor asserted the dignity of man against man. Man is the antagonist against which human dignity must always be defended; not against Puritanism, not against Nazism or communism, or McCarthyism, not against the Germans or the Russians or the Chinese, not against the Middle Ages or the Roman Empire. As long as we identify the evil in the world with some particular creed or with some other people remote in time or place, we flatter ourselves and cheapen the dignity and greatness of those who resist evil. The Germans, we say, or the Russians are inhuman beasts who trample humanity in the mud. We would never do such a thing. Belsen is in Germany. Salem Village is in the seventeenth century. It is a comforting and specious thought. It allows us to escape from the painful knowledge that has informed the great religions, knowledge incidentally that the Puritans always kept before them, the knowledge that all of us are capable of evil. The glory of human dignity is that any man may show it. The tragedy is that we are all equally capable of denying it.

WENDY SCHISSEL

Re(dis)covering the Witches in
Arthur Miller's The Crucible:
A Feminist Reading

Arthur Miller's *The Crucible* is a disturbing work, not only because of
the obvious moral dilemma that is irresolutely solved by John Proctor's
death, but also because of the treatment that Abigail and Elizabeth receive
at Miller's hands and at the hands of critics. In forty years of criticism
very little has been said about the ways in which *The Crucible* reinforces
stereotypes of *femme fatales* and cold and unforgiving wives in order to assert
apparently universal virtues. It is a morality play based upon a questionable
androcentric morality. Like Proctor, *The Crucible* "[roars] down" Elizabeth,
making her concede a fault which is not hers but of Miller's making: "It
needs a cold wife to prompt lechery,"[1] she admits in her final meeting with
her husband. Critics have seen John as a "tragically heroic common man,"[2]
humanly tempted, "a just man in a universe gone mad,"[3] but they have
never given Elizabeth similar consideration, nor have they deconstructed
the phallologocentric sanctions implicit in Miller's account of Abigail's fate,
Elizabeth's confession, and John's temptation and death. As a feminist reader
of the 1990s, I am troubled by the unrecognized fallout from the existential
hu*man*ism that Miller and his critics have held dear. *The Crucible* is in need
of an/Other reading, one that reveals the assumptions of the text, the author,
and the reader/critic who "is part of the shared consciousness created by
the [play]."[4] It is time to reveal the vicarious enjoyment that Miller and his

From *Modern Drama*, vol. 37, no. 3 (Fall 1994): pp. 461–473. © 1994 by University of Toronto
Press.

critics have found in a cathartic male character who has enacted their sexual and political fantasies.

The setting of *The Crucible* is a favoured starting point in an analysis of the play. Puritan New England of 1692 may indeed have had its parallels to McCarthy's America of 1952,[5] but there is more to the paranoia than xenophobia—of Natives and Communists, respectively. Implicit in Puritan theology, in Miller's version of the Salem witch trials, and all too frequent in the society which has produced Miller's critics is gynecophobia—fear and distrust of women.

The "half dozen heavy books" (36) which the zealous Reverend Hale endows on Salem "like a bridegroom to his beloved, bearing gifts" (132) are books on witchcraft from which he has acquired an "armory of symptoms, catchwords, and diagnostic procedures" (36). A 1948 edition of the 1486 *Malleus Maleficarum* (*Hammer of Witches*), with a foreword by Montague Summers, may have prompted Miller's inclusion of seventeenth-century and Protestant elucidations upon a work originally sanctioned by the Roman Church.[6] Hale's books would be "highly misogynic" tomes, for like the *Malleus* they would be premised on the belief that "'All witchcraft comes from carnal lust which in women is insatiable.'"[7] The authors of the *Malleus*, two Dominican monks, Johan Sprenger and Heinrich Kraemer, were writing yet another fear-filled version of the apocryphal bad woman: they looked to Ecclesiasties which declares

> the wickedness of a woman is all evil ... there is no anger above the anger of a woman. It will be more agreeable to abide with a lion and a dragon, than to dwell with a wicked woman ... from the woman came the beginning of sin, and by her we all die. (25:17, 23, 33)

The Crucible is evidence that Miller partakes of similar fears about wicked, angry, or wise women; even if his complicity in such gynecophobia is unwitting—and that is the most generous thing we can accord him, a "misrecognition" of himself and his reputation-conscious hero John as the authors of a subjectivity[8] which belongs exclusively to men—the result for generations of readers has been the same. In Salem, the majority of witches condemned to die were women. Even so, Salem's numbers were negligible[9] compared with the gynocide in Europe: Andrea Dworkin quotes a moderate estimate of nine million witches executed at a ratio of women to men of as much as 100 to 1.[10] Miller assures us in one of his editorial and political (and long and didactic) comments, that despite the Puritans' belief in witchcraft, "there were no witches" (35) in Salem; his play, however, belies his claim, and so do his critics.

The Crucible is filled with witches, from the wise woman/healer Rebecca *Nurse* to the black woman Tituba, who initiates the girls into the dancing which has always been part of the communal celebrations of women healers/ witches.[11] But the most obvious witch in Miller's invention upon Salem *his*tory is Abigail Williams. She is the consummate seductress; the witchcraft hysteria in the play originates in *her* carnal lust for Proctor. Miller describes Abigail as *"a strikingly beautiful girl . . . with an endless capacity for dissembling"* (8–9). In 1953, William Hawkins called Abigail "an evil child";[12] in 1967, critic Leonard Moss said she was a "malicious figure" and "unstable";[13] in 1987, June Schlueter and James Flanagan proclaimed her "a whore,"[14] echoing Proctor's "How do you call Heaven! Whore! Whore!" (109); and in 1989, Bernard Dukore suggested that "if the *'strikingly beautiful'* Abigail's behaviour in the play is an indication, she may have been the one to take the initiative."[15]

The critics forget what Abigail cannot: "John Proctor . . . took me from my sleep and put knowledge in my heart!" (24). They, like Miller, underplay so as not openly to condone the "natural" behaviour of a man tempted to adultery because of a young woman's beauty and precociousness, her proximity in a house where there is also an *apparently* frigid wife, and the repression of Puritan society and religion. Abigail is a delectable commodity in what Luce Irigaray has termed a "dominant scopic economy."[16] We are covertly invited to equate John's admirable rebellion at the end of the play—against the unconscionable demands of implicating others in a falsely acknowledged sin of serving that which is antithetical to community (the Puritans called that antithesis the devil)—with his more self-serving rebellion against its sexual mores. The subtle equation allows Miller not only to project fault upon Abigail, but also to make what is really a clichéd act of adultery on John's part much more interesting. Miller wants us to recognize, if not celebrate, the individual trials of his existential hero, a "spokesman for rational feeling and disinterested intelligence" in a play about "integrity and its obverse, compromise."[17] Mary Daly might describe the scholarly support that Miller has received for his fantasy-fulfilling hero as "The second element of the Sado-Ritual [of the witch-craze] . . . [an] erasure of responsibility."[18]

No critic has asked, though, how a seventeen-year-old girl, raised in the household of a Puritan minister, can have the knowledge of how to seduce a man. (The only rationale offered scapegoats another woman, Tituba, complicating gynecophobia with xenophobia.) The omission on Miller's and his critics' parts implies that Abigail's sexual knowledge must be inherent in her gender. I see the condemnation of Abigail as an all too common example of blaming the victim.

Mercy Lewis's reaction to John is another indictment of the sexual precociousness of the girls of Salem. Obviously knowledgeable of John and

Abigail's affair, Mercy is both afraid of John and, Miller says, *"strangely titillated"* as she *"sidles out"* of the room (21). Mary Warren, too, knows: "Abby'll charge lechery on you, Mr. Proctor" (90), she says when he demands she tell what she knows about the "poppet" to the court. John is aghast: "She's told you!" (80). Rather than condemning John, all these incidents are included to emphasize the "vengeance of a little girl" (79), and, I would add, to convince the reader who is supposed to sympathize with John (or to feel titillation himself) that no girl is a "good girl," free of sexual knowledge, that each is her mother Eve's daughter.

The fact is, however, that Salem's young women, who have been preached at by a fire and brimstone preacher, Mr. Parris, are ashamed of their bodies. A gynocritical reading of Mary Warren's cramps after Sarah Good mumbles her displeasure at being turned away from the Proctor's door empty-handed is explainable as a "curse" of a more periodic nature:

> But *what* does she mumble? You must remember, Goody Proctor. Last Month—a Monday, I think—she walked away, and I thought my guts would burst for two days after. Do you remember it? (58)

The "girls" are the inheritors of Eve's sin, and their bodies are their reminders. Though, like all young people, they find ways to rebel—just because adolescence did not exist in Puritan society does not mean that the hormones did not flow—they are seriously repressed. And the most insidious aspect of that repression, in a society in which girls are not considered women until they marry (as young as fourteen, or significantly, with the onset of menses), is the turning of the young women's frustrations upon members of their own gender. It is not so strange as Proctor suggests for "a Christian girl to hang old women!" (58), when one such Christian girl claims her position in society with understandable determination: "I'll not be ordered to bed no more, Mr. Proctor! I am eighteen and a woman, however single!" (60). Paradoxically, of course, the discord only serves to prove the assumptions of a parochial society about the jealousies of women, an important aspect of this play in which Miller makes each woman in John's life claim herself as his rightful spouse: Elizabeth assures him that "I will be your only wife, or no wife at all!" (62); and Abigail makes her heart's desire plain with "I will make you such a wife when the world is white again!" (150). To realize her claim Abigail has sought the help of voodoo—Tituba's and the court's—to get rid of Elizabeth, but not without clear provocation on John's part.

Miller misses an opportunity to make an important comment upon the real and perceived competitions for men forced upon women in a patriarchal society by subsuming the women's concerns within what he knows his audience will recognize as more admirable communal and idealistic concerns. The eternal triangle motif, while it serves many interests for Miller, is, ultimately, less important than the overwhelming nobility of John's Christ-like martyrdom; against that the women's complaints seem petty indeed, and an audience whose collective consciousness recognizes a dutifully repentant hero also sees the women in his life as less sympathetic.[19] For Abigail and Elizabeth also represent the extremes of female sexuality—sultriness and frigidity, respectively—which test a man's body, endanger his spirit, and threaten his "natural" dominance or needs.

In order to make Abigail's seductive capability more believable and John's culpability less pronounced, Miller has deliberately raised Abigail's age ("A Note on the Historical Accuracy of This Play") from twelve to seventeen.[20] He introduces us to John and Abigail in the first act with John's acknowledgement of her young age. Abby—the diminutive form of her name is not to be missed—is understandably annoyed: "How do you call me child!" (23). We already know about his having "clutched" her back behind his house and "sweated like a stallion" at her every approach (22). Despite Abigail's allegations, Miller achieves the curious effect of making *her* the apparent aggressor in this scene—as critical commentary proves. Miller's ploy, to blame a woman for the Fall of a good man, is a sleight of pen as old as the Old Testament. There is something too convenient in the fact that "legend has it that Abigail turned up later as a prostitute in Boston" ("Echoes Down the Corridor"). Prostitution is not only the oldest profession, but it is also the oldest evidence for the law of supply and demand. Men demand sexual services of women they in turn regard as socially deviant. Miller's statement of Abigail's fate resounds with implicit forgiveness for the man who is unwittingly tempted by a fatal female, a conniving witch.

Miller's treatment of Abigail in the second scene of Act Two, left out of the original reading version and most productions but included as an appendix in contemporary texts of the play, is also dishonest. Having promised Elizabeth as she is being taken away in chains that "I will fall like an ocean on that court! Fear nothing" (78)—at the end of the first scene of Act Two—John returns to Abigail, alone and at night. The scene is both anticlimactic and potentially damning of the hero. What may have begun as Miller's attempt to have the rational John reason with Abigail, even with the defense that Elizabeth has adjured him to talk to her (61)—although that is before Elizabeth is herself accused—ends in a discussion that is dangerous to John's position in the play.

Miller wants us to believe, as Proctor does *"seeing her madness"* when she reveals her self-inflicted injuries, that Abigail is insane: "I'm holes all over from their damned needles and pins" (149). While Miller may have intended her madness to be a metaphor for her inherent evil—sociologists suggest that madness replaced witchcraft as a pathology to be treated not by burning or hanging but by physicians and incarceration in mental institutions[21]—he must have realized he ran the risk of making her more sympathetic than he intended. Miller is intent upon presenting John as a man haunted by guilt and aware of his own hypocrisy, and to make Abigail equally aware, even in a state of madness, is too risky. Her long speech about John's "goodness" cannot be tolerated because its irony is too costly to John.

> Why, you taught me goodness, therefore you are good. It were fire you walked me through, and all my ignorance was burned away. It were a fire, John, we lay in fire. And from that night no woman dare call me wicked any more but I knew my answer. I used to weep for my sins when the wind lifted up my skirts; and blushed for shame because some old Rebecca called me loose. And then you burned my ignorance away. As bare as some December tree I saw them all—walking like saints to church, running to feed the sick, and hypocrites in their hearts! And God gave me strength to call them liars, and God made men to listen to me, and by God I will scrub the world clean for the love of Him! (150)[22]

We must not forget, either, when we are considering critical commentary, that we are dealing with an art form which has a specular dimension. The many Abigails of the stage have no doubt contributed to the unacknowledged view of Abigail as siren/witch that so many critics have. In Jed Harris's original production in 1953, in Miller's own production of the same year (to which the later excised scene was first added), and in Laurence Olivier's 1965 production, Abigail was played by an actress in her twenties, not a young girl. The intent on each director's part had to have been to make Abigail's lust for John believable. Individual performers have consistently enacted the siren's role:

> The eyes of Madeleine Sherwood, who played Abigail in 1953, glowed with lust ... [but] Perhaps the most impressive Abigail has been that of Sarah Miles in 1965. A "plaguingly sexy mixture of beauty and crossness" ... Miles "reeks with the cunning of suppressed evil and steams with the promise of suppressed passion."[23]

Only the 1980 production of *The Crucible* by Bill Bryden employed girls who looked even younger than seventeen. Dukore suggests that Bryden's solution to the fact that John's "seduction of a teenage girl half his age appears not to have impressed (critics) as a major fault" was "ingenious yet (now that he has done it) obvious."[24]

Abigail is not the only witch in Miller's play, though; Elizabeth, too, is a hag. But it is Elizabeth who is most in need of feminist reader-redemption. If John is diminished as Christian hero by a feminist deconstruction, the diminution is necessary to a balanced reading of the play and to a revised mythopoeia of the paternalistic monotheism of the Puritans and its twentieth-century equivalent, the existential mysticism of Miller.

John's sense of guilt is intended by Miller to act as salve to any emotional injuries given his wife and his own conscience. When his conscience cannot be calmed, when he quakes at doing what he knows must be done in revealing Abigail's deceit, it is upon Elizabeth that he turns his wrath:

> Spare me! You forget nothin' and forgive nothin'. Learn charity, woman. I have gone tiptoe in this house all seven month since she is gone. I have not moved from there to there without I think to please you, and still an everlasting funeral marches round your heart. I cannot speak but I am doubted, every moment judged for lies, as though I come into a court when I come into this house. (54–55)

What we are meant to read as understandably defensive anger—that is if we read within the patriarchal framework in which the play is written—must be re-evaluated; such a reading must be done in the light of Elizabeth's logic—paradoxically, the only "cold" thing about her. She is right when she turns his anger back on him with "the magistrate sits in your heart that judges you" (55). She is also right on two other counts. First, John has "a faulty understanding of young girls. There is a promise made in any bed" (61). The uninitiated and obviously self-punishing Abigail may be excused for thinking as she does (once again in the excised scene) that he is "singing secret hallelujahs that [his] wife will hang!" (152). Second, John *does* retain some tender feelings for Abigail despite his indignation. Elizabeth's question reverberates with insight: "if it were not Abigail that you must go to hurt, would you falter now? I think not" (54). John has already admitted to Abigail—and to us—in the first act that "I may think of you softly from time to time" (23), and he does look at her with *"the faintest suggestion of a knowing smile on his face"* (21). And John's use of wintry images of Elizabeth and their home in Act Two—"It's winter in her yet" (51)—echoes the imagery used by Abigail in Act One.[25] John is to Abigail "no wintry man," but one whose "heat" has drawn her to her window to see him looking up (23). She is the one who describes Elizabeth as "a cold, snivelling woman" (24), but it is Miller's favoured imagery for a stereotypically frigid wife who is no less a witch (in patriarchal lore) than a hot-blooded sperm-stealer like Abigail. Exacerbating all of this is the fact that John lies to Elizabeth about having been alone with Abigail in Parris's house; Miller would have us believe that John lies to save Elizabeth pain, but I believe he lies out of a rationalizing habit that he carries forward to his death.

Miller *may* want to be kind to Elizabeth, but he cannot manage that and John's heroism, too. Act Two opens with Elizabeth as hearth angel singing softly offstage to the children who are, significantly, never seen in the play, and bringing John his supper—stewed rabbit which, she says, "it hurt my heart to strip" (50). But in the space of four pages Miller upbraids her six times. First, John "is not quite pleased" (49) with the taste of Elizabeth's stew, and before she appears on stage he adds salt to it. Second, there is a "certain disappointment" (50) for John in the way Elizabeth receives his kiss. Third, John's request for "Cider?" made "*as gently as he can*" (51) leaves Elizabeth "*reprimanding herself for having forgot*" (51). Fourth, John reminds Elizabeth of the cold atmosphere in their house: "You ought to bring flowers in the house . . . It's winter in here yet" (51). Fifth, John perceives Elizabeth's melancholy as something perennial: "I think you're sad *again*" (51, emphasis added). And sixth, and in a more overtly condemning mood, John berates Elizabeth when he discovers that she has allowed Mary Warren to go to Salem to testify: "It is a fault, it is a fault, Elizabeth—you're the mistress here" (52). Cumulatively, these criticisms work to arouse sympathy for a man who would *season* his meal, his home, and his *amour*, a man who is meant to appeal to us because of his sensual awareness of spring's erotic promise: "It's warm as blood beneath the clods" (50), and "I never see such a load of flowers on the earth. . . . Lilacs have a purple smell. Lilac is the smell of nightfall" (51). We, too, are seasoned to believe that John really does "[aim] to please" Elizabeth, and that Elizabeth is relentless in her admonishing of John for his affair, of which she is knowledgeable. It is for John that we are to feel sympathy when he says, "Let you look to your own improvement before you go to judge your husband more" (54). Miller has informed us of several ways in which Elizabeth could improve herself.

Neil Carson claims that "Miller intends the audience to view Proctor ironically" in this scene; Proctor, he says, is "a man who is rationalising in order to avoid facing himself," and at the beginning of Act Two "Proctor is as guilty as any of projecting his own faults onto others."[26] While I find much in Carson's entire chapter on *The Crucible* as sensitive a criticism of the play as any written, I am still uncomfortable about the fact that a "tragic victory" for the protagonist[27] necessarily means an admission of guilt for his wife—once again, it seems to me, a victim is being blamed.

No critic, not even Carson, questions Miller's insistence that Elizabeth is at least partly to blame for John's infidelity. Her fate is sealed in the lie she tells for love of her husband because she proves him a liar: "as in *All My Sons*," says critic Leonard Moss, "a woman inadvertently betrays her husband."[28] John has told several lies throughout the play, but it is Elizabeth's lie that the critics (and Miller) settle upon, for once again the lie fits the stereotype—

woman as liar, woman as schemer, woman as witch sealing the fate of man the would-be hero.

But looked at another way, Elizabeth is not a liar. The question put to her by Judge Danforth is "is [present tense] your husband a lecher!" (113). Elizabeth can in good conscience respond in the negative for she knows the affair to be over. She has no desire to condemn the man who has betrayed her, for she believes John to be nothing but a "good man ... only somewhat bewildered" (55). Once again, though, her comment condemns her because an audience hears (and Miller perhaps intends) condescension on her part. The patriarchal reading is invited by John's ironic response: "Oh, Elizabeth, your justice would freeze beer!" (55). What seems to be happening is that Goody Proctor is turned into a goody two-shoes, a voice of morality. Why we should expect anything else of Elizabeth, raised within a Puritan society and a living example of its valued "good woman," escapes me. I find it amazing that the same rules made but not obeyed by "good" men can be used to condemn the women who do adhere to them.

The other thing which Miller and the critics seem unwilling to acknowledge is the hurt that Elizabeth feels over John's betrayal; instead, her anger, elicited not specifically about the affair but about the incident with the poppet, following hard upon the knowledge of Giles Corey's wife having been taken, is evidence that she is no good woman. Her language condemns her: "[Abigail] is murder! She must be ripped out of the world!" (76). Anger in woman, a danger of which Ecclesiastes warns, has been cause for locking her up for centuries.

After Elizabeth's incarceration, and without her persistent logic, Miller is able to focus on John and his sense of failure. But Elizabeth's last words as she is taken from her home are about the children: "When the children wake, speak nothing of witchcraft—it will frighten them. *She cannot go on*. . . . Tell the children I have gone to visit someone sick" (77–78). I find it strange that John's similar concerns when he has torn up the confession—"I have three children—how may I teach them to walk like men in the world, and I sold my friends?" (143)—should be valued above Elizabeth's. Is it because the children are boys? Is it because Elizabeth is expected to react in the maternal fashion that she does, but for John to respond thus is a sign of sensitive masculinity? Is it because the communal as defined by the Word is threatened by the integrity of women? And why is maintaining a name more important than living? At least alive he might attend to his children's daily needs—after all, we are told about the sad situation of the "orphans walking from house to house" (130).[29]

It would be foolish to argue that John does not suffer—that, after all, is the point of the play. But what of Elizabeth's suffering? She is about to lose her husband, her children are without parents, she is sure to be condemned to death as well. Miller must, once again, diminish the threat that Elizabeth offers to John's martyrdom, for he has created a woman who does not lie, who her husband believes would not give the court the admission of guilt "if tongs of fine were singeing" her (138). Miller's play about the life and death struggle for a *man's* soul, cannot be threatened by a woman's struggle. In order to control his character, *Miller* impregnates her. The court will not sentence an unborn child, so Elizabeth does not have to make a choice. Were she to choose to die without wavering in her decision, as both John and Miller think she would, she would be a threat to the outcome of the play and the sympathy which is supposed to accrue to John. Were she to make the decision to live, for the reasons which Reverend Hale stresses, that "Life, woman, life is God's most precious gift; no principle, however glorious, may justify the taking of it" (132), she would undermine existential integrity with compromise.

I am not reading another version of *The Crucible*, one which Miller did not intend, but rather looking at the assumptions inherent in his intentions, assumptions that Miller seems oblivious to and which his critics to date have questioned far too little. I, too, can read the play as a psychological and ethical contest which no one wins, and of which it can be said that both John and Elizabeth are expressions of men and women with all their failings and nobility, but I am troubled by the fact that Elizabeth is seldom granted even that much, that so much is made of Elizabeth's complicity in John's adultery, and that the victim of John's "virility,"[30] Abigail, is blamed because she is evil and/or mad. I do want to question the gender stereotypes in the play and in the criticism that has been written about it.

Let me indulge finally for a moment in another kind of criticism, one that is a fiction, or more precisely, a "crypto-friction" that defies "stratifications of canonical thought" and transgresses generic boundaries of drama/fiction and criticism.[31] Like Virginia Woolf I would like to speculate on a play written by a fictional sister to a famous playwright. Let us call Arthur Miller's wide-eyed younger sister, who believes she can counter a scopic economy by stepping beyond the mirror, *Alice* Miller. In Alice's play, Elizabeth and John suffer equally in a domestic problem which is exacerbated by the hysteria around them. John does not try to intimidate Elizabeth with his anger, and she is not described as cold or condescending. Abigail is a victim of an older man's lust and not inherently a "bad girl"; she is not beautiful or if she is the playwright does not make so much of it. Her calling out of witches would be explained by wiser critics as the result of her fear and her confusion, not her lust. There is no effort made in Alice's play to create a hero at the expense of the female characters, or a heroine at the expense of a male character. John is no villain, but—as another male victim/hero character, created by a woman, describes himself—"a trite, commonplace sinner,"[32] trying to right a wrong he admits—without blaming others.

Or, here is another version, written by another, more radical f(r)ictional sister, *Mary* Miller, a real hag. In it, all the witches celebrate the death of John Proctor. The idea comes from two sources: first, a question from a female student who wanted to know if part of Elizabeth's motivation in not pressing her husband to confess is her desire to pay him back for his betrayal; and second, from a response to Jean-Paul Sartre's ending for the film *Les Sorcières de Salem*. In his 1957 version of John Proctor's story, Sartre identifies Elizabeth "with the God of prohibiting sex and the God of judgment," but he has her save Abigail, who tries to break John out of jail and is in danger of being hanged as a traitor too, because Elizabeth realizes "'she loved [John].'" As the film ends, "Abigail stands shocked in a new understanding."[33]

In Mary Miller's version Elizabeth is not identified with the male God of the Word, but with the goddesses of old forced into hiding or hanged because of a *renaissance* of patriarchal ideology. Mary's witches come together, alleged seductress and cold wife alike, not for love of a man who does not deserve either, but to celebrate life and their victory over male character, playwright, and critics, "'men in power' ... who create and identify with the roles of both the victimizers and the victims," men who Mary Miller would suggest "vicariously enjoyed the women's suffering."[34]

NOTES

1. Arthur Miller, *The Crucible* (New York, 1981), 137. The play was originally published in 1953, but all further references to *The Crucible* are to the 1981 Penguin edition, and will be noted parenthetically in the text.

2. June Schlueter and James K. Flanagan, *Arthur Miller* (New York, 1987), 68.

3. Neil Carson, *Arthur Miller* (New York, 1982), 61.

4. Sandra Kemp, "'But how describe a world seen without self?' Feminism, fiction and modernism," *Critical Quarterly* 32:1 (1990), 99–118: 104.

5. Miller's interest in the Salem witchcraft trials predated his confrontation with McCarthyism (see E. Miller Budick, "History and Other Spectres in *The Crucible*," *Arthur Miller*, ed. Harold Bloom (New York, 1987), 127–28, but it is also clear from the Introduction to Miller's *Collected Plays* Vol 1 (New York, 1957) that he capitalized upon popular response and critical commentary which linked the two. Miller has been, it seems, a favoured critic on the subject of Arthur Miller.

6. In 1929 George L. Kittredge published a work called *Witchcraft in Old and New England* (Cambridge) in which he remarked that "the doctrines of our forefathers differed [in regard to witchcraft] from the doctrines of the Roman and Anglican Church in no essential—one may safely add, in no particular" (21). In *Gyn\Ecology: The Metaethics of Radical Feminism* (Boston, 1978), Mary Daly says that during the European witch burnings—she does not deal with the Salem witch trials—Protestants "vied with and even may have surpassed their catholic counterparts in their fanaticism and cruelty" (185–86).

7. Cited by Peter Conrad and Joseph W. Schneider, *Deviance and Medicalization: From Badness to Sickness*, expanded edition (Philadelphia, 1992), 42.

8. Chris Weedon, *Feminist Practice and Poststructuralist Theory* (Oxford, 1987), 30–31.

9. "Nineteen women and men and two dogs were hanged, one man was pressed to death for refusing to plead, and 150 were imprisoned" (see Schlueter and Flanagan, 72).

10. "Remembering the Witches," *Our Blood: Prophecies and Discourses on Sexual Politics* (London, 1982), 16–17. See also the 1990 National Film Board production, *The Burning Times*, directed by Donna Read, which declares the European executions for witchcraft to have been a "women's holocaust." Of the nine million people the film numbers among the burned, hanged, or otherwise disposed of, 85 per cent, it reports, were women.

11. *The Burning Times* discusses at length the place of women healers in Third-World cultures.

12. From Hawkins's review of the play in *File on Miller*, ed. Christopher Bigsby (London, 1988), 30.

13. Leonard Moss, *Arthur Miller* (New York, 1967), 60, 63.

14. Schlueter and Flanagan, 69.

15. Bernard Dukore, *"Death of a Salesman" and "The Crucible": Text and Performance* (Houndmills, Basingstoke, Hampshire and London, 1989), 50.

16. Luce Irigaray, "This Sex Which Is Not One," *New French Feminisms: An Anthology*, ed. Elaine Marks and Isabelle de Courtivron (Amherst, 1980), 101.

17. The only critic I have read who has made comments even remotely similar to my own regarding Abigail is Neil Carson. In a 1982 book he remarks that "Abigail is portrayed as such an obviously bad piece of goods that it takes a clear-eyed French critic to point out that Proctor was not only twice the age of the girl he seduced, but as her employer he was breaking a double trust" (75). Despite his insight, when it comes to explaining the effect of Miller's omission of detail regarding the early stages of the affair, he does not, I think, realize its full implications. He says that "Proctor's sense of guilt [seems] a little forced and perhaps not really justified," but I think the choice was deliberately made so as to minimize John's guilt and emphasize his redemption as an existential man. Conversely, Abigail is more easily targeted (as the critics prove) for her active role in her seduction.

18. Daly, 187.

19. Carol Billman ("Women and the Family in American Drama," *Arizona Quarterly* 36: 1 [1980], 35–48) discusses the study of "everyman" made in the family dramas of O'Neill, Williams, Albee, and Miller (although she does not mention *The Crucible*): "women necessarily occupy a central position, [but] little attention is paid to their subordination or suffering.... Linda Loman [and I would add Elizabeth Proctor] ... suffers at least as much as her husband" (36–7). Victoria Sullivan and James Hatch, as well, have complained about the standards of review: "'*a complaining female protagonist is automatically less noble than Stanley Kowalski or Willy Loman ... [only] men suffer greatly*'" (quoted in Billman, 37, emphasis added).

20. Carson, 66. In a play that is historically accurate in so many ways, it is significant to note that the affair between John and Abigail was invented by Miller (Dukore, 43).

21. Conrad and Schneider, 43.

22. I think that whether or not one sees the irony as intentional on Abby's part, she becomes more sympathetic. If intentional we can agree with her realization that John's hypocrisy was least when he was seducing her; he is a commonplace lecher. If Abigail is not cognizant of the extent of the irony of what she is saying, then she truly is too young—or too emotionally disturbed—to understand the implications of what she is doing.
Carson again comes close to making a very astute judgment about Abigail's awareness of events going on around her: "It seems clear that we are to attribute at least a little of Abby's 'wildness' and sensuality to her relationship with John, and to assume that the 'knowledge' which Proctor put in Abigail's heart is not simply carnal, but also includes some awareness

of the hypocrisy of some of the Christian women and covenanted men of the community" (68). Carson's insight, however, is limited by his belief in the "'radical' side of Proctor's nature," something with which modern audiences are sure to identify. The problem here is that the focus is once more removed from Abigail's plight to her vicarious participation in one more of John Proctor's admirable traits, for his "is not a simple personality like that of Rebecca Nurse" (68).

23. Dukore, 102.

24. Ibid., 95.

25. One critic, who celebrates John's "playfulness" and who does not want his description of John as a liar to be taken in a pejorative sense, suggests that John and Abigail share a kindred spirit: "The physical attractiveness of Abby for John Proctor is obvious in the play, but, I think, so is the passionate imagination which finds its outlet in one way in her and in another in Proctor" (William T. Liston, "John Proctor's Playing in *The Crucible*," *Midwest Quarterly: A Journal of Contemporary Thought* 20:4 (1979), 394–403: 403). John is a liar—that is part of his guilt—and to suggest that Abigail offers John something that Elizabeth does not condemns Elizabeth and exonerates John even more than Miller intends.

26. Carson, 69–70.

27. Ibid., 75.

28. Leonard Moss, *Arthur Miller*, revised edition (Boston, 1980), 40, emphasis added.

29. I think it significant that the orphans are but one of the wasted possessions unattended to in Salem. The next part of the same sentence mentions abandoned cattle bellowing and rotted crops stinking. Miller has described a material and contemporary world.

30. Richard Hayes, "Hysteria and Ideology in *The Crucible*," *Twentieth Century Interpretations of "The Crucible*," ed. John H. Ferres (Englewood Cliffs, 1972), 34. I find it interesting and instructive that a 1953 review of the play uses the term to describe Arthur Kennedy's portrayal of John Proctor.

31. Aritha Van Herk, *In Visible Ink (crypto-frictions)* (Edmonton, 1991), 14.

32. Charlotte Brontë, *Jane Eyre* (Harmondsworth, 1984), 160.

33. Eric Mottram, "Jean-Paul Sartre's *Les Sorcières de Salem*," *Twentieth Century Interpretations of "The Crucible*," 93, 94.

34. Daly, 215.

THOMAS P. ADLER

Conscience and Community in
An Enemy of the People
and The Crucible

"It's all clear to me now, finally at this late hour. They had their script. I
had mine. Theirs: 'Confess, lie, and you'll live.'"
Tema Nason, *Ethel [Rosenberg]: The Fictional Autobiography* (1990)

When the Wooster Group, one of the more controversial of the experimental
theatrical troupes active during the 1970s and 1980s, incorporated segments
of *The Crucible* (1953) into their performance piece entitled *LSD (... Just
the High Points ...)* (1984), Arthur Miller's threat of legal action eventually
forced the project to be withdrawn from the stage. Even though the excerpts
included from Miller's work were reduced first from forty-five minutes to
twenty-five minutes and then later to ten minutes—and that recited virtually
in gibberish—the dramatist objected on the grounds that such a treatment
might be regarded as a parody, which violated his initial intention, rather than
an homage, and so might somehow preclude a serious New York revival of
his play. Not only does Miller's action provide a fascinating case study in the
ongoing debate over who "owns" or maintains interpretive authority over the
written text when it becomes a performance text—the author or the director—
it also evidences what might seem a peculiar paradox. As David Savran notes,
"By insisting on his own interpretation, Miller has, ironically, aligned himself
with the very forces that *The Crucible* condemns, those authorities who

From *The Cambridge Companion to Arthur Miller*, Christopher Bigsby, ed., pp. 86–100. © 1997
by Cambridge University Press.

exercise their power arrogantly and arbitrarily to ensure their own continued political and cultural dominion."[1] The creators of *LSD* had, in fact, signaled this in their greatly reduced version by uttering "accidental lines" from Miller's work which were then "silenced by the buzzer" in order to demonstrate the "enforced suppression" (*Wooster*, p. 193) that their performance piece, itself concerned with victimization and cultural oppression, experienced because of the playwright's objections. Yet, in 1961, Miller had raised not the least demur when Bernard Stambler reproduced much of his dramatic text verbatim in the libretto to his and composer Robert Ward's operatic version (which went on to win the Pulitzer Prize for Music).

An additional irony presents itself in that, immediately before writing *The Crucible*, Miller, in adapting *An Enemy of the People* (1950), had subjected Ibsen's 1882 play to his own interpretation. As Gerald Rabkin comments, Miller himself "*has* changed textuality by not hesitating to revise his dramatic texts *after* initial production . . . and he was not constrained by the playwright's intentionality in his version of Ibsen's *An Enemy of the People*, which eliminated all unsympathetic ambiguity from [Dr. Thomas] Stockmann's character."[2] Essentially, Miller removes what he saw as potentially a protofascist strain in Stockmann's espousal of an evolving aristocracy of leaders with broad powers to mould community standards. In his autobiography, *Timebends*, Miller justifies his alteration of Ibsen's original by remarking upon the discomfort he "felt with one or two of its implications. Though Dr. Stockmann fights admirably for absolute license to tell society the truth, he goes on to imply the existence of an unspecified elite that can prescribe what people are to believe," concluding that it "is indefensible in a democratic society, albeit the normal practice, to ascribe superior prescience to a self-elected group."[3]

Apart from the shadings in the protagonist's character and Miller's introduction of more colloquial language, the alterations between original and adaptation might be accounted minimal; perhaps the most significant, given the political climate of the 1950s in which he wrote, is the addition of a speech by Stockmann's brother Peter, the town's mayor, which suggests how, sensing some internal threat to its stability, even a democracy might rationalize the adoption of totalitarian tactics in the name of preserving security and avoiding revolution: "Now, God knows, in ordinary times I'd agree a hundred percent with anybody's right to say anything. But these are not ordinary times" (*An Enemy of the People*, p. 89). In the Preface to his adaptation of *An Enemy of the People*—which he terms "a new translation into spoken English" (p. 12) and which lasted originally for only thirty-six performances—Miller isolates those qualities that to his way of thinking make Ibsen "really pertinent today," chief among them being "his insistence, his utter conviction, that he is going to say what he has to say, and that the audience, by God, is going to listen," and his belief in the dramatist's "right to entertain with his brains as well as his heart," that is, "the stage [as] *the* place for ideas" (pp. 7–8). Regardless of whether this accurately articulates Ibsen's characteristic contribution, *Enemy* is very much in the nature of a dramatized debate. The question it poses is: what is the nature of good government, and, when, if ever, does adherence to abstract principles, either in support of or in revolt against a lawfully constituted government, become an extreme that cannot be tolerated if individual rights and the community are to be protected?

The bureaucrats in power in this Norwegian town, led by Peter Stockmann, define an authoritarian, hierarchical, homogeneous ideal, in which the individual remains subordinate to the state, tolerance extends only to non-dissenters of like mind, and basic rights, such as free speech, can be abrogated at will or whim for expediency's sake, all in the name of maintaining indispensable "moral authority." The radical challenge to this theory of government comes from Dr. Thomas Stockmann, who envisions a more representative society in which those outside the traditional governing class are somehow brought within the net, in order that their "ability, self-respect, and intelligence" can be nurtured. To make his point about an ideal form of participatory democracy—a kind of Deweyan deliberative community—in which an enlightened electorate is empowered by the very act of its participation, the doctor dons the mayor's hat, his "official insignia," that can, unlike a crown, be worn by whomever the people choose. At this point, he thinks they will unquestioningly support his self-assumed mission of purifying the town's fetid waters, which are symbolic of a deeper "pestilence" of intolerance and suppression rotting the society.

In *The Quintessence of Ibsenism*, G. B. Shaw not only pinpointed as Ibsen's chief structural innovation the introduction of "discussion" into the drama, but delineated as foremost in Ibsen's agenda the destruction of ideals, that is, of those lies that prevent one's living in and accepting unadorned reality. In fact, the progress of numerous Shavian protagonists as various as Major Barbara and St. Joan is an emphatically educative one similar to the pattern he had detected at work in Ibsen: from idealism or illusion, through disillusionment, to reality. The doctor in *Enemy*, with his credo of "blow[ing] up every lie we live by" (*An Enemy of the People*, p. 66), gives ample proof of this Shavian art of destroying ideals, most startlingly of the notion that "the majority is always right." Perhaps following the lead of John Stuart Mill, who proclaimed in *On Liberty* (1859) that "No government, by a democracy or a numerous aristocracy, either in its political acts or in the opinions, qualities, and tone of mind, ever did or could rise above mediocrity, except in so far as the Many have let themselves be guided (which in their best times they have always done) by the counsels and influence of a more highly gifted and instructed One or Few,"[4] Thomas Stockmann asserts that, in fact, "the majority is always wrong" (*An Enemy of the People*, p. 94). Since majority rule results in a leveled-down, lowest common denominator of "meatheads," the enlightened "*one* must know" the truth—and by implication lead—"before many can" (p. 95). So Stockmann, branded a "criminal" and a "traitor" by the majority, must become at least a gadfly if not a revolutionist.

Although Miller leaves the basic tenet underlying the doctor's actions unchallenged, he does (as Rabkin noted) present a less flawed Stockmann than Ibsen. In both works, the idealistic doctor naively believes that people will always go with the truth, even when doing so threatens their material well-being; and so when he reveals that the town's medicinal baths feed on polluted springs, he confidently expects they will be rebuilt using tax dollars. Yet, though he might leave a patient half-bandaged while he runs off to make his case, or rant about having the walls scrubbed to remove the moral filth after Peter's visit, or mistakenly think the townspeople will confer upon him sainthood for carrying on his crusade, Miller's protagonist is never quite so "muddleheaded" as Ibsen portrayed him as being. For Miller has deliberately removed certain tendencies that he feared would be found racist by his audiences—such as an intimation about eugenics and biological engineering to breed a superior governing class—arguing that it would be "inconceivable" for Ibsen ever to have intended that to be the case. Rather, again like Mill, Ibsen argues for "'the aristocracy of character, of will, of mind—that alone can free us'" (p. 10).

Miller's Stockmann, nevertheless, is still generously over-endowed with a messiah complex. He embraces as a form of solitary martyrdom the designation "enemy of the people" (Miller's mob, in fact, is even darker than Ibsen's and linked more nearly with the American public of the Cold War fifties), and his missionary zeal perhaps verges on madness. Along with specifically likening himself to Galileo, the doctor identifies himself with Christ; the bribes that he is offered if he will compromise his position seem akin to Satan's temptations of Jesus in the wilderness. In response to the townspeople "crucifying their hero," he will gather around himself a "school of twelve" disciples—in this instance, young people with free and independent minds—whom he and his daughter Petra, who with her sincerely espoused doctrine of work represents the hope for the future, will instruct. And, like Christ, he is betrayed, both by his brother/enemy (à la Cain and Abel) as well as by the representative of the liberal press. Undoubtedly alluding to his own fellow liberals who buckled under to outside pressure, Miller condemns the unprincipled editor Hovstad, who ultimately temporizes and sells out for financial security, because he "DIDN'T DARE." Very handily, Miller can find in Ibsen's original text a profoundly ironic commentary on the contemporary political situation of paranoia and persecution when Dr. Stockmann muses about "go[ing] to America" where "the spirit must be bigger" and "at least there must be more room to hide" (p. 101).

The lessened ambiguity in Miller's handling of Dr. Stockmann may be linked to another facet of Ibsen's writing that his literary descendant could well have pointed to, and assuredly found congenial: an antithetical mode of thinking. In *Enemy* this is configured as an absolute opposition between society and the individual, the majority and the minority, power and truth. The tendency to privilege one side of the binary over the other results not only in didacticism but in what some would construe as dogmatism. This makes for a moral system that is generally more Manichaean than nuanced in nature. Miller, while insisting vehemently on the individual's "need, if not holy right, to resist the pressure to conform" to society (*Timebends*, p. 324)—which would appear to signal a totally relativistic or pluralistic perspective—still remains a moral absolutist. As he writes in his preface to *Enemy*, "At rock bottom, then, the play is concerned with the inviolability of objective truth" (*An Enemy of the People*, p. 9). What Miller, in fact, found most perplexing and frightening about the late forties and early fifties "was not only the rise of 'McCarthyism' . . . but something which seemed much more weird and mysterious. It was the fact that a political, objective, knowledgeable campaign from the far Right was capable of creating not only a terror, but a new subjective reality, a veritable mystique which was gradually assuming even a holy resonance."[5] What seems most to have disturbed him, then, was a confusion of the relative with the absolute, so that "subjective reality" could be foisted off as "objective truth."

Although it initially ran for only 197 performances when it opened on Broadway, *The Crucible* has become Miller's most frequently produced play. (At this writing, a new film version starring Daniel Day-Lewis and Winona Ryder is before the cameras in Massachusetts.) Since increasingly most audiences will no longer remember the particular sociopolitical situation of anti-Communism that reached its apogee in the House Un-American Activities Committee hearings, Miller has made the claim that "if I hadn't written *The Crucible* that period would be unregistered in our literature on any popular level," and that it continues to be the work that he "feel[s] proudest" of "because I made something lasting out of a violent but brief turmoil."[6] Partial proof of that "lasting" quality might be found, Miller muses, in the appeal the work exerts at times of political upheaval, when audiences around the world seem to have taken it to heart as "either a warning of tyranny on the way or a reminder of tyranny just past" (*Timebends*, p. 348). Yet from Miller's personal perspective as a writer, that tumultuous period in America's history—which saw him being denied a passport in 1954 to travel to the play's Brussels premiere and being found in contempt of Congress in 1957 (though never imprisoned) for his refusal to incriminate friends by naming names of Communist sympathizers—evidences a phenomenon every bit as troubling as the demand for ideological purity: a deep-seated fear of the artist's power and influence. As Miller would formulate it in his autobiography years later,

"The overwhelmingly significant truth, I thought, as I still do, was the artist-hating brutality of the Committee and its envy of its victims' power to attract public attention and to make big money at it besides" (*Timebends*, p. 242.).

In *An Enemy of the People*, the literal text which is read, and which to Miller's way of thinking passes the test of "objective truth," is comprised of the scientific report that Dr. Stockmann receives through the mails that confirms the fact of bacterial pollution and that he then shares with the public authorities and the Norwegian press, expecting them to receive its evidence unquestioningly and move to the same conclusion as he has about an ethically appropriate course of action. In Puritan New England, as C. W. E. Bigsby provocatively suggests, those wielding religious and political power claim to possess an authorized text requiring "a singular reading of the world, a reality constituted by those who claim to possess or interpret the Word."[7] In fact, to study the witch trials themselves necessarily "becomes," as Bernard Rosenthal claims, "a textual problem—one of narration, of weighing competing narratives against each other for their reliability."[8] To a large extent, this proves true of Miller's play as well, for in *The Crucible* there are several texts that are "read" and either interpreted or misinterpreted. First, the playwright himself reads and finds an analogy between two historical texts: that of Salem at the time of the witch-hunt in 1692; and that of America in the McCarthy era of the 1950s. Abigail, as we shall see, likewise reads the "text" of the Puritan community and its believers, just as both she and Elizabeth will turn the body of John Proctor—its gestures, its expressions—into a text to be read; if Abigail, for example, finds love and loneliness in his face and interprets his "blush" as evidence of continuing sexual temptation, Elizabeth interprets it as shame and embarrassment over his character flaw.

Although Miller begins his "Note on the Historical Accuracy" of *The Crucible* by stating emphatically "This play is not history" (*Collected Plays*, p. 224), it most definitely constitutes a reading of history, with the playwright explicitly rendering his personal interpretation in the narrative interludes—available to readers of the text but not to audiences in the theatre—that he intersperses within the dialogue. In these, he not only expresses his value judgments upon the Puritan community, but also establishes the lineage for those strains he finds still alive in the America of his time. Employing the mythic opposition between civilization and the wilderness, he pictures a society on the edge of a "virgin forest [that] was the Devil's last preserve and home to marauding Indian tribes"; its "parochial snobbery" over their moral destiny—the conviction "that they held in their steady hands the candle that would light the world"—exacerbated by (as Paul Boyer and Stephen Nissenbaum have confirmed)[9] dissension over religious leadership, property rights, economic change, sexual repression, and the movement "toward greater individual freedom," all of which helped fuel persecution of the Other as a way to forestall a fractious dissolution. The Puritan theocracy, in short, had to be built upon an ideology of "exclusion and prohibition" in order to survive (*Collected Plays*, p. 228). Those who felt the least rebellion against the Establishment were almost forced, then, to channel their own guilt into accusations demonizing the Other. Several commentators have suggested that when Miller comes to set up the conflict between the Puritan theocracy and the authority of individual conscience in *The Crucible*, he might be distorting aspects of the former in order unswervingly to espouse the latter. E. Miller Budick, for instance, points to the "moral arrogance" of what she designates as "Miller's own narrator" in dredging up "his Puritan forbears' ethical deficiencies," while Edmund Morgan believes that the dramatist has set up Puritanism as a straw man or escape hatch that allows audiences to transfer their own moral inadequacies to its "benighted and outworn creed."[10]

One inheritance from Puritanism, Miller suggests, is the continuing application of religious categories to political actions, so that the nation is seen as having a "mission." Another is categorizing things in terms of "diametrically opposed absolutes," so that "a political policy is equated with moral right, and opposition to it with diabolical malevolence." As a consequence, "in America, any man who is not reactionary in his views is open to the charge of alliance with the Red hell" (*Collected Plays*, p. 249). If, in Salem, Miller discerned at work a "cleansing" through a "projection of one's own vileness onto others in order to wipe it out with their blood," in 1950s America he sadly found "a public rite of contrition ... an obligatory kowtow before the state, the century's only credible god" (*Timebends*, pp. 337, 395). So the McCarthy hearings, "profoundly ritualistic" in themselves, become, in Miller's reading of the two historical periods, "a surreal spiritual transaction that connected Washington to Salem." The analogy at the base of Miller's political allegory has, however, not gone unquestioned, particularly by those who would argue that whereas there really never had been any witches in Salem, there most assuredly were Communists to be ferreted out. For his part Miller replied that anyone denying the existence of witches in 1692 would have been guaranteed a short life.

The first significant prop that Miller introduces into his play is a stack of books. When the Reverend Hale, summoned from Beverly to Salem to help in the initial investigation of witchcraft, enters, he comes onto the stage carrying several "heavy" tomes on demonology "weighted [down] with authority." He goes on to describe their contents: "Here is all the invisible world, caught, defined, and calculated. In these books the Devil stands stripped of all his brute disguises. Here are all your familiar spirits—your incubi and succubi; your witches that go by land, by air, and by sea; your wizards of the night and of the day" (*Collected Plays*, p. 253). To argue that specters inhabiting an "invisible world" can be scrutinized and measured as if they were subject to sensory perception appears somewhat akin to Lear's error that qualitative emotions can be quantified and precisely verbalized, or Othello's misguided demand for the "ocular proof" of one's honor or dishonor. By the play's last act, a chastened and much less assured Hale concludes "we cannot read His [God's] will" (p. 320). As James Martine notices, Hale appears without his books when he ministers to the condemned in jail,[11] although he now preaches—perhaps as a salve to the guilt he feels concerning his responsibility for those already executed—that it would be preferable to lie, to confess to witchery, and live rather than to die a martyr's death, since for him "life" is an absolute value, superseding even morality. Among the other authorities, Judge Danforth will admit that "witchcraft is *ipso facto*, on its face and by its very nature, an invisible crime, is it not? Therefore, who may possibly be witness to it?" (*Collected Plays*, p. 297)—though that gives him no pause in investigating and condemning solely on the basis of spectral evidence. As Reverend Parris reemphasizes, "We are here, Your Honor, precisely to discover what no one has ever seen" (p. 300).

Versions of the word "see," in fact, recur frequently in the play, keeping before the audience this question of seeing the unseen, of reading or misreading the evidence. The workings of this verbal patterning become clear almost from the play's opening moments, as the townspeople claim to see not only things visible to the eye but spectral appearances as well. If Parris can claim to have seen one of the girls "naked" in the woods during Tituba's ceremony, another will claim to have seen his daughter Betty "fly." Only the wise old Rebecca Nurse, who has "seen" children's games before, can discern how such happenings can be accommodated to reasonable explanation: the girls are going through "their silly seasons, and when it comes on them they will run the Devil bowlegged keeping up with their mischief" (p. 247). By the end of Act One, fearful, to the point of hysteria, of being punished for transgressing religious and social codes in the forest, and subject to the power of suggestion, Abigail and Betty let forth a veritable crescendo of accusations which links together the notion of seeing with the naming of a half-dozen accused, as each girl claims in a frenzied sort of litany that she "saw" so-and-so with the Devil. It takes Giles Corey, who will be pressed to death, and John Proctor, hanged for witchcraft, to break the chain and refuse to name names—as Miller and others, like his fellow playwright Lillian Hellman, refused to do when called to testify before the Congressional committee.

Proctor, from early on, challenges authority that coerces through terror, saying he "likes not its smell" (p. 246)—being particularly galled by the contemptuous way the Reverend Parris exercises his domination through fire-and-brimstone threats and through materialistic showiness in golden candlesticks that seem to Proctor almost idolatrous; in short, he "sees no light of God" (p. 273) shining through Parris's actions, which he finds deeply disturbing since the tenets of Puritanism posit an outward sign of inward grace.

If the authorities, both religious and civil, insist on their ability to perceive and interpret the unseen, Abigail, in "reading" the Puritan community, claims a universal disjunction between the visible and the invisible, the seen and the unseen. Pointing to her seduction by John Proctor in words perhaps intended to evoke the biblical tree of the knowledge of good and evil in the Garden, she exclaims: "John Proctor ... took me from my sleep and put knowledge in my heart. I never knew what pretense Salem was. I never knew the lying lessons I was taught by all these Christian women with their covenanted men! And now you bid me tear the light out of my eyes?" (p. 241). Essentially, then, these outwardly god-fearing and self-righteous people recall for her the "whited sepulchers" of scripture. The word "pretense," in the sense of falsity or lie, also ramifies (like the word "see") throughout the play, beginning with Abigail's early confession that what was reputed to be witchcraft "were sport," later echoed by Mary Warren's "it were pretense" but redefined in the eyes of Proctor and his supporters as "fraud."

In an additional scene that Miller inserted between Acts One and Two late in the initial Broadway run (but that most critics, like Gerald Weales, judge "not an obligatory scene, either dramatically or thematically"[12]), the playwright clarifies both Abigail's motives and the reasons why she sees the adultery as a positive act from the point of view of her own psychological development. Since it is perhaps the most self-revelatory of Abigail's speeches, casting her in a somewhat more sympathetic light, it bears glossing for what it adds to the verbal motif of "pretense": "It were a fire you walked me through, and all my ignorance was burned away ... I used to weep for my sins when the wind lifted up my skirts; and blushed for shame because some old Rebecca called me loose. And then you burned my ignorance away. As bare as some December tree I saw them all—walking like saints to church, running to feed the sick, and hyprocrites in their hearts!" (*The Crucible: Text and Criticism*, p. 150). The "fire" of their passion becomes for her, then, the crucible that she claims effected her growth from ignorance to experience, just as the trial will be the crucible that burns Proctor down to his essential elements. If the repressive and closed Puritan society somehow made her conclude that her sexual stirrings were shameful and peculiar to herself alone, Abigail discovered in the sexual act that these were normal and universal human feelings, that if she was depraved, then underneath they were all depraved, only acting as if they were among the elect whom God had saved. To lie—to appear on the surface to be what one is not (the Shakespearean motif of "seems" vs. "is" appears applicable here)—is perhaps the greatest among the sins, and her appointed mission in life becomes to reveal this flaw.

Although one impetus behind both *An Enemy of the People* and *The Crucible* would seem to be a challenge to a hegemonic world order that demonizes the other, the outsider who rebels, some recent criticism cogently demonstrates that, in his handling of the women characters in the later play, Miller falls prey, however unwittingly, to some of the very same patriarchal attitudes he appears to be criticizing. Wendy Schissel, for example, argues not only that Tituba, Parris's black slave from Barbados, has been made a scapegoat, but that Miller has objectified Abigail and Elizabeth by casting them as "extremes of female sexuality—sultriness and frigidity, respectively—which test a man's body, endanger his spirit, and threaten his 'natural' dominance or needs"; consequently, the text "reinforces stereotypes of *femme fatales* and cold-unforgiving wives" in order to cater to men's "vicarious enjoyment [of] a cathartic male character who has enacted their sexual and political fantasies."[13] John, in truth, does tend to blame the victim of his lust for seducing him, quick to openly name Abigail as "whore" rather than himself as "adulterer"; and if it is Elizabeth who ultimately verbalizes the judgment upon herself as "cold," John has intimated at this rationalization for his betrayal all along. The Establishment itself criminalizes sexual desire, reading the women's bodies as the source of sin and shame; feminine power is interpreted as dangerous in the eyes of a "Puritanism [that] transforms risky sexuality into witchcraft."[14] The first women accused of witchcraft exist on the margins of a society where class strata and property holdings were increasingly noticed. And Tituba refuses to be bound by the restrictive Puritan interpretation of the Devil, reading him in the more expansive role of trickster and source of community vibrancy: "Devil, him be pleasureman in Barbados, him be singin' and dancin' in Barbados . . . you riles him up 'round here . . . but in Barbados he be just as sweet" (*Collected Plays*, p. 313). As Ann Scarboro remarks, apart from the too easy one-dimensionality of Tituba's characterization, complete with pidgin English, Miller does grant "her a subtle power by making her a critic of the Puritans' devil."[15]

Miller found the germ for the adulterous relationship in what seemed to him a peculiar reference in the trial records to the Proctors' servant girl having been expelled from the house; to make it more theatrically viable, he raised Abigail's age from eleven to seventeen, at the same time lowering Proctor's from the sixties to the thirties. Even so, several commentators have doubted Miller's success at making the adultery integral to the larger plot and the development of his protagonist's character. Yet Miller focuses on it almost from the beginning, and it becomes a central motivation for the characters. Although John claims that any "promise" made to Abigail was purely an animal act, that they "touched" momentarily in a physical way without any deeper commitment, Abigail insists that he desires her still and is hypocritical in continuing to "bend" to Elizabeth and act out of duty to her. Unsuccessful in supplanting Elizabeth in Proctor's hearth and heart, a vindictive Abigail will wreak vengeance on her by naming her as a witch in hope of finally displacing her. John's guilt over the brief affair, his seeing the sexual sin as an indication of utter depravity, his unwillingness to forgive himself, and his need to be punished are what drive much of the later action. When he decides, in the almost Shakespearean cadences that close Act Two, to reveal his lechery publicly, he exalts that now all "our old pretense will be ripped away"—both the lies about witchcraft and any mask of personal godliness—so that "we are only what we always were, but naked now" (*Collected Plays*, p. 284). Whereas Abigail centers his "goodness" in his bringing her out of innocence into experience, John sees a larger social role and responsibility, arguing that to fail to bring the community out of ignorance, that is, out of its self-imposed condition of blindness to what is ripping it apart, would be the greatest sin and a failure truly worthy of damnation.

Elizabeth is set apart from all the play's other major characters in that she is the only one who understands, from the very beginning, that however much she may be able to read the physiognomy of the body as text, she cannot read another's heart—in fact, must not presume to read the heart of the other. If it perhaps will always remain true that she can never totally forget John's adultery, neither, however, will she judge, instructing her husband that "the magistrate sits in your heart" (p. 265). Though she "sees" evidence of John's continued interest in Abigail (his being in a room alone with her, his hesitancy in revealing their adultery, his failure to revoke the promise made in bed), she knows that judgment, like forgiveness, must come from the self. That the only goodness which counts is interior to the individual is forcefully brought home when Elizabeth redefines the nature of her own goodness, so that it coincides not with others' interpretation of it but rather with the dictates of her own heart. Under questioning by Hale as to whether she believes in the existence of witches and the minister's utter shock when she answers no, she insists on the priority of her knowledge of her own moral character rather than others' reading of it: "I cannot think the Devil may own a woman's soul, Mr. Hale, when she keeps an upright way, as I have. I am a good woman, I know it; and if you believe I may do only good work in the world, and yet be secretly bound to Satan, then I must tell you sir, I do not believe it" (p. 276). Her husband situates Elizabeth's goodness in her inability to lie, which would seem to set her completely apart from the hypocritical Puritan community as defined by Abigail.

Yet in that moment of greatest tension, when asked in court under oath whether John is the lecher he has already, without her knowledge, confessed himself to being in order to save her, she does lie out of love, not just to protect his honor but to validate her belief that only the individual can "read" and then name his or her own good or evil. Is to lie in this instance, then, not an act of love? Is the refusal to specify the guilt of others, to name names (whether in Salem in the 1690s or in America in the 1950s) not an act of love? Her lie is not, as Schissel worries it might be interpreted, an "act of betrayal," nor evidence of her as "schemer" ("Re(dis)covering the Witches," p. 468), but arises instead from moral conviction. Even though her confession of herself as a "cold wife" who prompted John's lechery seems an overly-judgmental act of self-limitation, it cannot subjectively be faulted for, as she says, "I have read my heart" (*Collected Plays*, p. 323). Her doubt, nevertheless, that she was ever worthy to *be loved* by John, which apparently resulted in a less than total giving of self, is perhaps on the personal level analogous to the larger Puritan conviction of depravity, a fettering belief in one's unworthiness to be saved. Elizabeth's refusal finally to sit in judgment upon the other, though John might initially interpret it as an indication of emotional distance, sets her apart from other Miller protagonists such as Chris Keller in *All My Sons* and Biff Loman in *Death of a Salesman*. In each case, they do judge the father and find him wanting, not in the abstract but for having failed to fulfill their expectations as a moral exemplar. When the fathers act on that accusation by committing suicide, then the surviving sons must live on with their guilt over having brought the father, however justifiably, to the bar of judgment.

In the play's final act, John Proctor makes a series of decisions, some of them reversing earlier ones, manifesting the existential nature of Miller's *Crucible*. When John had first confessed to his sin of lechery, he did so both to alleviate his guilt and to save his wife's life, since he trusted that the Court would see the vindictiveness at the base of Abigail's charges. Now it would, he rationalizes, given his "private" sin, be more "honest" (that is, a closer approximation of outer and inner) to lie and live. When he signs the confession to being in the devil's company, he does so not only because he deems himself unworthy to die a saint's death, for to do so would be (in a culmination of that verbal pattern) a "pretense," but also because, perceiving an apparent discrepancy between their moral character and his, he refuses to falsely name and incriminate others. Yet only moments later, John tears up his confession when he realizes that the text will be made public and taken as evidence that he claims others to be in Satan's power, thus blackening their good names. Furthermore, he destroys the written "lie" because, though it would save his life, it would ruin both his own good name and that of his children. For the notion of one's name assumes a talismanic power in Miller: an outward sign of an inner integrity. Proctor must judge and answer only to himself: human conscience is the final authority, autonomous in all things. Even the law must, in fact, be violated when it comes into conflict with the dictates of a rightly formed conscience. Miller himself identifies the "real and inner theme" of *The Crucible* as "the handing over of conscience to another, be it woman, the state, or a terror, and the realization that with conscience goes the person, the soul immortal, and the name" (*Collected Plays*, p. 47).

So Proctor finally does what Elizabeth has been goading him into doing all along: whereas before others had appropriated his identity and (re)constructed it according to their own agenda, now he takes charge of his destiny and in that moment discovers his identity. Perceiving a threat to his "sense of personal dignity," he "evaluates himself justly," to use Miller's phrases from his essay "Tragedy and the Common Man." Freed from excessive emphasis on human imperfection and redeemed by having placed others outside himself first, John is defined not by the "shame" that Hale (mis)reads in the act; rather, as Elizabeth affirms, "He have his goodness now" (*Collected Plays*, p. 329), which can never be taken from him. As Miller understands his protagonist's conflict, Proctor is "a man who is confronted with the opportunity, the possibility of negating himself, of calling true what he knows is half-truth ... he's being asked by the court to condemn himself to a spiritual death. He can't finally do it. He dies a physical death, but he gains his soul, so to speak, he becomes his rebellion" (Roudané, *Conversations*, p. 158). So ultimately John can unhesitatingly mount the gibbet like the other scapegoat/saints in this community, the text of whose iconic bodies can now be read as martyrs to the tyranny of a patriarchal system that has come unhinged. Like every man who "need[s] to leave a thumbprint somewhere in the world" (*Collected Plays*, p. 29), he can now inscribe his name justly in the family and in the society—in short, on the text that is history. Elizabeth stands listening to the drum rolls of the executioners, bathed in light from "the new sun," reading the text rightly across the ages, as she had always done.

NOTES

Since *An Enemy of the People* is not included in the *Collected Plays*, page references are to the Penguin edition (New York, 1977). Also, the additional scene Miller wrote for *The Crucible* does not appear in the standard edition; it can be found as an Appendix to the play in Gerald Weales (ed.), *The Crucible*: Text and Criticism (New York: Penguin, 1977), pp. 148–52.

1. David Savran, *The Wooster Group, 1975–1985: Breaking the Rules* (Ann Arbor: UMI Research Press, 1986), p. 219.

2. Gerald Rabkin, "Is There a Text on This Stage?: Theatre/Authorship/Interpretation," *Performing Arts Journal* 26/27 (1985): 158.

3. Arthur Miller, *Timebends* (New York: Grove Press, 1987), pp. 323–24.

4. John Stuart Mill, *On Liberty*, ed. David Spitz (New York: Norton, 1975), pp. 62–63.

5. *Arthur Miller's Collected Plays*, vol. 1 (New York: Viking Press, 1957).

6. In Matthew C. Roudané (ed.), *Conversations with Arthur Miller* (Jackson: University Press of Mississippi, 1987), pp. 179, 360.

7. C. W. E. Bigsby, *Modern American Drama, 1945–1990* (Cambridge: Cambridge University Press, 1992), p. 96.

8. Bernard Rosenthal, *Salem Story: Reading the Witch Trials of 1692* (Cambridge: Cambridge University Press, 1993), p. 27.

9. Paul Boyer and Stephen Nissenbaum, *Salem Possessed: The Social Origins of Witchcraft* (Cambridge, MA: Harvard University Press, 1974).

10. E. Miller Budick, "History and Other Spectres in Arthur Miller's *The Crucible*," *Modern Drama* 28.4 (1985): 538; Edmund S. Morgan, "Arthur Miller's *The Crucible* and the Salem Witch Trials: A Historian's View," in John M. Wallace (ed.), *The Golden and Brazen World: Papers in Literature and History 1650–1800* (Berkeley: University of California Press, 1985), p. 187.

11. James J. Martine, *The Crucible: Politics, Property, and Pretense* (New York, Twayne, 1993), p. 30.

12. Gerald Weales (ed.), *The Crucible*: Text and Criticism, p. 154.

13. Wendy Schissel, "Re(dis)covering the Witches in Arthur Miller's *The Crucible*: A Feminist Reading," *Modern Drama* 37.3 (1994): pp. 464, 461.

14. Iska Alter, "Betrayal and Blessedness: Explorations of Feminine Power in *The Crucible, A View from the Bridge*, and *After the Fall*," in June Schlueter (ed.), *Feminist Rereadings of Modern American Drama* (Rutherford, NJ: Fairleigh Dickinson University Press, 1989), p. 123.

15. Ann Scarboro, "Afterword" to Maryse Conde, *I, Tituba, Black Witch of Salem*, trans. Richard Philcox (New York: Ballantine, 1994) p. 222.

ARTHUR MILLER

The Crucible *in History*
The Massey Lecture, Harvard University

I̤t would probably never have occurred to me to write a play about the Salem witch trials of 1692 had I not seen some astonishing correspondences with that calamity in the America of the late forties and early fifties. There were other enticements for me in the Salem period, however, most especially the chance it offered to write in what was for me a practically new language, one that would require new muscles.

I was never a scholar or an historian, of course; my basic need was somehow to respond to a phenomenon which, with only small exaggeration, one could say was paralysing a whole generation and in an amazingly short time was drying up the habits of trust and toleration in public discourse. I refer, of course, to the anti-communist rage, that threatened to reach hysterical proportions and sometimes did. I can't remember anyone calling it an ideological war but I think now that that is what it amounted to. Looking back at the period, I suppose we very rapidly passed over anything like a discussion or debate, and into something quite different, a hunt not just for subversive people but for ideas and even a suspect language. The object, a shock at the time, was to destroy the least credibility of any and all ideas associated with socialism and communism, whose proponents were assumed to be either knowing or unwitting agents of Soviet subversion. An ideological war is like guerrilla war, since the enemy is first of all an idea whose proponents are not

From *Arthur Miller: The Crucible in History and Other Essays*, pp. 3–55. © Arthur Miller, 2000.

in uniform but are disguised as ordinary citizens, a situation that can scare a lot of people to death.

I am not really equipped to deliver a history of Cold War America, which, like any other period, is packed with passionately held illusions and ideas distorted on all sides by fear. Suffice to say it was a time of great, no doubt unprecedented fear; but fear, like love, is mostly incommunicable once it has passed. So I shall try to limit myself, as far as possible, to speak of events as they struck me personally, for those are what finally created *The Crucible*.

One knew that Congressional investigations of subversion had been going on since the thirties. The Dies Committee, beginning with Nazi subversion in America, ended up with a never-ending and often silly investigation of communists. But the country in the thirties was not under external threat and nobody seemed to take seriously any menace from an American Communist Party that could hardly elect a dog-catcher. From my perspective, what changed everything was the victory of the Chinese communists in 1949. Inevitably, the Chinese reds were seen as all but an arm of the expansionist post–Second World War Soviet machine, and a look at the map would indeed show that an enormous new part of the planet had turned red.

'Who Lost China!' almost instantly became the Republican mantra. Who were the traitors inside the Democratic administrations going back to Roosevelt that had sold out our favourite Chinese, Chiang Kai-shek? This, I think, was the first notable injection of the idea of treason and foreign agents into domestic political discourse. To me the simplicity of it all was breathtaking. There had to be left-wing traitors in government, otherwise how could the Chinese—who, as everyone knew, loved Americans more than anybody—have turned against the pro-American Chiang Kai-shek in favour of a Soviet agent like Mao Tse-tung?

All I knew about China in 1949 was what I had read in Edgar Snow and Jack Belden and Teddy White and other American reporters. What it amounted to was that the Nationalist regime was feudal and thoroughly corrupt and that the reds were basically a miserably exploited peasantry which at long last had risen up and thrown their exploiters into the sea. I thought it was a great idea. In any event, the idea of our 'losing' China seemed the equivalent of a flea losing an elephant. Nevertheless there was a growing uproar in and out of Congress. One read that the China Lobby, a wealthy support group backing Chiang Kai-shek's efforts to return to Beijing from Taiwan, was reportedly paying a lot of the bills, and that Senator McCarthy was one of their most effective champions. The partisan political manipulation of a real issue was so patent that President Truman could dismiss the Republican scare as a 'red herring'. But it is an indication of its impact on the public mind that he soon had to retreat and institute a Loyalty Board of his own to investigate the allegiance of government employees.

The Chinese Revolution was always central to the fear of the reds and remained so to the end of McCarthy's magical sway over the country. For example, when at long last Edward R. Murrow, CBS's chief correspondent, finally decided to take on the Senator, who by then had been weakened by the puncturing of his own overblown exaggerations, McCarthy was given air-time to respond to Murrow's barbs, and facing the camera simply displayed a wall-sized map of Russia, and then expanded it until it showed China alongside, saying in effect, Here is Russia, and now they have the teeming land-mass of China added on. Then, with his usual hambone, through-the-nose foreboding, he turned straight into the camera and announced, 'Edward R. Murrow is a card-carrying member of the American Civil Liberties Union!' It no longer worked—most star-turns have a certain limited shelf-life; but even at the time it was striking how the Chinese reds were so incendiary to the prevalent fearfulness.

To call the ensuing atmosphere paranoid is not to say that there was nothing real in the American–Soviet stand-off. To be sure I am far more willing than I was then, owing to some experiences of my own with both sides, to credit both American and Soviet leaderships with enough ignorance of each other to have ignited a third world war. But if there was one element that lent the conflict a tone of the inauthentic, the spurious and the invented it was the swiftness with which all values were being forced in a matter of months literally to reverse themselves. I recall some examples.

Death of a Salesman opened in February of 1949 and was hailed by nearly every newspaper and magazine. Parenthetically, I should add that two exceptions come to mind, one Marxist the other ex-Marxist: the Marxist being the *Daily Worker*, which found the play defeatist and lacking militant protest; and the ex-Marxist Mary McCarthy, who seemed outraged by the idea of elevating it to the status of tragedy and just hated it in general, particularly, I thought, because it was so popular. As all participants in the higher dispensation understood, the mark of real tragedy was that it always closed in two weeks. Anyway, several movie studios wanted it and it was finally Columbia Pictures that bought it, and engaged a great star, Frederick March, to play Willy.

In something like two years or less, as I recall, with the picture finished, I was asked by a terrified Columbia to sign an anti-communist declaration in order to ward off picket lines, which the American Legion was threatening to throw across the entrances of theatres showing the film. In the numerous phone calls that followed, the air of panic was heavy. It was the first intimation of what would soon follow. I declined to make any such statement which frankly I found demeaning; what right had any organization to demand anyone's pledge of loyalty? I was sure the whole thing would soon go away, it was just too outrageous.

But instead of the problem disappearing, the studio, it now developed, had actually made another film, a short which was to be shown with *Salesman*. This was called *The Life of a Salesman* and consisted of several lectures by City College School of Business professors. What they boiled down to was that selling was basically a joy, one of the most gratifying and useful of professions, and that Willy was simply a nut. Never in show-business history has a studio spent so much good money to prove that its feature film was pointless. I threatened to sue (on what basis I had no idea) but of course the short could not be shown lest it bore the audience blind. But in less than two years *Death of a Salesman* had gone from being a masterpiece to being a heresy, and a fraudulent one at that.

In 1948, '49, '50, '51, I had the sensation of being trapped inside a perverse work of art, one of those Escher constructs in which it is impossible to make out whether a stairway is going up or down. Practically everyone I knew, all survivors of the Great Depression of course, as well as the Second World War, stood somewhere within the conventions of the political left of centre; one or two were Communist Party members, some were sort of fellow travellers, as I suppose I was, and most had had one or another brush with Marxist ideas or organizations. I have never been able to believe in the reality of these people being actual or putative traitors any more than I could be, yet others like them were being fired from teaching or jobs in government or large corporations. The surreality of it all never left me. We were living in an art form, a metaphor that had no long history but had suddenly, incredibly enough, gripped the country. In today's terms, the country had been delivered into the hands of the radical Right, a ministry of free-floating apprehension toward absolutely anything that never happens in the middle of Missouri. It is always with us, this anxiety, sometimes directed toward foreigners, Jews, Catholics, fluoridated water, aliens in space, masturbation, homosexuality, or the Internal Revenue Department. But in the fifties any of these could be validated as real threats by rolling out a map of China. And if this seems crazy now it seemed just as crazy then, but openly doubting it could cost you.

So I suppose that in one sense *The Crucible* was an attempt to make life real again, palpable and structured. One hoped that a work of art might illuminate the tragic absurdities of an anterior work of art that was called reality, but was not.

Again, it was the very swiftness of the change that lent it this surreality. Only three or four years earlier an American movie audience, on seeing a newsreel of—let's say—a Russian soldier or even Stalin saluting the Red Army, would have applauded, for that army had taken the brunt of the Nazi onslaught, as most people were aware. Now they would have looked on with fear or at least bewilderment, for the Russians had become the enemy of mankind, a menace to all that was good. It was the Germans who, with amazing rapidity, were turning good. Could this be real? And how, mentally, to deal with, for example, American authorities removing from books in German schools any mention of the Hitler decade?

In the unions, communists and their allies, who had been known as intrepid organizers, were now to be shorn of union membership and turned out as seditious. Harry Bridges, for example, the idol of West Coast longshoremen, whom he had all but single-handedly organized, would be subjected to court trial after court trial to drive him out of the country and back to his native Australia as an unadmitted communist. Academics, some of them prominent in their fields, were especially targeted, many forced to retire or simply fired for disloyalty. Some of them were communists, some were fellow travellers and, inevitably, a certain number were simply unaffiliated liberals refusing to sign one of the dozens of humiliating anti-communist pledges being required by terrified college administrations.

The sweep went not only very wide but also very deep. By 1950 or thereabouts there were subjects one would do better to avoid, and even words that were best left unspoken. The Spanish Civil War, for example, had quickly become a hot button. That war, as some of you may not recall, resulted from an attack in 1936 by the military upon the democratically elected socialist government. After three years of terrible fighting, in which the Luftwaffe's planes and Mussolini's troops gave him crucial help, the fascist General Franco took power. Spain would become the very symbol of the struggle against fascism; but more and more one heard, after about 1950, that Franco's victory was actually a not unworthy triumph of anti-communists. This, despite the common belief through the forties that, had Franco been thrown-back, opening Hitler's whole Atlantic flank to hostile democrats rather than allied fascists, his war against Europe might well have had to be postponed, if not aborted.

Again, it was the swiftness of this change that made it so fictional to me. Occasionally these sudden turnarounds were rather comical, which didn't help one's sense of reality.

One day in 1950 or thereabouts, a stranger called, asking to come and see me about some matter he preferred not to talk about on the phone, and dropping as one of his bona fides that he had fought in Spain. I figured he was in trouble politically and must be really desperate to imagine I could help him. (A few ill-informed people still imagined I had some clout of this kind.) He arrived at my Brooklyn Heights house, a bright youngish fellow carrying a briefcase. We chatted for a few minutes and then got down to business. From his briefcase he unfolded a desk-sized map of a Texas oilfield, and pointing at various black dots explained that these were oil wells in which he was selling stock. When I confessed surprise that an idealistic anti-fascist fighter should end up as an oil-stock salesman, he asked, 'Why not?' and with a touch of noble sincerity added, 'Once the workers take over they're going to need oil!' This was a harbinger of the wondrous rationalizations that I would have cause to recall as our future arrived. But I really should add that while all this was new to us it was a very old story in many other places where dictatorships had come and gone, where people had long since learned how to laugh internally without creasing a cheek.

My view of things as uneasily 'fictional' turned out not to be entirely unwarranted; some six or seven years later, in one of the more elaborate episodes of my experience, I would be cited for contempt of Congress for refusing to identify writers I had met at one of the two communist writers' meetings I had attended many years before. Normally, these citations resulted in a routine Federal Court trial which wound up in half an hour with an inevitable conviction. But my lawyer, Joseph L. Rauh, Jr, brought in a former senator, Harry M. Cain of Washington, who had been head of the Loyalty Board under Eisenhower, to testify as an expert witness that my plays showed no signs of having been written under communist discipline. Until then, 'expert witnesses' had always been FBI men or ex-communists. Cain had a very different and curious history: a decorated Korean War veteran and fierce anti-communist, he had been a sidekick of McCarthy's and a weekly poker partner. But disillusionment had worn him down when, as head of the Loyalty Board, he had had to deal with an amazing load of letters arriving each morning from people suspecting employers or employees, neighbours, friends, relatives and the corner grocer of communist sympathies. The idea of the whole country spying on itself began to depress him, and looking down from his office window he had the overwhelming idea of a terrified nation out there—and worse, that some substantial fraction of it had become quite literally crazed.

The breaking point for him came with a series of relentlessly persistent letters from a Baltimore postman complaining of having been fired for disloyalty. What bothered him was the handwriting, which was barely literate. Communists were bad people but they were rarely illiterate. Finally, Cain invited the man to his office and soon realized that the accusations were simply not credible; this led him to wonder about the hundreds of other accusations he had been regularly forwarding to the FBI with little or no examination. At last he went directly to Eisenhower and told him he was convinced that the Loyalty Board itself was incompatible with political liberty. The next morning he found himself fired. It seems that handling all that disloyalty had infected him, too.

That was still six or seven years on. My brushes with this fictional world I would soon inhabit went back to 1947, when *All My Sons*, as the result of protests by the Catholic War Veterans, was removed from the US Army's theatrical repertoire in Europe. It was deemed a threat to soldiers' morale, since it told the story of a manufacturer selling defective parts to the Air Force. In a few years an ex-officer in that theatrical troupe wrote to inform me that not only had *All My Sons* been banned, but also an order had come down that no other play written by Arthur Miller was to be produced by the Army. As far as the Army was concerned, I had simply disappeared as an American writer.

But you never know—sometimes a bad experience can turn out to be useful. In the late sixties, as President of International Pen, the London-based, worldwide writers' organization, I would find myself commiserating with Soviet, Chinese, Czech, Hungarian writers, and those in other Communist countries who had seen their names obliterated from the rosters of living authors. Of course the so-called Socialist Bloc was far from alone in this practice; the South African Apartheid regime was probably more ruthless as a censor, not to mention the long list of right-wing, fascistic Latin American regimes. If there was a unique element in the American repression, it was the widespread assumption that it didn't exist. The demonization of the Left had been so thorough as to justify what in effect was its illegalization and then its disappearance, and without the government or many people admitting that it was not simply the zeitgeist that had sort of blown it away.

But it is impossible, certainly in this short time, to convey properly the fears that marked that period. Nobody was being shot, to be sure, although some were going to jail, where at least one, a man named William Remington, was murdered by an inmate hoping to shorten his sentence for having killed a communist. Rather than physical fear it was the sense of impotence, which seemed to deepen with each passing week, of being unable to speak simply and accurately of the very recent past when being left-wing in America, and for that matter in Europe, was simply to be alive to the dilemmas of the day. To be sure, I had counted myself a radical since my years in college and had tried and failed to read *Das Kapital*; but the Marxist formulations had certainly given shape to my views on politics—fundamentally that to understand a political phenomenon you had to look for the money. (Which is also why businessmen understand Marxism better than anybody.) It also meant that you believed capitalism was quite possibly doomed, but during and after the Great Depression there were times when not to believe that would have put you in a political minority. I may have dreamed of a socialism where people no longer lived off another's labour, but I had never met a spy.

As for the very idea of willingly subjecting my work not only to some party's discipline but to anyone's control, my repugnance was such that, as a very young and indigent writer, I had turned down fairly lucrative offers to work for Hollywood studios because of a helpless revulsion at the thought of someone other than myself literally owning the paper I was typing on. It would not be long, perhaps four or five years, before the fraudulence of

Soviet cultural claims was as clear to me as it should have been earlier. But I would never have found it believable, either in the fifties or later, that with its thuggish self-righteousness and callous contempt for artists' freedoms, the unabashed Soviet way of controlling culture could be successfully exported to America. The possible exception, perhaps, might be Madison Avenue advertising agencies where ideological control over artists is taken for granted as a condition of employment. In any case, to believe in that danger generally I would have had to share a bed with the Republican Right.

Which is not to say that there was no sincerity in the fears people felt in the fifties, and—as in most things human—much cynicism as well, if not corruption. The moral high ground, as in most things human, was wreathed in fog. But the stubborn fact remained that some greatly talented people were being driven out of the country to live and work in England, screenwriters like Carl Foreman and Donald Ogden Stewart, actors like Charlie Chaplin and Sam Wanamaker, who, incidentally, in his last years led the campaign to build the replica of Shakespeare's theatre on the Thames. I no longer recall the total number of our political exiles, but it was more than too many and too disgraceful for a nation prideful of its democracy.

Writing now, almost half a century later, with the Soviet Union in ruins, China rhetorically fending off capitalism even as in realty it adopts a market economy, Cuba wallowing helplessly in the Caribbean, it is not easy to convey to a contemporary audience the American fear of a masterful communism. When Khrushchev in 1956 bellowed out from his United Nations seat, 'We are going to bury you!', shivers went up a lot of spines but not only because Soviet missiles were pointed our way. It was also on account of something that only ever incidentally referred to external threats—our American triumphalism. This tendency, almost as old as the country, was always a bit too triumphal for the facts: our cyclical depressions, our corrosive racism, our mystification toward so many foreign things. To put it bluntly, there has always been for a great many people a lurking fear of falling in this country, of the bottom suddenly and reasonlessly dropping out. Perhaps it is that the causes of our recurring crises were never really understood, but merely passed in the fullness of time. After all, in the late forties there were millions of Americans still alive—myself among them—who had experienced the complete collapse of our banking system, the near-total destruction of our vaunted Navy at Pearl Harbor and the continuing persistence of high unemployment despite so many measures to combat it. Boastful though politicians might be, in the fifties, as always, most people were a lot less naive than really to believe in America's social invulnerability. And now, worse yet, a new militant certainty was suddenly in the air, and one which seemed to have no self-doubts worth mentioning. The quickness with which Soviet-style regimes had taken over eastern Europe and then China was breathtaking for a lot of people, and I believe it stirred up a fear in Americans of our own ineptitudes, our mystifying inability, despite our fantastic military victories, to control the world whose liberties we had so recently won back from the Axis powers.

So, the fears on which the anti-communist crusade was raised transcended the immediate political situation. They also went deeper than politics, right down into sex. Again, it is wise to remember that the Right was not only afraid of communism but also and even more so, if on a different level, of homosexuality. This, oddly enough, became real to me on a certain day in 1977 when I arrived at the Franco-Belgian border crossing without my passport.

The Belgian National Theatre, in 1952, had been the first European theatre to put on *The Crucible*, an exciting prospect in those times when it was still quite uncommon for American plays to be done in Europe at all. The theatre, along with the Belgo-American Association, a business group, invited me to attend the premiere. In the company of Montgomery Clift, whom I was at the time trying to help through a misconceived off-Broadway production of *The Seagull*, I took the subway downtown to renew my outdated passport. I had read, of course, of people being denied passports by the State Department, but by 1952 it had still not dawned on me that I might be one of them, and so I chatted away with Monte about *The Seagull* as I waited to be called up to the clerk. I showed him the telegram from the Belgo-American Association, and requested the renewal within the week so that I could get to Brussels for the premiere on Saturday evening, five days hence.

Three days passed with nothing from the State Department. I had my lawyer call the Passport Division. He was soon informed that I was not going to Brussels at all. It had been decided that my presence abroad was not in the best interests of the United States, nothing more, nothing less, and no passport was to be issued to me. And I had even begun to brush up on my high-school French!

I soon learned that in Brussels a faintly farcical situation had developed—and I should say that farce was always a step away from many of the tragedies of the period. Since the play was the first and practically the only artistic evidence Europe had seen of resistance to what was considered a fascistic McCarthyism, the applause at the final curtain was intense and insistent, and since the newspapers had announced that I had accepted the invitation to be present, there were calls for the author. These went on and on until the American ambassador felt compelled to stand and take a bow. A species of insanity was spreading everywhere. Here was the ambassador, an officer of the State Department, acknowledging applause for someone deemed by that department too dangerous to be present. It must surely have struck some of the audience as strange, however, that an author would be wearing a wide diplomatic sash diagonally across his chest, and next morning's papers had loads of fun with the scene, which, of course, could hardly have advanced the best interests of the United States. And naturally those inclined to do so saw this shot at me as one more proof that America was launched on the road to fascism.

Twenty-five years passed like an afternoon, and my wife, Inge Morath, and I were in Paris when the invitation came to attend the twenty-fifth anniversary of that first production of *The Crucible* in Belgium. We soon found ourselves nearing the France-Belgium border on our way to the celebratory production at the Belgian National Theatre. The Douane is passing down the aisle inspecting passports. My European-born wife takes hers out of her bag, and I now realize that it never occurred to me, being an American, to bring a passport since, after all, the Belgians and the French are as close as Jersey and Manhattan and both speak French! Luckily, the Douane officer was a theatre buff and recognized me and let us through, but warned that with the recent outbreak of terrorism in Germany especially, controls had been stiffened at all borders and I would absolutely have to have a passport to get back into France.

As I noted in my autobiography, *Timebends*, the American Consul General, Rossiter, attended the theatre's reception for me that afternoon, and in passing offered to be of help, should I need any, during our short stay in Brussels. Leaping at this I asked if I could perhaps get a duplicate passport, and explained what had happened. Twenty-four hours was a drastically short time to expect a passport to be issued but we had to leave for Germany the next day. Rossiter, unflustered, said he could arrange it if I supplied the usual photos. I couldn't help contrasting this behaviour with what I had experienced twenty years earlier from the State Department, but kept the thought to myself.

Next day, photos in hand, I walked into the consulate. Half a dozen or more employees looked up from their desks and applauded! Rossiter's office door opened and he appeared, noting, I was sure, the flummoxed if pleased look on my face. I heartily thanked him and he said, 'Come inside, if you have a minute. I'll explain why you got it so fast.'

In the fifties, he said, he had spent some six years trying to get his Foreign Service job back after being fired for some unexplained breach which, he was told, marked him as a security risk. With the State Department refusing any further explanation, and the inevitable inference of communist sympathies threatening his future in or out of government, he borrowed money and mortgaged his house to mount a lawsuit against the Department, demanding an exposition of this obscure charge.

At long last he was granted a hearing before his accusers and a judge, our final ambassador to South Vietnam, Graham Martin. No friend of the Left, he was last seen helping to load pro-American Vietnamese onto escaping helicopters the day Saigon fell. Scott McCleod, the ultimate sniffer-outer of security risks, proceeded to tell his story. Rossiter had for a couple of years shared an apartment in Cairo with a known homosexual, period. His continued employment by the State Department could not be tolerated.

Rossiter's turn came. Arriving in Cairo, young and unmarried, on his first post as a fledgling diplomat, he was given a list of available apartments, one of which he picked. Not knowing Cairo, his choice was blind. Thus, he lived a couple of years with his fellow officer who, on strict guard against revealing sexual proclivities that would certainly mean the end of his career, had been careful enough to keep Rossiter from suspecting them. Indeed, this hearing was the first time Rossiter had heard that his co-tenant was homosexual. Ambassador Martin now turned to McCleod and asked if he had anything more; McCleod thought not. The ambassador restored Rossiter to his position, ordered his lost salary repaid to him with interest, and that was that.

'So when you asked me to help with your passport,' Rossiter told me, 'I remembered your problems with the Department, and thought I'd speed things up.' Sometimes things work out, if you live long enough.

What this story says about the level of anxiety about security is obvious, but some of the elements aren't. In succeeding years real traitors would indeed be exposed; in the eighties, one of them sold the Navy's entire secret communications codes, another sold the names of all the CIA's collaborators in the world, and so on. But I recall no mention in these real cases of the culprits being left-wingers or homosexuals. They were all good old boys, apparently, and if one, like Aldrich Ames, who sold the Navy codes, sported high-end jaguars and Mercedes and was a known alcoholic living far beyond his salary, these were indulgences that any successful American would be inclined to allow himself in pursuit of the good life. What is important to remember is that the sale of one's country, in these cases to Russia, never caused the eruption of any generalized fears in the press or public. One need not look far for the reason; these men had no ideology beyond the money-lust. Which leads inexorably to the conclusion that more than actual subversives were the target of the red-hunt; rather it was the *idea* they represented that was so frightening. We were indeed in an ideological war.

I should explain what I mean by the cynicism and corruption of the red-hunt. By 1956, when the House Un-American Activities Committee subpoenaed me, the tide was going out for the committee, which was finding it more and more difficult to make front pages. However, the news of my forthcoming marriage to Marilyn Monroe was too tempting to be passed by. That our marriage had some connections with my being subpoenaed was confirmed when Chairman Walters of the HUAC sent word to Joseph Rauh, my lawyer, that he would be inclined to cancel my hearing altogether if Miss

Monroe would consent to have a picture taken with him. The offer having been declined, the good chairman, as my hearing came to an end, proceeded to entreat me to write less tragically about our country. This lecture cost me some $40,000 in lawyer's fees, a year's suspended sentence for Contempt of Congress, and a $500 fine. Not to mention about a year of inanition in my creative life.

But back to the late forties and early fifties; my fictional view of the period, my sense of its unreality was, like any impotence, a psychologically painful experience. A very similar paralysis at a certain point descended on Salem. In both places, to keep social unity intact, the authority of leaders had to be hardened and words of skepticism toward them constricted.

A new cautionary diction, an uncustomary prudence was swiftly inflecting our way of talking to one another. In a country that a bit more than a quarter of a century earlier had given three million votes to Eugene Debs, a socialist presidential candidate, the very word socialism was all but taboo. Words had gotten fearsome. As I would learn directly from students and faculty in Ann Arbor on a 1953 reporting visit for *Holiday Magazine*, students were actually avoiding renting rooms in the houses run by the Housing Co-operative for fear of being labelled communist, so darkly suggestive was the word 'Co-operative'. On hearing this even I was amazed. For one thing, the 'Housing Co-operative' had had a rather noble ring in the despairing thirties; a number of home-owners, unable to make tax or mortgage payments had had to abandon their buildings, and they had been boarded up. Along came some students who had simply gone in and squatted, taking down the boards, cleaning the places up, fixing roofs, painting walls, and charging next to nothing for rooms. It had been a refreshing moment of action in a paralysed hour, and now the very name they had given it was dangerous to utter. But there was more.

The faculty head of orientation at the university told me, in a rather cool, uninvolved manner, that the FBI was enlisting professors to report on students voicing left-wing opinions, and—some more comedy—they had also engaged students to report on professors with the same views. When I published these facts in *Holiday*, the Pontiac division of General Motors threatened to withdraw all advertising from the magazine if I ever appeared in it again; Ted Patrick, its editor, promptly badgered me for another piece, but I didn't know the reason why for some years.

It was a time—as I would only learn decades later from my FBI record obtained under the Freedom of Information Act—when the FBI had shadowed a guest of mine from a dinner party in my Brooklyn Heights house. The guest's name was blacked out and I have been puzzling ever since about his possible identity. The point is that reading my FBI record in the seventies I was not really surprised to learn this. In the fifties everybody over forty believed their phone was being tapped by the FBI, and they were probably right. What is important here is that none of this was secret; most everybody had a good idea of what was happening, but, like me, felt helpless to reverse it. And to this moment I don't think I can adequately communicate the sheer density of the atmosphere of the time, for the outrageous had so suddenly become the accepted norm.

In the early fifties, for example, along with Elia Kazan, who had directed *All My Sons* and *Death of a Salesman*, I submitted a film script to Harry Cohn, head of Columbia Pictures. It described the murderous corruption in the gangster-ridden Brooklyn longshoreman's union, whose leadership a group of rebel workers was trying to overthrow. Cohn read the script and called us to Hollywood, where he simply and casually informed us that he had first had the script vetted by the FBI, and that they had seen nothing subversive in it. On the other hand, however, the head of the AFL motion picture unions in Hollywood, Roy Brewer, had condemned it outright as totally untrue communist propaganda, since, quite simply, there were no gangsters on the Brooklyn waterfront. Cohn, no stranger to the ways of gangsterism, having survived an upbringing in the tough, famously crime-ridden 'Five Points' area of Manhattan, opined that Brewer, quite naturally, was only trying to protect fellow AFL union leader, Joe Ryan, head of the Brooklyn longshoremen. Brewer also threatened to call a strike of projectionists in any theatre daring to show the film, no idle threat since he controlled their union. Ryan, incidentally, would shortly go to Sing Sing prison for gangsterism. But that was not yet.

Meanwhile, Cohn offered his solution to our problem with Brewer: he would produce the film if I would agree to make one simple change—the gangsters in the union were to be changed to communists. This would not be easy; for one thing, I knew all the communists on the waterfront and there was a total of two of them. (Both of whom, incidentally, in the following decade became millionaire businessmen.) And so I had to withdraw the script, which prompted an indignant telegram from Cohn: 'As soon as we try to make the script pro-American you pull out.' One understood not only the threat in those words but also the cynicism: he certainly knew it was the Mafia that controlled waterfront labour. Nevertheless, had I been a movie writer in Hollywood my career would have ended with that refusal to perform this patriotic idiocy. I have to say that there were days when I wondered if we would end up with an unacknowledged, perhaps even comfortable American fascism.

But the theatre had no such complications, no blacklist—not yet anyway—and I longed to respond to this climate of fear if only to protect my sanity. But where to find a transcendent concept? As I saw it, the difficulty was that we had grown so detached from any hard reality I knew about. It had become a world of signals, gestures, loaded symbolic words, and of rites and rituals. After all, the accusations of Communist Party membership aimed at film writers, actors and directors never mentioned treasonous acts of any sort; what was in their brains was the question, and this created a kind of gestural phantom-land. I did not think of it this way at the time but looking back, as I have said, I think we had entered an ideological war, and in such wars it is ideas and not necessarily actions that arouse anger and fear. And this was the heart of the darkness—that the belief had flourished rather quickly that a massive, profoundly organized conspiracy was in place and carried forward mainly by a concealed phalanx of intellectuals, including labour activists, teachers, professionals of all sorts, sworn to undermine the American government. And it was precisely the invisibility of ideas that was helping to frighten so many people. How could a play deal with this mirage world?

There was a fundamental absurdity in the Salem witch-hunt, of course, since witches don't exist, but this only helped relate it more to what we were going through. I can't recall the date anymore, but to one of the Un-American Committee hearings several Hollywood writers brought piles of their film scripts for the committee to parse for any sign of Marxist propaganda. Of course there would hardly be anything that provocative in a Hollywood movie of the time but in any case the committee refused to read the scripts, which I imagined was a further humiliation for the writers. But what a cruel irony that these terribly serious Party members or sympathizers, in an attempt to prove themselves patriotic Americans, should feel compelled to demonstrate that their work was totally innocuous!

Paranoia breeds paranoia, of course, but below paranoia there lies a bristling, unwelcome truth, a truth so repugnant as to produce fantasies of persecution in order to conceal its existence. For example, the unwelcome truth denied by the Right was that the Hollywood writers accused of subversion were not a menace to the country, or even bearers of meaningful change. They wrote not propaganda but entertainment, some of it of a mildly liberal cast to be sure, but most of it mindless, or when it was political, as with Preston Sturges or Frank Capra, entirely and exuberantly un-Marxist. In any real assessment, the worst they could do was contribute some money to Party coffers. But most Hollywood writers were only occasionally employed, and one doubted their contributions could have made any difference to a party so completely disregarded by the American public and so thoroughly impregnated by the FBI into the bargain. Yet, they had to be portrayed as an imminent danger to the Republic.

As for the Left, its unacknowledged truth was more important for me. If nobody was being shot in our ideological war but merely vivisected by a headline or two, it struck me as odd—if understandable—that the accused were mostly unable to cry out passionately their faith in the ideals of socialism. There were attacks on the committees' right to demand that a citizen reveal his political beliefs, yes; but on the idealistic canon of their own convictions, the defendants were largely mute. It was a silence, incidentally, which in the public mind probably tended to confirm the committees' characterization of them as conspirators wrapping themselves in darkness. In the artists' defence, the committees instantly shut down as irrelevant any attempts to explicate their ideas, any idealistic displays. But even outside, in public statements beyond the hearings, the accused relied almost wholly on legalistic defences rather than the articles of the faith in which they unquestionably believed. The rare exception, like Paul Robeson's forthright declaration of faith in socialism as a cure for racism, was a rocket that momentarily lit up the sky. But even this, it must be said, was dimmed by his adamant refusal to recognize, at least publicly, what he knew to be the murders of two Soviet Jewish artists, his good friends, under Stalin's anti-Semitic decrees. It was one of the cruel twists of the time that while he would not, in Washington, display his outrage at the murders of his friends, he could, in Moscow, choose to sing a song in Yiddish which the whole public knew was his protest against Soviet anti-Semitism.

In short, the disciplined avoidances of the Left betrayed a guilt which the Right had found a way to exploit. A similar guilt seems to reside in all sorts of American dissidents, from Jehovah's Witnesses to homosexuals, no doubt because there is indeed an unacknowledged contempt in them toward the cherished norms of the majority. It may be that guilt, perhaps, helps account to some important degree for the absence in our theatre of plays that in any meaningful way confronted the deepening hysteria, which after all was the main event in our culture. Here was a significant part of a whole generation forced to the wall and hardly a word about it written for the stage. But it may simply have been the difficulty of finding a dramatic locution, a working symbolization that might illuminate the complex fog of the unspoken in which we were living—the smoke signals from all sides were hardly declarations of what they really stood for.

To put it bluntly, the pockets of both sides were stuffed with hidden agendas. On the Right there was, quite simply, their zeal to bring down finally in disgrace the last vestiges of New Deal attitudes, particularly those dreadful tendencies in Americans to set limits around the more flagrant excesses of unbridled capitalism and when in distress to look to government for help. Instead, the Right's advertised goal was the defence of liberty against communism, which, in translation, meant that the poor had no one to blame but themselves.

What the Left were not saying was that they were in truth dedicated to replacing capitalism with a society based on Marxist principles, and this could well mean the suppression of non-Marxists for the good of mankind. Instead, they were simply espousing constitutional protections against self-incrimination. Thus, the fresh wind of a debate of any real substance was not blowing through these hearings, or these terrible years. And so the result was miasma, and on the Left, the guilt of the wholly or partially insincere. The Right, of course, with its professional innocence as the warden of hallowed old virtues in whose defence it is convinced it is forever being persecuted, is always a stranger to guilt, sure as ever that it represents the genuine, if incoherent and stifled, wishes of the majority.

How to express all this, and much more, on a stage? I began to despair of my own paralysis. I was a fisherman without a hook, a seaman without a sail.

On a lucky afternoon I happened upon a book, *The Devil in Massachusetts*, by Marion Starkey, a narrative of the Salem witch-hunt of 1692. I knew this story from my college reading more than a decade earlier, but now in this changed and darkened America it turned a completely new aspect toward me, namely the poetry of the hunt. Poetry may seem an odd word for a witch-hunt but I saw now that there was something of the marvellous in the spectacle of a whole village, if not an entire province, whose imagination was literally captured by a vision of something that wasn't there.

In time to come the very notion of equating the red-hunt with the witch-hunt would be condemned by some as a deception. There were certainly communists and there never were witches. But the deeper I moved into the 1690s the further away—drifted the America of the 1950s, and rather than the appeal of analogy I found something somewhat different to draw my curiosity and excitement.

First of all, anyone standing up in the Salem of 1692 who denied that witches existed would have faced immediate arrest, the hardest interrogation and quite possibly the rope. Every authority from the Church in New England, the kings of England and Europe, to legal scholars like Lord Coke not only confirmed their existence but never questioned the necessity of executing them when discovered. And of course there was the authority of the Bible itself and the words of Saul which had commanded, 'Thou shalt not suffer a witch to live.' To deny witches was to deny the existence of the Devil's age-old war against God, and this in effect left God without an opposite, and stripped him of his first purpose—which was to protect the Christian religion and good order in the world. Without Evil what need was there for Good? Without the Devil's ceaseless plotting who needed God? The existence of witches actually went to prove the existence of God's war with Evil.

Indeed, it became obvious that to dismiss witchcraft was to forego any understanding of how it came to pass that tens of thousands had been murdered as witches in Europe, from Scandinavia across to England, down through France and Spain. Likewise, to dismiss any relation between that episode and the hunt for subversives was to shut down an insight into not only the remarkably similar emotions but also the numerous identical practices, of both officials and victims.

Of course there were witches, if not to most of us then certainly to everyone in Salem; and of course there were communists, but what was the content of their menace? That to me became the issue. Having been deeply influenced as a student by a Marxist approach to society—if less so as I grew older—and having known any number of Marxists and numerous sympathizers, I could simply not accept that these people were spies or even prepared to do the will of the Soviets in some future crisis. That such people had thought to find some hope of a higher ethic in the Soviet was not simply an American but a worldwide irony of catastrophic moral proportions, for their like could be found all over Europe and Asia. But as the fifties dawned they were stuck with the past they had chosen or been led into. Part of the surreality of the great anti-Left sweep of that decade was that it picked up a lot of people for exposure and disgrace who had already in their hearts turned away from a pro-Soviet past but had no stomach for naming others who had merely shared their illusions. In short, then, the whole business for me remained what Truman had called it initially—not a moral crusade but a political red herring.

Nevertheless, the hunt had captured some significant part of the American imagination and its power demanded respect. And turning to Salem was like looking into a petri dish, a sort of embalmed stasis with its principal moving forces caught in stillness. One had to wonder what the human imagination fed on that could inspire neighbours and old friends suddenly to emerge overnight as hell's own furies secretly bent on the torture and destruction of Christians. More than a political metaphor, more than a moral tale, *The Crucible*, as it developed for me over the period of more than a year, became the awesome evidence of the power of human imagination inflamed, the poetry of suggestion, and finally the tragedy of heroic resistance to a society possessed to the point of ruin.

In the stillness of the Salem courthouse, surrounded by the miasmic swirl of images of the 1950s but with my head in 1692, what the two eras had in common was gradually gaining definition. In both was the menace of concealed plots, but most startling were the similarities in the rituals of defence, the investigative routines. Three hundred years apart, both prosecutions were alleging membership of a secret disloyal group. Should the accused confess, his honesty could only be proved in precisely the same way—by naming former confederates, nothing less. Thus, the informer became the very axle of the plot's existence and the investigation's necessity.

Finally, in both eras, since the enemy was first and foremost an idea, normal evidentiary proof of disloyal actions was either de-emphasised, left in limbo, or not required at all, and indeed finally, actions became completely irrelevant. In the end, the charge itself, suspicion itself, all but became the evidence of disloyalty. Most interestingly, in the absence of provable disloyal actions both societies reached for very similar remedies.

Something called the 'Attorney General's List' was promulgated, a list of communist front organizations, membership in which was declared not so much illegal as good reason to suspect subversive conduct or intentions. If membership in an organization could not be called illegal it could at least be made disgusting enough to lose you your job and reputation. One might wonder whether many spies would be likely to join communist fronts, but liberals very possibly might, and indeed had done so at various turns in the road, frequently making common cause with the Left and with communists during the New Deal period a decade earlier.

The witch-hunt in 1692 had a not dissimilar evidentiary problem, but a far more poetic solution. Most suspected people named by others as members of the Devil's conspiracy, had not been shown to have actually *done* anything—neither poisoning wells, setting barns on fire, sickening cattle, aborting babies or calves, nor somehow undermining the virtue of wives (the Devil having two phenomenally active penises, one above the other, as everybody knew). Rather than acts, these suspect folk need only have had the bad luck to have been 'seen' by witnesses consorting with the Devil. The witnesses might be dismally addled hysterics, but they might also be sober citizens who'd somehow gotten themselves suspected of practising witchcraft and could only clear themselves by confessing and naming co-conspirators. But, as in the fifties, there was a supply of non-hysterical lawyers in and around the witch-hunt, as well as Harvard-educated ministers. And, as accusations piled up, one obvious fact became more and more irritating for them: as they well knew, the normal fulcrum of any criminal prosecution, namely acts, deeds, crimes, and witnesses thereto, was simply missing. As for ordinary people, devout and strictly literal about Biblical injunctions as they might be, they still clung to the old habit of expecting some sort of proof of guilt, in this case of being an accomplice to the Devil.

To the rescue came not an Attorney General's List, but a piece of poetry smacking of both legalistic and religious validity—it was called 'Spectral Evidence'. Spectral Evidence, in normal jurisprudence, had been carefully excluded from the prosecutorial armoury by judges and lawyers, as being manifestly open to fabrication. But now, with society under this hellish attack, the fateful decision was made to allow it in, and the effect was the bursting of a dam. Suddenly, all the prosecution need do was produce a witness who claimed to have seen, not an accused person, but what was called his familiar spirit—his living ghost as it were—in the act of poisoning a pig or throwing a burning brand into a barn full of hay. You could be at home asleep in your bed but your spirit could be crawling through your neighbour's bedroom window to feel up his wife. The owner of that wandering spirit was thereupon obliged to account to the court for his crime. With the entrance of Spectral Evidence the air quickly filled with the malign spirits of those identified by good Christians as confederates of the Beast, and with this, of course, the Devil himself really did dance happily into Salem village and proceeded to take the place apart.

In no time at all people in Salem began *looking* at each other with new eyes, and *hearing* sounds from neighbours' throats that they had never heard before, and *thinking* about each other with new and far deeper insights than their former blind innocence toward one another had allowed them. And now, naturally, so many things that had been hidden or befogged suddenly burst open and made sense. Why, for instance, had London annulled all property deeds, flinging people at each other's throats in fights over boundary lines? Why was the congregation forever turning in on itself in fierce doctrinal confrontations and bitter arguments with ministers who one after another had had to flee the contentiousness of Salemites? Clearly, it was the Devil who had been creeping into people's ears and muddling their brains to set them against each other. But now, now at last, with the Lord's help they had the gift of seeing through darkness, the afflicted children had opened up their eyes to the plot in which unknowingly, like innocent birds in a net, they were all caught. Now, with the admission of Spectral Evidence, they could turn to the traitors among them and run them to their deaths.

I spent some ten days in the Salem courthouse reading the crudely recorded trials of the 1692 outbreak, and it was striking how totally absent was any least sense of irony, let alone humour. I can't recall if it was the provincial governor's nephew or son who with a college friend had come from Boston to watch the strange proceedings. At one point both boys burst out laughing at some absurd testimony: they were promptly jailed, and were saved only by friends galloping down from Boston with a bribe for a guard who let them escape from a very possible hanging.

Irony and humour were not exactly conspicuous in the fifties either. I was in my lawyer's office one afternoon to sign some contract and a lawyer in the next office was asked to come in and notarize my signature. While this man was stamping pages, I continued a discussion with my lawyer about the Broadway theatre, which at one point I said was corrupt, that the art of theatre had been totally displaced by the bottom line, which was all that really mattered anymore. Looking up at me, the notarizing lawyer said, 'That's a communist position, you know.' I started to laugh until I saw the constraint in my lawyer's face, and despite myself I quickly sobered up.

I am glad, of course, that I managed to write *The Crucible* but looking back I have often wished I'd had the temperament to do an absurd comedy, which is what the situation so often deserved. There is something funny in the two sophisticated young Bostonians deciding to trot down to Salem to look in on the uproar among the provincials, and failing to realize that they had entered a new age, a new kind of consciousness. Now, after more than three-quarters of a century of fascination with the great snake of political and social developments, I can see more than a few occasions when a lot of us were confronted by the same sensation of having stepped into another age.

Sometime around 1939–40, with the long Spanish Civil War finished and Franco ensconced, a new European war coming closer, and the decade-long Depression lifting at last, the Hollywood studios began flushing out writers in New York for duty on the West Coast. One recruiter sent by Warner Brothers was named, incredibly enough, Colonel Joy. The Colonel was determined to fill boxcars with writers for shipment west. Most of these 'junior writers' were young and were being tempted with a salary of $250 a week, a pittance by Hollywood standards but munificent from the point of view of the deprived denizens of Union Square, Brooklyn and the Bronx. I was acquainted with four or five writers who were packing their bags, a couple of them contributors to and one editor of *New Masses* magazine, a communist weekly. I was young and naive enough to ask this editor, who also had ambitions as a playwright, why he was going west. 'Don't you realize how many people movies reach?' he replied. But with what were they being reached? I wondered. He then mentioned a recent film with John Garfield, the title of which I no longer recall. 'Didn't you see him standing at that bar and saying, "I fought in Spain"? You realize how many people heard that?' It was an action picture, I recalled, and the line had come out of nowhere and gone nowhere.

'But you know what they'd probably make of that?' I said. 'That he'd had a prizefight in Spain; or a fistfight; or maybe even fought on the Franco side. About one in five hundred would know he was referring to the Abe Lincoln Brigade and the Loyalist cause.' I was too timid to ask if he would be going west if the salary was $35 a week instead of $250. There is no conflict of principle and interest that we humans cannot find a way to rationalize, as Molière should have taught us three centuries ago, and I mention this incident now only to reaffirm that the so-called militant Left was born to mothers like anybody else.

My disbelief in the crusade, as it was coming to be called, against communism, was in some important part the product of this same skepticism toward the idealism of the crusaders. (Nevertheless, of course, I continued to genuflect toward the shibboleths of the Left, a habit that dies hard.) But I had made a similar misidentification of the new direction of the wind as the fifties dawned, and worse yet, continued making it.

A young film producer whom I didn't know asked me to write a script for a film about what was then called juvenile delinquency. A mystifying, unprecedented outbreak of gang violence had exploded all over New York. The city, in return for a good percentage of profits, had contracted with this producer to open police stations, schools and so on to his camera. I spent the summer of 1955 in Brooklyn streets with two violent gangs and wrote an outline, which, incidentally, was much praised by the priests leading the city's main Catholic youth organization. I was ready to proceed with the script when an attack on me as a disloyal lefty was opened in the *New York World Telegram*. The cry went up that the city must cancel its contract with the producer so long as I was the screenwriter. A hearing was arranged, attended by some twenty-two city commissioners, including the police, fire, welfare and not least the sanitation departments, as well as two judges.

At the long conference table there also sat a lady in sneakers and a sweater who produced a thick folder of petitions and statements I had signed, going back to my college years, provided to her, she said, by the House Un-American Committee. I defended myself, I thought I was making some sense when the lady began literally screaming that I was killing the boys in Korea. She meant me personally, as I could tell from the froth at the corners of her mouth, the fury in her eyes, and her finger pointing straight into my face. The vote was taken and came up one short of continuing the city's collaboration, and the film was killed that afternoon. As we were filing out, the two judges came up and offered their sympathy. I always wondered whether the crucial vote against me came from the sanitation department. But it was not a total loss; the suffocating sensation of helplessness before the spectacle of the impossible coming to pass would soon help in writing *The Crucible*.

As I indicated in my autobiography, the impossible coming to pass was not merely an observation made at a comfortable distance but a blade cutting directly into my life. This was especially the case with Elia Kazan's decision to co-operate with the House Un-American Activities Committee. Again, the surrounding fears felt even by those with the most fleeting of contacts with any communist-supported organization were running high enough to break through long associations and friendships. Kazan, after all, had been a member of the Party a mere matter of months, and even that link had ended years before. And the Party, moreover, had never been illegal nor was membership in it. Yet this great director, left undefended by Twentieth Century Fox executives, his longtime employers, was told—as he related to me—that if he refused to name people whom he had known in the Party years earlier—actors, directors and writers—he would never be allowed to direct another picture in Hollywood. This was before the era of independently financed movies, and such a threat meant the end of his career in films.

Of course, these names were already known to the committee through other testifiers and FBI informants, but exactly as in Salem—or Russia under the Czar and the Chairman, and in China, Inquisition Spain, Revolutionary France or any other place of revolution or counter-revolution—conspiracy was the name for all opposition. And the reformation of the accused, quite logically, could only be believed when he gave up the names of his co-conspirators. Only this ritual of humiliation, the breaking of his pride and independence, could finally win the accused re-admission into the community. Whether his repentance was wholly or partially sincere, or wholly or partially cynical, was another question; as was indeed, whether his accusers had one eye on the next election. But whatever the case the process inevitably did produce in the accused a new set of political, social and even moral convictions more acceptable to the state whose fist, as it were, had been shoved into his face, with his utter ruin promised should he resist.

Seen up close, however, it was all even more complicated; some confessors experienced genuine relief from the secret burden carried by the outsider, and worse yet, from the obligation of continuing support for eroded, half-believed radical credos of their Depression youth. There was even a certain gratitude for having been forced to emerge from the guilt-ridden shadows into the American light, where accepted opinion and openness prevailed, into the blessed country of the majority which never knows guilt.

As described in *Timebends*, I had stopped by Kazan's house in the country in 1952 after he had called me several times to come and talk, an unusual invitation, when he had never been inclined to indulge in talk unless it concerned work. So I had suspected from his dark tone that it must have to do with the Un-American Committee, which was rampaging through the Hollywood ranks then. Since I was on my way up to Salem for research on a play that I was still unsure I would write, I called at his house, which was on my route. As he laid out his dilemma and his decision to comply with the committee (which he had already done, as it turned out) it was impossible not to feel his anguish, old friends that we were. But the crunch came when I felt fear, that great teacher, that cruel revealer. For it swept over me all at once that had I been one of his comrades he would have spent my name along with others as part of the guarantee of his reform. Even so, oddly enough, I was not filling up with hatred or contempt for him; his suffering was too palpable for that. It was the whole hateful procedure which had brought him to this, and I believe it made the writing of *The Crucible* all but inevitable. For even if one could grant him sincerity in his new-found crusading anti-communism, the concept of an America where such self-discoveries were mandated, pressed out of people, was outrageous and a frightening contradiction of any concept of personal liberty.

Is all this of some objective importance in our history, this destruction of bonds between people? I think it may be, however personal it may appear. It is a fact, after all, that Kazan's testimony against former associates created a far greater shock than anyone else's. Lee Cobb's similar testimony and Jerome Robbins' co-operation with the committee seemed hardly to matter. And it rudely surprised even people who had had no connection of their own with the Left. It is impossible to be sure about this, but it may be, at bottom, that he had been loved more than any other, that he had attracted far greater affection from writers, actors and others with whom he had worked over the years, and so what was overtly a political act was sensed to have been a betrayal of love. This, perhaps, is what unhinged so many and would continue to do so for the next half century, for since they know, consciously or not, that loyal love is dangerously conditional for them as well, it is alarming to see it proved to be so, no matter what its political justifications.

It is very odd and significant, I think, that in the uproar set off by the awarding earlier this year of an Oscar to Kazan for Life Achievement by the Motion Picture Academy, one heard no mention of the name of any member of the House Un-American Committee. One doubted whether the thought so much as occurred to many people that the studio heads at the time had ignominiously collapsed before the committee's insistence that they institute a blacklist of artists in the movie industry, something they had once insisted was too dishonourable to do and a violation of democratic norms to boot. Half a century had passed since his testimony, but Kazan now bore very nearly the whole onus of the era, quite as though he had manufactured its horrors all by himself, when in fact he was surely its victim, however notable—a characterization which, for opposite reasons, both he and those he had named would vociferously deny.

Since you, or some of you, are historians, I have emphasised history in these remarks, but I doubt if I'd have actually written the play had the question of language not so powerfully drawn me on. The trial record in Salem courthouse, a photocopy of which I was allowed to borrow, had been written by ministers in a primitive shorthand. This condensation gave emphasis to a gnarled, densely packed language which suggested the country accents of a hard people. (A few years on, Laurence Olivier would stage his London production using the gruff Northumberland accent.) In any event, to lose oneself day after day in that record of human delusion was to know a fear not perhaps for one's safety precisely, but of the spectacle of perfectly intelligent people giving themselves over to a rapture of such murderous credulity. It was as though the absence of real evidence was itself a release from the burdens of this world; in love with the invisible they moved behind their priests, closer to that mystical communion which is anarchy and is called God. Evidence, in contrast, is effort; leaping to conclusions is a wonderful pleasure, and for a while there was a highly charged joy in Salem, for now that they could see through everything to the frightful plot that was daily being laid bare in court sessions, their days, formerly so eventless and long, were swallowed up in hourly revelations, news, surprises. *The Crucible*, I think, is less a polemic than it might have been had it not been filled with wonder at the protean imagination of man.

I suppose the pithiness of the language and the directness of its imagery were its main attractions. 'What do you say, are you not a witch?' 'No, I know it not, if I were to die presently.'

'Why, it is false,' an accused responds to a charge, 'I know not of it any more than the child that was born tonight.'

One of my most useful sources was the 1867 two-volume history of the trials by Charles W. Upham, who had been Mayor of Salem, albeit nearly a century and a half after the catastrophe. But there were still some seventeenth-century houses, and a number of descendants of participants in the Delusion, as he called it, whose traditions helped him to see obscure connections in court testimony and to draw detailed maps showing where many of the participants' vanished homes had once stood, as well as lanes and byways, long grown over, where people had once moved cattle and goods. It is rather an amazing book, full of canny insights drawn from obscure contradictions in the testimony and also letters of the era. He was able, for example, to deconstruct a deposition, phonetically written, allegedly by one James Carr, a simple farmer, accusing a Mrs Bradley of witchcraft, and to show that in fact it was written by none other than the perfectly literate Thomas Putnam, the same man who was behind so many false accusations, some of which resulted in the deaths of the accused. More, by mouthing the spelling Putnam used, Upham could guess at the way certain words were pronounced a century and a half earlier. '"Corsely",' he writes, 'no doubt shows how the word was then spoken. "Angury" was, with a large class of words now dissyllables, then a trisyllable. "Tould", "spaking", ... are spelled just as they were then pronounced".'

From this and other accusatory depositions I was able to begin sounding the language of 1692 Salem on my own tongue, and they ultimately informed my dialogue. I came to believe, incidentally, that they spoke in a kind of brogue with a Scottish flavour. In any case, with the ample history at my elbow it struck me that Shakespeare's string of long plays might be explained by his having the books to dip into whenever he got stuck for more story. Of course it is never quite that easy; any history is so packed with important characters that their merging into compound personalities, along with the condensation of events, becomes the main order of business. And in the end a new history emerges whose 'truths' may be related to the original facts but do not really replicate them.

The Crucible straddles two very different worlds to make them one, but in the usual sense of the word it is not history but rather a moral, political and psychological construct that floats on the fluid emotions of both eras. As a commercial entertainment the play failed, of course. To start with there was the title: nobody knew what a crucible was. Most of the critics, as sometimes does happen, never caught on to the play's ironical substructure, and the ones who did were nervous about validating a work that was so unkind to the same sanctified procedural principles as underlay the then-current hunt for reds. Some old acquaintances gave me distant nods in the theatre lobby on opening night, and even without air-conditioning the house was noticeably cool. (It reminded me of a remark, allegedly a real one, uttered by a famous Broadway producer of the twenties, Max Gordon, whose play about Napoleon had just flopped. 'I hope I croak before I put on another play where the guy writes with a feather!')

But the problem was also with the temperature of the production. The director, Jed Harris, a great name in the theatre of the twenties, thirties, and into the forties, had decided that the play, which he believed a classic, should be staged like what he called a Dutch painting. In the Dutch paintings of groups everyone is always looking front. We knew this from the picture on the wooden boxes of Dutch Masters cigars. Unfortunately, on a stage such rigidity can only lead an audience to the exits. It would be several years before a gang of young actors, setting up chairs in the ballroom of the McAlpin Hotel, fired up the audience and convinced the critics—and the play at last took off and soon found its place in the world. There were cheering reviews this time, but I couldn't help noting that by then McCarthy was dead. The public fever on whose heatwaves he had spread his wings, had subsided, and more and more people were finding it possible to look into the dying embers and read the terrible message in them.

It is said that no one would buy land in Salem for a hundred years. The very ground was accursed. Salem's people, in the language of the time, had broke charity with one another. But the Devil, as he usually does after such paroxysms, has had the last laugh. Salem refuses to fade into history.

A few years ago the foundations of an old colonial era church in a town near Salem began to sag. The contractor engaged to make repairs dug out some of the loose stones and crawled underneath to inspect matters. There he discovered what looked to him like barely buried human skeletons. Harvard scientists were called in and confirmed that the remains of some twenty-two people were under the church. Now, no one has ever known exactly where the gibbet was located in Salem and the bodies of the twenty-two people hanged there for practising witchcraft have never been found. Moreover, according to one legend they were denied Christian burial as their ultimate punishment.

The scientists wanted to remove the skeletons and try to identify them, but some aged parish leaders, descendants not only of the witchcraft victims but no doubt their persecutors as well, were adamantly opposed. The younger church members were all for it but decided to wait until the elders had passed away rather than start a ruckus about the matter. In short, even after three centuries, the thing, it seems, cannot find its serene, just and uncomplicated end. And oddly enough, something very similar occurred in Salem three hundred years before. After the hunt had blown itself out—after Cotton Mather, having whipped up the hysteria to the point of murder, had finally conceded that supporting the admission of Spectral Evidence had been his dreadful mistake—the legislature awarded, not to all but to some of the victims' families, a few pounds damages along with a mild apology . . . Sorry we hanged your mother, and so forth. But in the true Salem style of solemn bewilderment, this gesture apparently lacked a certain requisite chaos, and so they also included reparations to some informers whose false accusations had gotten people hanged. Victims and victimizers, it was all the same in the end. I suppose it was just the good old American habit of trying to keep everybody happy.

The Crucible is my most-produced play, here and abroad. It seems to be one of the few surviving shards of the so-called McCarthy period. And it is part of the play's history, I think, that to people in so many parts of the world its story seems so like their own. It was in the mid-seventies—dates at my age take on the viscosity of poached eggs—but in any case, I happened to be at my publishers', when another Grove Press author came in. Her eyes filled with tears at our introduction, and she hastened to explain: she was Yuen Cheng, author of Life and Death in Shanghai, the story of her six-year solitary confinement under the Cultural Revolution. It seems that on her release, an old friend, a theatre director, took her to see a new production of his in Shanghai of The Crucible—she had heard of neither the play nor its author. Listening to it, the interrogations sounded so precisely the same as the ones she and others had been subject to under the Cultural Revolutionaries that she couldn't believe a non-Chinese had written it. And picking up the English text she was amazed, she said, not least by the publication date, which of course was more than a decade before the Cultural Revolution. A highly educated woman, she had been living with the conviction that such an outrageous perversion of just procedure could only happen in the China of a debauched revolution! I have had similar reactions from Russians, South Africans, Latin Americans and others who have endured dictatorships, so universal is the methodology of terror portrayed in The Crucible. In fact, I used to think, half-seriously—and it was not far from the truth—that you could tell when a dictator was about to take power in a Latin American country or when one had just been overthrown, by whether The Crucible was suddenly being produced in that country.

The net result of it all I suppose, is that I have come, rather reluctantly, to respect delusion, not least of all my own. There are no passions quite as hot and pleasurable as those of the deluded. Compared to the bliss of delusion, its vivid colours, blazing lights, explosions, whistles and sheer liberating joys, the search for evidence is a deadly bore. In Timebends, I have written at some length about my dealings with Soviet cultural controllers when, as International President of Pen, I would attempt to impress its democratic values upon them in their treatment of writers. Moving about there, and in

East Germany, Hungary, Czechoslovakia in communist times, it was only by main force that I could dredge up memories of my old idealism which I had attached to what in reality had turned out to be little more than a half-feudal society led by an unelected elite. How could this possibly be? I can only think that a man in a rushing river will grasp at any floating thing passing by.

History, or whatever piece of its debris one happens to connect with, is a great part of the answer. For me it was my particular relation to the collapse of key institutions in the Great Depression, the sometimes scary anti-Semitism I kept running into and the Left's thankful condemnation of it; the Spanish Civil War and the all-but-declared pro-fascist sympathies of the British, and Roosevelt's unacknowledged collaboration with their arms blockade of the Republic, the so-called Non-Intervention Policy. Indeed, on Franco's victory, Roosevelt would tell Secretary of the Interior Harold Ickes, according to Ickes' autobiography, that his Spanish policy was 'the worst mistake I ever made'. In a word, out of the great crash of '29 America and the world seemed to awaken to a new sense of social responsibility, something which to the young seemed very much like love. My heart was with the Left if only because the Right hated me enough to want to kill me, as the Germans amply proved. And now, of course, the most blatant and most foul anti-Semitism is in Russia, leaving people like me filled not so much with surprise as a kind of wonder at the incredible amount of hope there once was, and how it disappeared and whether in time it will ever come again, and attached, no doubt, to some new illusion.

So there is hardly a week that passes when I don't ask the unanswerable— what am I now convinced of that will turn out to be ridiculous? And yet one can't forever stand on the shore; at some point, even filled with indecision, skepticism, reservation and doubt, you either jump in or concede that life is forever elsewhere. Which I dare say was one of the major impulses behind the decision to attempt *The Crucible*.

Salem village, that pious, devout settlement at the very edge of white civilization, had displayed—three centuries before the Russo-American rivalry and the issues it raised—what can only be called a kind of built-in pestilence nestled in the human mind, a fatality forever awaiting the right conditions for its always unique, forever unprecedented outbreak of distrust, alarm, suspicion and murder. And for people wherever the play is performed on any of the five continents, there is always a certain amazement that the same terror that had happened to them or that was threatening them, had happened before to others. It is all very strange. On the other hand, the Devil is known to lure people into forgetting precisely what it is vital for them to remember—how else could his endless reappearances always come with such marvellous surprise?

May 1999

TERRY OTTEN

The Crucible *to*
A Memory of Two Mondays

Miller's next stage work was not his own play but an adaptation of Ibsen's *An Enemy of the People*. His admiration for Ibsen long established, he responded positively when Robert Lewis, Frederic March, and March's wife, Florence Eldridge, encouraged him to undertake the project. In addition to his respect for Ibsen's playwriting, Miller was attracted because he shared with the others involved in the effort a fear of growing pro-fascist sentiment that he thought Ibsen's play could question. The producer of the play, a wealthy Swedish businessman, Lars Nordenson, worked directly with Miller in producing the script, translating Ibsen into pidgin English, which Miller then reworked. Miller attributed the play's failure (it was restaged for a short run at Lincoln Center in 1971) not only to "Broadway's historic allergy to uplift masked as entertainment" but to Lewis's direction, which "encouraged a certain self-indulgent picturesqueness and choreographical quality," especially when "March stood over the townspeople with arms outspread like Christ on the cross" (*T*, 324).

The truth is more likely that Miller essentially misread the play as primarily "a teaching play" and "a message work" (*T*, 324). Miller wrote an essay entitled "Ibsen's Warning" in which he argues that *Enemy of the People* "is far more applicable to our nature-despoiling societies than to even turn-of-the-century capitalism, untrammelled and raw as Ibsen knew it to be."

From *The Temptation of Innocence in the Dramas of Arthur Miller*, pp. 60–93. © 2002 by the Curators of the University of Missouri.

Emphasizing the play's polemical importance, he went on to say that "perhaps nature takes on even more of a pure moral value where religion itself has vanished into scepticism."[1] He seems largely to have ignored Ibsen's subtle irony and the near-comic incongruities with which Ibsen at times undercuts his idealistic hero, Dr. Thomas Stockmann. Miller claims that he was attacked for making Ibsen "a front for the Reds" by critics who "sprang to the defense of Ibsen's purity without bothering to read him" (*T*, 325). In truth, as David Bronson argues, Miller did make Ibsen's ambiguous protagonist into something of "a mouthpiece" and "a package of virtue,"[2] in some respects inviting the criticism the play evoked. Inspired by a political agenda, fearful like others of a rising McCarthyism, he tended to sacrifice Ibsen's more ambivalent view of Stockmann and to revert to his own earlier, more simplistic depiction of the moral idealist. When he found the inspiration for his next play buried in the historical records of the Salem witch trials, his image of the idealistic hero took on far greater complexity and richness. In the midst of a growing perspective of the fascist challenge to democratic principles, he discovered a character far more suited to his own tragic vision.

In *The Crucible* Miller again explores American culture in the perspective of tragedy, this time in the historical context of the McCarthy era. Like *All My Sons*, the play is constructed on a conspiracy of silence in which characters do not divulge the truth about others—or, more importantly, about themselves—and gradually fall prey to a deceit so pervasive as to be believed. "I was motivated in some great part by the paralysis that had set in among many liberals who . . . were fearful of being identified as covert Communists if they should protest too strongly," Miller has recently recalled. "Gradually, all the old political and moral reality had melted like a Dali watch. Nobody but a fanatic . . . could really say all that he believed."[3] Employing the historical context of the Salem witch trial like a Greek dramatist exploiting the mythic past, Miller reconstructs the historical moment in the present, transforming documentary records into modern tragedy.

In his well-known study *Historical Drama: The Relation of Literature and Reality*, Herbert Lindenberger acknowledges that in a strict sense historical dramas do not constitute a genre at all. But, he goes on to say, they "prove a special opportunity to examine the transitions between imaginative literature and the external world" by making "a greater pretense at engaging in reality than do writings whose fictiveness we accept from the start."[4] That grounding in reality no doubt explains the attraction Arthur Miller felt in writing about the Salem witch trials in *The Crucible*, excepting perhaps his early work *The Golden Years*, his most historically based drama. Inspired by a chance reading of Marion Starkey's *The Devil in Massachusetts*, Miller renewed an interest in the Salem trials that he had first experienced as an undergraduate at the University of Michigan (*T*, 330). As a consequence of his reading, Miller discovered in the trials a sort of "objective correlative," connecting him not only to the political inquisitions of the McCarthy era, in which he was increasingly embroiled, but also to something deeper—that same strain of American Puritanism that runs across American literature from Jonathan Edwards to Hawthorne to Faulkner and O'Neill. In his autobiography he recalls researching at the Historical Society in Salem in the spring of 1952 and seeing woodcuts and etchings of the 1692 trials; these exposed in him "a familiar inner connection with witchcraft and the Puritan cult, its illusions, its stupidities, and its sublimity too. . . . I felt strangely at home with these New Englanders." He remembers seeing in them "the same fierce idealism, devotion to God, tendency to legislate reductiveness," and "longings for the pure and intellectually elegant argument" he found in his Jewish heritage (*T*, 42). His personal affinity with characters and themes in the historical records and the corresponding political realities of the late forties and early fifties merged to form the matrix of what has become his most performed play and one of the most frequently staged works in modern drama. Recently adapted as an opera by William Bolcom and successfully made into a film in 1996, the drama has also sold in excess of six million paperback books. Despite the cool reception to the premiere on Broadway, "I don't think there has been a week in the past forty-odd years when it hasn't been on a stage somewhere in the world," Miller has recently written.[5]

By employing historical texts, Miller attempts to project his own experience and personal beliefs without violating the truth of the historical matter he surveyed. How a playwright manipulates and transforms the historical record of course determines the legitimacy of a play as historical drama. On one hand, as Niloufer Harben states, a playwright should "be free to approach his subject imaginatively," making "minor alterations such as transpositions of time and place, the telescoping of events and imposing of artistic form and movement." On the other hand, artistic license must be "controlled by an overriding respect for what is actually there in the evidence." Within its contexts, Lindenberger observes, historical drama assumes a protean character and may accommodate conventional and recognized genres such as tragedy or romance. In Miller's hands the historical play becomes a vehicle for modern tragedy in *The Crucible*, carefully sustaining the aura of the historical period but also projecting onto it the political realities of a dark era of modern American history and transfiguring an abbreviated reference to one John Proctor into an existential drama of self-discovery.[6]

To underscore the meaning of Miller's achievement, we might consider his play in juxtaposition with another drama written in the same period, Robert Bolt's *A Man for All Seasons*. Such a comparison is by no means arbitrary or tangential to the issues raised in this study, for despite the differing cultural and historical contexts out of which they wrote their plays, both Miller and

Bolt attempted to employ historical drama to characterize a modern tragic figure. After Bolt's stage drama *A Man for All Seasons*, based on the controversy between Sir Thomas More and Henry VIII, won wide acclaim in London in 1960–1961 and enjoyed a run of 637 performances in New York, it was turned into a highly successful screenplay in 1966—the movie won six Academy Awards. Although it gained its extensive popularity in the sixties, the work was first performed as a radio play in 1954, interestingly only a year following the opening of *The Crucible*. The close chronology does not constitute the major similarity between Bolt's and Miller's texts, however. Both writers attempt to describe a modern protagonist, specifically a hero of self; both depict him as a reluctant character who tries to evade martyrdom of any sort; despite a concern with recreating an accurate historical context, both playwrights conceive of personal character rather than political or economic factors as the chief determinant in the action; and, unlike Bertolt Brecht, whose historical play *Galileo* was staged just two weeks before the original stage production of *A Man for All Seasons*, both Bolt and Miller are less concerned with historical process than with the plight of the individual in a historical moment.[7]

Furthermore, the two playwrights both briefly flirted with communist ideology before writing their plays; perhaps more importantly, both saw their works as responses to the growing anticommunist sentiment in the West in the postwar period, especially in the United States. Miller's first unpublished dramas (*No Villain or They Too Arise, Honors at Dawn*, and *The Great Disobedience*) were strongly Marxian in character, and of course Miller was already feeling the heat of the McCarthy hearings at the time he seriously began to work on *The Crucible*, though he had considered writing about the witch trials much earlier in his career. Bolt, as William Free points out, had experienced and abandoned an early commitment to Marxism as well, emphasizing instead the capacity of the individual to color "the events which the forces of history determine." In the inevitable comparison with Brecht, some critics with Marxist leanings especially criticized Bolt's failure to, in Kenneth Tynan's words, "reveal [More's] convictions. . . . Mr. Bolt tells us nothing about More's convictions or how he came to embrace them." Such criticism echoes the objections of critics of Miller's play, like Eric Bentley and Tom Driver, that the American dramatist's "quasi-Marxist stamp" made his plays "mere partisan critique," lacking the profundity of more authentic Marxian dramas by Brecht or Pirandello. But the criticism is ill-directed in reference to both writers, for neither Bolt nor Miller embraced Marxism to any significant degree. Although both accepted the reality of historical determinism in the shaping of events, they saw the individual caught in the historical moment as capable of independent, if ill-fated, choice. As Christopher Bigsby has written, for Miller, drama exists in "the nexus between determinism and free will."[8]

To be sure, despite the obvious similarities, *The Crucible* and *A Man for All Seasons* do differ in essential ways. Miller's use of a seemingly minor historical character certainly contrasts with Bolt's focus on one of the major shaping figures of the Renaissance. Miller is somewhat less bound by historical records than Bolt in developing his hero, though Bolt certainly uses considerable freedom in constructing his text. Miller found his play's center, he writes in *Timebends*, in a relatively abbreviated account of the breakdown of the Proctor marriage and in Abigail Williams's effort to discredit Elizabeth Proctor, as recorded in Charles W. Upham's *Salem Witchcraft* (*T*, 337). Assuming the artistic license accorded an author of historical drama, Miller created a fictional character riveted to a distinct historical frame but imbued with the traits of a modern existential hero. Borrowing especially from R. W. Chambers's biography of More, Bolt, too, took the liberty to remodel his historical hero, making him into a "man for all seasons."[9] But the dramatic distinction between the two creations is the discrimination between heroism given and heroism earned, and the difference indicates the potential of historical drama in the twentieth century to produce both eloquent melodrama and modern tragedy.

As noted earlier, any attempt to define tragedy brings with it certain risks, as Miller's own commentaries on the subject surely suggest. On one hand, definitions tend to be reductive and exclusionary of works that can be wrongfully tainted as inferior because they do not measure up to some formulaic pattern; on the other hand, generic paradigms may well exaggerate the value of a work solely on the grounds that it fits a given model. Nonetheless, without some attempt at definition, no critical distinctions can be drawn— so the risk must be taken. For my purposes I again wish to employ the description of tragedy offered by the eminent Shakespearean scholar Robert Heilman, as discussed in the previous chapter. In an early but often-cited essay entitled "Tragedy and Melodrama: Speculations on Generic Form," Heilman summarizes the differences between tragedy and melodrama:

> In melodrama, man is seen in his strength or in his weakness; in tragedy, in both his strength and his weakness at once. In melodrama, he is victorious or he is defeated; in tragedy, he experiences defeat in victory, or victory in defeat. In melodrama, man is simply guilty or simply innocent; in tragedy his guilt and his innocence coexist. In melodrama, man's will is broken, or it conquers; in tragedy, it is tempered in the suffering that comes with, or brings about, new knowledge.[10]

These distinctions identify the major contrasts between Bolt's and Miller's plays and account for much of the durability and, arguably, superiority of Miller's forceful drama. To refine the distinction noted we can collapse the major differences between a melodramatic and tragic character to this: A melodramatic character is "whole," in Heilman's terms, whereas a tragic hero is "divided." A "whole" character is weak or strong, innocent or guilty; a tragic character is both weak and strong, innocent and guilty.

At no point does Bolt's Sir Thomas More display weakness of character, though he is of course physically vulnerable. Bolt so elevates his character that when he first introduces him, he says, "the life of his mind . . . illuminated his body." And every character who encounters More, from King Henry to his beloved Daughter Meg, acknowledges his goodness and moral firmness. Moreover, if More is wholly good, his antagonist, Cromwell, is entirely evil. In Heilman's definition, the ultimate antagonist in a true tragedy is the self, but in *A Man for All Seasons*, Cromwell plays the conventional "bad guy," a "dockside bully" whose threats More easily dismisses as "terrors for children . . . an empty cupboard: to frighten children in the dark."[11] Cromwell is More's opposite, not his own other self; and lacking any of Cromwell in himself, More remains "whole." He instinctively recognizes Cromwell's crass Machiavellian devotion to political cunning, and at every turn he battles his enemy with the untarnished weapon of his moral purity. In short, More's innocence is never seriously jeopardized, not by Wolsey's argument of accommodation, not by the Spanish ambassador Chapuy's appeal of loyalty to the "Church," not by his loyal friend Norfolk's pragmatism or Cromwell's bullying threats or Henry's pleading, not even by the loving concerns of his son-in-law, Roper, or, above all, his beloved wife, Alice, or daughter, Meg—against every threat or temptation, he stands foursquare.

John Proctor, on the other hand, is clearly a divided character, driven by the counter-demands of "impulse" and "imperative," to again use Heilman's terms. Having succumbed to lust for Abigail Williams, he has sinned against his own values. Miller makes use of the brief reference to Proctor in recorded documents to place him in a historical context ripe for tragedy. According to Miller, the witch trials occurred at a time when "the idea of exclusion and prohibition" essential to theocratic ideology was being undermined by a sense that "the repressions of order were heavier than seemed warranted by the dangers against which the order was organized" (*C*, 6). Desperate to maintain tight control, the theocratic system asserted its absolutism, generating a historical conflict between what Heilman calls the "imperative" for order and an "impulsive" will to power, a reflection of the Nietzschean dialectic of Apollonian and Dionysian principles described in *The Birth of Tragedy*. The conflict that results resides not alone in the society but more essentially in the self, as Miller conceives it, in John Proctor. Unlike Bolt's hero, Miller's endures a profound internal conflict that generates the tragic crisis in the play. Proctor is "a damaged man," Miller has said, at odds with himself as much as with the external forces that endanger him: "The most important thing is that Proctor is not to be heroic."[12] In the Massey Lecture of 1999, Miller relates Proctor's reluctance to speak out to the silence of the Left during the McCarthy era, which "bespoke a guilt that the Right found a way to exploit" (*E*, 285).

Although Miller, like Bolt, modified the historical accounts (reducing the number of girls in the "crying out," making Abigail Williams older and Proctor younger, limiting the judges to the primary characters Hathorne and Danforth), he claims in a brief headnote that "the fate of each character is exactly that of his historical model" and that the characters "play a similar—and in some cases exactly the same—role as in history." He adds that "little is known about most of the characters. . . . They may therefore be taken as creations of my own, drawn to the best of my ability in conformity with their known behavior" (*C*, 2). *The Crucible* thereby fulfills the definition of a historical play, as discussed earlier, and moves it toward the dimensions of tragedy.

Predictably some postmodern theorists have assaulted Miller's conception of "heroism" that simply does not mesh with the cynicism attached to much current theory. In his deconstructionist reading of *The Crucible*, for example, Joseph Valente calls the play "a contradictory form of dramatic praxis," an "unwitting" portrayal that "purchases the legitimacy of its protest against . . . one witch hunt with its assistance in perpetuating [an]other." In fact, Miller knowingly creates the drama of a flawed hero. At one point Miller characterizes Proctor by describing him in terms of "the concept of unity" accepted by the physical sciences, "in which positive and negative are attributes of the same force, in which good and evil are relative, ever-changing, and always point to the same phenomenon" (*C*, 31). It is More's innocence that attests to his heroism; it is Proctor's lack of innocence that affirms his. That is, Proctor is capable of both good and evil. In an interview with Robert Lee Feldman on Nazi war criminals, Miller mirrors the distinction between melodrama and tragedy expressed by Heilman, observing that melodrama occurs in a play that "is primarily between a perfectly good and a perfectly evil personality" and embodies "a conflict between people rather than within people."[13] In this regard *The Crucible* portrays a tragic figure.

Unlike Bolt's hero, Proctor "is a sinner," Miller writes, and "not only against the moral fashion of the time, but against his own vision of decent conduct"—he "has come to regard himself as a kind of fraud" (*C*, 19). Whereas More, like Proctor, attempts to evade martyrdom, he does so only because he wills to save his life, not because he deems himself unworthy. Bolt describes him as "a man with an adamantine sense of his own self. He knew where he began and left off."[14] Proctor, however, exposes "deep hatred of himself"; he tells Mary Warren in a fit of rage, "Now Hell and Heaven grapple on our backs, and our old pretense is ripped away. . . . [W]e are only what we always were, but naked now" (*C*, 76). He shouts at Danforth, "A fire, a fire is burning! I hear the boots of Lucifer, I see his filthy face. It is my face, and yours, Danforth!" (111). He finds in Danforth a mirror image of his own criminality. In contrast, there is no such mirror for More, no other self to reflect his own capacity for evil. Yet, ironically, it is Proctor's consciousness of his complicity that generates his authenticity as a tragic figure, for it provides the necessary "Other" that defines the measure of his heroism, a heroism gained by contesting the spurious innocence he first tries to claim and insure.

Even in the trial scene in act 3, though hounded by guilt, Proctor casts the blame on Abby, labeling her "whore" and "a lump of vanity." He acts neither heroically nor tragically. Only after fully acknowledging his own culpability can he assume the mantle of tragic hero. So it is that when Elizabeth attempts to blame her own frigidity for his adultery and its consequences, claiming "You take my sins upon you, John," Proctor, "in agony," can respond, "No, I take my own, my own!" (C, 127).

Furthermore, even though Rebecca Nurse and other admirable characters recognize Proctor's essential goodness just as More's compatriots recognize More's nobility, Miller does not diminish his guilt. Like the other girls, Mercy Lewis both fears and is "strangely titillated by John Proctor," implying Proctor's sexuality as much as her moral looseness (C, 20). And his guilt is already known or assumed when the play opens. Abby's inability to secure a new position after being discharged by Elizabeth suggests that Proctor's adultery is already suspected by the community. Proctor's brutish treatment of Mary Warren also hints at his guilt. Her insistence that she will "not stand for whipping any more!" (56) suggests that she has been victimized by him before. And Proctor's spurning of the saintly Rebecca Nurse's plea that he clasp Reverend Parris's hand and heal the breach between them gives further evidence of his quick temper and vengefulness.

Above all, despite his avowed attempt to free himself from Abby, Proctor is apparently attracted to her even after she leaves his house. Abby tells him at the beginning of the play that she is drawn at night by "a sense of heat, John, and yours has drawn me to the window, and I have seen you looking up, burning in your loneliness"—and he must confess, "I may have looked up" (C, 21–22). In her intense feminist reading, Wendy Schissel charges Miller with "blaming the victim" and accuses Miller and his critics of experiencing "vicarious enjoyment . . . in a cathartic male character who has enacted their sexual and physical fantasies."[15] But Miller in fact uses Abby to expose, not conceal or excuse, Proctor's guilt, and he uses Elizabeth to reinforce rather than exonerate Proctor's culpability. Elizabeth tells her defensive husband with cutting truth, "She has an arrow in you yet, John Proctor, you know it well!" (59). Even when Abby admits to him that she and the others were dancing in the woods when Betty Parris took fright, he smiles widely at her and says half-flirtatiously, "Ay, you're wicked, yet, aren't y'!" (20). She reminds him that "John Proctor took me from my sleep and put knowledge in my heart! . . . You loved me, John Proctor, and whatever sin it is, you love me yet!" Significantly, he does not deny her claim but rather "turns abruptly to go out" (22).

Seven months after Abby's departure, in the very present of the play, Elizabeth catches Proctor dissembling, committing the same offense he condemns the theocratic leaders of employing. She reminds him that he said he saw Abby in a crowd but then later inadvertently admitted he talked with her alone. His anger at being found out in his deceit only verifies his guilt. According to Schissel, "we are meant to read" this as "understandably defensive anger," but in fact we are truly "meant to read it" exactly as Miller writes it, to show that Elizabeth is right in her condemnation of Proctor. Miller carefully does not let Proctor off the hook in the scene, as Schissel contends. Furthermore, by dropping Abby from act 4 (and excluding her from act 2), Miller emphasizes the internal crisis in Proctor and avoids diminishing his guilt by shifting blame onto Abby in the final scenes. Rather he places the full weight of responsibility onto Proctor himself. It is worth noting that until Proctor finally owns up to his own duplicity, it is Elizabeth who provides the moral focus in the play, a point given forceful emphasis in Joan Allen's portrayal of Elizabeth in the 1996 film adaptation. In Allen's interpretation, as Boston Globe film critic Jay Carr writes, Proctor's resolute wife "never courts his approval—or, more importantly, ours. She's cold . . . but she's honorable and she's right."[16] When Proctor tells Elizabeth, "I come into a court when I come into this house!" she rightly responds, "The magistrate sits in your heart that judges you" (*C*, 52). Elizabeth insists that he tell the court of the fraud, whereas he fears standing alone as accuser and, perhaps more than he realizes, wants to protect Abby. And there is clearly irony when Proctor accuses Hale of cowardice for letting Elizabeth be jailed when he himself has played the coward all along by denying his affair with Abby. When Proctor does go to court to expose the lies, he acts less out of principle than the need to protect Elizabeth, more out of fear than a sense of justice. However, in Bolt's play, Sir Thomas More acts courageously from the beginning; his heroism is a given. Proctor becomes a tragic hero despite himself.

Ostensibly, More, too, attempts to avoid martyrdom. And like Proctor he tries every legal means of escape. When the bill is issued requiring a loyalty oath to Henry (certainly an intended reference to the McCarthy hearings, which also cast their shadow in Miller's play), More insists it is "God's part" to bring us to martyrdom, but "Our natural business is escaping—so let's get home and study this Bill."[17] But More is undoubtedly "the stuff" of martyrdom from his very first appearance on stage. He cannot not be a martyr, because nothing in him serves as a polar opposite to his absolute but existentially untested faith. Consequently, in the trial scene in *A Man for All Seasons*, More has nothing to confess, and so he can only be unjustly condemned. He suffers death because of Rich's perjury, not because he committed offenses against the legal code and certainly not against himself.

Proctor, though, knows that he "lusted, and there is promise in such sweat" (*C*, 102), confirming what Elizabeth had told him: "There is a promise made in any bed—" (58). Although he still tries to protect his innocence by taking cheap shots at Abby in court, noting that "she were twice this year put out of this meetin' house for laughter during prayer" (96), he must accept the consequences of his own actions as well as the injustice of the corrupt system. When he tries to escape martyrdom, therefore, he is motivated by his consciousness of his own unworthiness. Even to the very end, his self-judgment keeps him from playing the hero: "I cannot mount the gibbet like a saint. It is a fraud. I am not the man" (126). Not only does he not act heroically, he acts out of fear as well. Driven by self-preservation and self-judgment, he seemingly lacks More's capacity for heroism. "Let them that never lied die now to seek their souls," Proctor says of his condemned friends. "It is pretense for me . . ." (126). In his spirited attack on Tom Driver's position that Miller offers only "strident moralism" in defense of Proctor, E. Miller Budick notes that Proctor tries throughout not to acknowledge evil, including his own, and by his silence perpetuates it until the end of the drama when he discovers a morality "dependent upon recognizing and accepting" his own "humanness." Evil, Proctor finally comes to understand, "is more primary than the Devil who incorporates it," and it exists in the self. "Thus Miller puts the emphasis of his play on the importance of self-awareness, the recognition of evil within one's self, and the acknowledgment that this evil may be projected onto others through no fault of theirs."[18]

More attests to his heroic nature throughout the drama, so the action in the play turns not on self-discovery but on plot, which is in some respects the limitation of Miller's *All My Sons* and the earlier unpublished plays. When he therefore speaks eloquently to his family in the jail cell, More has already fully accepted his pending death without painful self-judgment. He represents a transcendent authority he has always claimed. Even when Meg offers up the greatest temptation, "doing the right deed for the wrong reason," in T. S. Eliot's famous phrase from *Murder in the Cathedral*,[19] More easily brushes it aside. Eliot's renowned play on the martyrdom of Thomas Becket is also an example of the history play as significant melodrama. Eliot forgoes the inner conflict to establish Becket's mythic heroism in language and deed, just as Bolt resorts to rhetoric and gesture to illuminate More. We never doubt for a moment that Becket will do the right deed for the right reason. In *The Crucible* the Fourth Tempter moves from static stage to dynamic reality. Miller gives us a historical figure in self-conflict, not an archetypal saint. We get tragedy in Miller, spectacle in Bolt and Eliot. More remains unchallenged; when Meg warns, "if you elect to suffer for it, you elect yourself a hero," More answers confidently, "we must stand fast a little—even at the risk of being heroes."[20] He endures no internal debate and suffers from no self-doubt.

But whereas Bolt depicts no conflict in More, Miller brings Proctor to a point of existential confrontation. He allows for the possibility of self-deception as Bolt never does. When Proctor seeks Elizabeth's forgiveness, she places the burden properly on him: "There be no higher judge under Heaven than Proctor is!" (*C*, 127)—a truth she ironically acquires because she has accepted responsibility for her own failure as a wife. Coming to the awareness that he must judge himself because he himself is responsible, Proctor must ask the existential question, "God in Heaven, what is John Proctor, what is John Proctor?" (127). Christopher Bigsby rightly concludes that the process that most concerns Miller "is clearly . . . self-betrayal."[21] And even to the end, as Proctor tries every avenue of escape, he betrays his own moral principles. It is guilt that both debilitates him and generates his heroism. More tries to evade his death by hiding in the tangle of the law; but once the law itself is violated, he willingly, almost eagerly, embraces his death. He would have been incapable of perjuring himself like Proctor does when he offers his false confession to save himself.

Proctor's heroism does not come so easily. It comes only when he discovers he will be "used" to compromise the fame of those truly martyred. Whereas the plot turns when Elizabeth lies to save Proctor, the essential "action in character" reaches the climax only when Proctor destroys the signed confession. In the first case Proctor is subject to another's action, in the second to his own. Michael J. O'Neal calls the tearing up of the confession "a bit of grandstanding."[22] But Miller makes a critical distinction between confessing orally and signing one's name—"How may I live without my name?" Proctor asks; "I have given you my soul" (*C*, 133). More secures his soul by not taking the oath; in confessing, Proctor willingly offers up his "soul," negating any claim of transcendence. But the signed "name" attests to the here and now. It is an existential emblem, a personal affirmation, not a symbol of transcendental glory. Finally, when More dies he remarks to the Headsman, "Friend, be not afraid of your office. You send me to God."[23] Proctor dies with no such trust in the hereafter or God—"I say—I say—God is dead!" (111). He sees not God's assurance, but at least some degree of self-worth: "for I do think I see some shred of goodness in John Proctor. Not enough to weave a banner with, but white enough to keep it from such dogs" (133). His modest existential victory illustrates once again Miller's often-repeated dictum that in tragedy the "birds come home to roost. . . . You've got to retrieve what you've spent and you've got to account for it somehow. I don't mean to God, I mean to yourself, or else you are totally incomplete always. . . . You get existential justice, where you do your best, but that's about it" (*AMC*, 201).

According to Heilman's definition, melodramas (or what he labels "disasters") such as *A Man for All Seasons* end "monopathically," because we the audience experience a single strong emotion—we feel pathos for a good man victimized by injustice or fate. Tragedy ends "polypathically," because although we feel sorrow at the protagonist's death, we also feel that justice has somehow been satisfied, that the tragic figure pays a price for his own choices even though he also may be the unjust victim of powers beyond his control. Furthermore, his suffering ultimately ennobles him—we rejoice that suffering leads to a self-awareness, and so we experience a paradoxical "victory in defeat." An innocent victim but an absolute hero, More is totally victorious over a degenerate system; a divided character, Proctor gains self-recognition only through self-confrontation and self-judgment. Unlike More he moves from something and to something, from paralyzing innocence to a morally energizing guilt. If the focus in *The Crucible* were only on the horrors of the system that produced the witch trials and congressional hearings, then the evil would be clearly identifiable and contained. In this regard, Proctor is undoubtedly the hero, the rebel against a repressive system. But Miller asks us to see another, more subtle, and profound drama, in which the protagonist is fighting personal betrayal as well. To believe in his heroism we must also believe in the gravity of his offense against others and his own values, or else the moral victory rings hollow. Miller attempts to make the guilt credible. Indeed, as Christopher Bigsby observes, it is Proctor's "guilt that creates the conditions for self-betrayal."[24]

Bolt presents historical narrative in the form of polished melodrama; Miller transforms historical narrative into modern tragedy. The distinction is important, for as Eric Bentley reminds us, although "there is melodrama in every tragedy," tragedy "is melodrama plus something."[25] Miller's play is not hospitable to historical or Marxian determinism because it insists that human beings choose and so must accept responsibility. Miller declares in the Massey Lecture that *The Crucible* taught him "that a kind of built-in pestilence was nestled in the human mind, a fatality forever awaiting the right conditions for its always unique, forever unprecedented outbreak of alarm, suspicion and murder" (*E*, 295). If characters are victims, they are the victims of themselves, not simply of class or economic forces or social imperatives or political oppression. Yet Miller also insists on a paradoxical, but not contradictory, belief in destiny, in the inevitability of the meeting at the crossroads where once more his modern Oedipus must face his fate and yet claim that, although Apollo has brought him to his place, he has been his own criminal and his own judge.

A View from the Bridge

A View from the Bridge germinated from a story Miller's friend Vinny Longhi heard about a longshoreman's betrayal of two brothers to immigration authorities. He wrote the play several years after hearing the tale, when Martin Ritt asked Miller if he had a one-act he might stage at the Cornet Theater with a group of talented young actors. One-acts were then virtually never performed in New York and Miller had none on hand, so he responded by transforming the story into a one-act play, which he first called *An Italian Tragedy*, in a period of only one or two weeks; he added to this offering *A Memory of Two Mondays*, a one-act autobiographical play he considered "a kind of elegy for my years in [an] auto parts warehouse" (*T*, 353). *A View* instinctively seemed to him especially appropriate for the genre—"it always seemed to me to be a one-act play" (*AMC*, 366). He clearly considered it a tragedy in the tradition of classic Greek dramas, which he noted were always one-acts:

> [E]verything that is said in the Greek classic play is going to advance the order, the theme, in manifest ways. There is no time for the character to reveal himself apart from thematic considerations.... So I began *A View From the Bridge* in its first version with a feeling that it would make a single, constantly rising trajectory, until the fall, rather like an arrow shot from a bow.... I wanted to reveal the method nakedly to everyone so that from the beginning of the play we are to know that this man can't make it, and yet might reveal himself somehow in the struggle. (*Conv.*, 366–67)

Intent upon avoiding "the spectacle of still another misunderstood victim" and the "psycho-romanticism" that he felt produced "mere sympathy" on stage (*TE*, 219), as he wrote in the introduction to the 1960 republication of the play, Miller wanted to construct a play stripped of any extraneous material that might retard the protagonist's inexorable movement to his fated end. The opening New York production failed, however, only to be successfully restaged in London scarcely a year later. The young English director Peter Brook told Miller that the original play was "too relentless in the sense that some of the life of the family, the neighborhood, had been squeezed out." Convinced that Brook was right, Miller modified the play, slightly expanding it to two acts, letting "that life back in, especially the dilemma as seen by the wife.... I could see on the stage that I could give those actors more meat, and let the structure take care of itself a little" (*Conv.*, 367).[26]

The revisions in the two-act version (reducing or altering some of the free verse into prose, especially in Alfieri's speeches; incorporating more of the Red Hook environment; amplifying the characterization of Beatrice and Catherine; using the boxing scene between Eddie and Rodolpho to climax the first act; intensifying the triangles of Eddie-Catherine-Beatrice and Eddie-Catherine-Rodolpho; and revising the ending) have inevitably created disagreement among critics about which text is better, although Miller chose the two-act version for the *Collected Plays*. It subsequently has been the essential text performed on stage, and so it is the basis of my discussion here.[27]

Although *A View* seems to extend Miller's already established themes— the quest for identity, the conflict between society and the individual, the loss of innocence, the theme of betrayal—some feel it marks a departure from his earlier work. According to Robert Heilman, Miller "deliberately made a turn away from victims . . . who can never be tragic, to the story of self-injuring personality," though Heilman goes on to say that because Eddie "never knows himself, [he] falls away from the tragic magnitude that he has when . . . he is doubly caught between an imperative and a destructive passion." John Orr goes so far as to call Eddie "unconditionally tragic," unlike Willy Loman and John Proctor, and claims the play possesses "the power of tragedy" lacking in *Death of a Salesman* and *The Crucible*. Alan Stambusky, on the other hand, labels it "a final abortive attempt to display the tragedy of the common man in classical terms. . . . Eddie lacks true nobility of motive." And John Styan contends that the revised text, with its emphasis on Beatrice and Catherine's awareness of the sexual crisis in Eddie, moves *A View* "away from the Greeks" and as well "away from the social drama, away from the Ibsen of the social plays—perhaps toward Chekhov." Clinton W. Trowbridge insists, though, that the play "shows a profound change in Miller's concept of fate," in that Eddie's "struggle is within, with a person that he can neither understand nor control," whereas in the earlier plays fate surfaces in the guise "of the social, economic or political forces in society."[28]

But in fact the drama's juxtaposing of counterforces operating within Eddie resembles the internal conflicts endured by Willy Loman and John Proctor in *Death of a Salesman* and *The Crucible*. Eddie's struggle to claim his name mirrors Willy's attempt to leave a thumbprint in the world and Proctor's effort to preserve his name; and it even echoes Mark Donegal's more simplistic quest for self-integrity in *The Half-Bridge*. Miller explores the psychological dimension with more intensity, perhaps, but the existential issue of self-identity had always been the driving motivation in his work. *A View* seemed to him inherently tragic in the Greek sense in its unwavering trajectory and inevitability, but he conceived of it, especially in the two-act version, as inextricably bound with a psychological and social determinism that seals Eddie's fate the more.

Miller has never considered his plays as narrowly deterministic, however. "Determinism," he has written, "is a contradiction of the idea of drama itself as drama has come down to us in its fullest development. . . . It is a process inconceivable without the existence of the will of man. His will is as much a fact as his defeat" (*TE*, 168). The two-act version, first performed in London in October of 1958, enhanced both the mythological thrust of the play and the psychosexual drama. As he writes in the 1960 introduction to the play, "The importance of [Eddie's] interior psychological drama was magnified to the size it would have in life. What had seemed like a mere aberration had now risen to a fatal violation of ancient law" (*TE*, 221). The three-storied tenement buildings in the London staging and the evocation of the Sicilian community of Red Hook established a closed and elementally threatening world. "On those fire escapes the neighbors appeared at the end like a chorus, and Eddie could call up to them, to his society and his conscience. . . . The splitting in half of the whole three story tenement . . . opened the mind to the size of the mythic story" (*T*, 431). Here, unlike in the New York opening, members of the tight-knit society walked the streets and stared down from fire escapes, and interrelationships formed rigid societal bounds. More mythical and symbolic than naturalistic, the environment spoke of undeniable forces against which Eddie vainly attempts to exist. Writes Miller, "once Eddie had been placed squarely in his social context, among his people, the mythlike feeling of the story emerged of itself, and he could be made more human and less a figure, a force" (*TE*, 222). Internally driven by the unrelenting impulse to possess his niece, Eddie pays ironic allegiance to the ancient code of the polis that ultimately denies him. Euripidean in its passionate intensity, the drama retains a Sophoclean nature as well. Hopelessly divided, Eddie acts under the insistence of incestuous desire while futilely trying to maintain order. As Steven Centola observes in his essay "Compromise as Bad Faith," the play reflects the Freudian dialectic between order and chaos, between "civilization and its discontents." Recognizing Eddie's inability to articulate his crisis, Miller employs a stage narrator as chorus to provide the moral perspective and interpret events for the audience, much like the Greek chorus served as liaison between stage and audience. A "minor" but "crucial" character, in Miller's words, Alfieri, the lawyer-narrator, "represents common sense in the way that Greek choruses did. That is, common sense in relation to excess" (*Conv.*, 262–63).[29] Yet as he well knows, Alfieri is as helpless to avert the pending tragedy as the chorus in *Oedipus the King* or Linda in *Death of a Salesman*. Alfieri compares himself to "another lawyer" in ancient times who "heard the same complaint and sat there as powerless as I, and watched it run its bloody course" (*VB*, 5). Possibly modeled on a young lawyer from a Neapolitan family Miller knew, Alfieri stands outside the action and yet gives us an "objective" view in language that Miller intended to be "above mere everyday language without giving him too stiff a quality" (*Conv.*, 158). Alfieri's often elevated and dignified tone contrasts with the harsh colloquialisms of the blue-collar community and provides a more dispassionate view that transforms the psychological and social realism into myth. In Donald Costello's words, Alfieri "mythologizes the tale" by expanding it beyond the personal, familial, and social into the "universal . . . beyond time and space."[30] Lawyers, of course, figure prominently in Miller's works, which so often center on literal or symbolic trials. In *A View* the contest between the legal system and the ancient code of the Sicilian community of Red Hook, and even more elementally between illicit impulse and communal imperative within Eddie himself, constitutes a universal and timeless moral conflict that Eddie Carbone can neither evade nor resolve. The title alludes to the bridge linking the view of contemporary culture with the past, Miller has noted; from this vantage point, Alfieri senses that in "a little neighborhood an ancient tragedy is being worked out. . . . The narrator's view . . . is looking at it all from the point of view of American civilization and that ancient one that is really down there" (*AMC*, 111).

Like Willy Loman, Eddie Carbone possesses an innocence born of self-ignorance, what Christopher Bigsby describes as a yearning for "a kind of adolescency"—and such a "yearning for innocence is not merely a symptom of its loss but the beginning of an implacable evil."[31] Once again, nothing is so potentially destructive as the temptation of innocence, and Eddie's vain attempt to secure his innocence provides the impetus for the tragedy he brings upon himself. Yet ironically, even Catherine unwittingly preys on his innocence, acquiring a measure of complicity in his destruction.

The stage directions often show Catherine as a seductive figure, bound by her own naive innocence. But Catherine projects an innocence that Iskar Alter rightly calls "the innocence that unwittingly kills,"[32] and consequently assumes a degree of responsibility for the tragic consequences, however unaware she may be. When she first appears before Eddie to show off a new dress, she runs her hands down her skirt, "turns for him," walks "him to the armchair" and "sits on her heels before him" (*VB*, 5–6). Later she lights Eddie's cigar, nearly burning her hand because she is so focused on him (20). When toward the end of the play Rodolpho asks, "Why are you so afraid of him?" (60), her long pause hints at something she fears to acknowledge. Her admission that "I can tell when he's hungry or wants a beer before he ever says anything. I know when his feet hurt, I mean I know him . . ." (61) constitutes a deeper confession than she intends or perhaps even understands. According to Albert Rothenberg and Eugene Shapiro, both Eddie and Catherine employ "projection, rationalization and repression" as defense mechanisms, and their "defensive patterns remain basically the same throughout the play, and they complement and intensify each other."[33] At one point Beatrice reminds Catherine, "You still walk around in front of him in your slip [and] . . . sit at the edge of the bathtub talkin' to him when he's shavin' in his underwear," and "when he comes home you sometimes throw yourself at him like you was twelve years old" (40). When she concludes "You're a grown woman, and you're in the same house with a grown man"

(40–41) and insists that Catherine say good-bye, Catherine's naïveté finally gives way to self-knowledge, and she "turns with some fear, with a discovery, to Beatrice" (41). Ignorance is not synonymous with genuine innocence for Miller, and in his view no one can ultimately claim innocence. We all live after the Fall. Even at the end, when Eddie's need to protest his innocence leads him to violate the communal code by reporting Rodolpho and Marco, Beatrice sounds the chord: "Whatever happened we all done it, and don't you ever forget it, Catherine" (82),[34] anticipating Dr. Hyman's remark in *Broken Glass* that "we get sick in twos and threes, not alone as individuals" (*BG*, 27). And even Beatrice's innocence is compromised by her urging Eddie to forget what has happened and her assuring him that he is not responsible for his actions. Her complicity of accommodation, of ignoring the truth and evading responsibility, cannot be excused. But as Steven Centola concludes, "Beatrice and Catherine's culpability does not mitigate Eddie's responsibility" even though "Miller does seem to suggest that Beatrice and Catherine cannot be excused for their insincerity."[35]

It is of course Eddie's need for innocence that propels the play to its tragic end, and his guilt cannot be diminished by making it somehow communal. Unwilling or unable to see his own culpability, he displaces it by targeting Rodolpho. But it remains uncertain whether or not even Rodolpho is blameless. To be sure, Eddie's accusation of Rodolpho as a homosexual is a ruse to conceal his own unacknowledged love for Catherine.[36] He tells Alfieri that Rodolpho "give me the heeby-jeebies the first moment I seen him" (*VB*, 69). Noting his effeminate traits and actions—his blond hair and too-high tenor voice,[37] his cooking and sewing, his "pointy" shoes—he tells Beatrice that Rodolpho is taunted by the other longshoremen who work with him. Eddie must believe in his rival's guilt to displace his own; yet we do not know that Rodolpho's intentions are totally innocent, not because of supposed homosexuality but because he may be using Catherine. Given the immigrant experience, there may be some credibility in Eddie's claim that Rodolpho wants to marry Catherine to secure his citizenship even if the accusation that Rodolpho is gay is totally spurious.

Nevertheless, from the beginning Eddie reveals a powerful sense of guilt even as he claims the role of defender of the communal code. When Beatrice first warns him to "leave [Catherine] alone," he responds with "open fright" and "in guilt walks out of the house" (*VB*, 38). Confidently judging his seventy-four-year-old Sicilian neighbor Vinny Bolzano for fingering his own uncle to immigration authorities (". . . a guy do a thing like that? How's he gonna show his face?" [18]), he seems horrified by Beatrice's insistence that he wants "somethin' . . . and you can never have her!" (83). Yet, as Miller states, "There is a sexual guilt operating" that is "combined with, and threaded through, the social situation" (*AMC*, 112). In fact the real crime for which he feels subconsciously guilty is not for the betrayal of Rodolpho and Marco, but a crime he never consummates. His love for Catherine turns from innocence as she grows up. It is not Catherine's innocence that is lost as she becomes Rodolpho's woman, of course, but Eddie's; and his struggle to retain that lost innocence leads him to tragic choice. If his guilty love for Catherine is a matter of pathos in that he is driven by forces beyond his control, his violation of the communal code is tragic in its implications. Eddie, some say, never acknowledges his culpability, never arrives at the self-recognition of a tragic hero, never chooses, and so lacks tragic stature. But when he informs on Rodolpho and Marco, he in fact does choose, translating the passive and private "sin" of his illicit love for Catherine into a wholly conscious and social act. When he tries to protect his innocence by imposing upon others the cost of violating his personal morality, he acts willfully. Trying to demand that others pay the price for his own offense, however unconsciously and, indeed, inevitably, he commits his real crime. Eddie is not, as Alan Stambusky argues, "a perfectly blameless character" any more than Oedipus can be excused because he fulfilled the destiny already marked out for him by fate.[38] Like Oedipus, he is the agent of his own destruction.

Christopher Bigsby, among others, argues that Eddie "has no choice," and "[w]here there is no choice there can be no culpability." In this sense, Eddie is a victim beyond judgment, "a psychological study of an individual who displaces his sexual passion into a concern with honor and family responsibility."[39] But, as Miller contends, the personal and social drama are so "threaded" that neither the impulse nor imperative can displace the other. Rather, the counterdemands placed on Eddie constitute tragic division and propel him to act, to choose. As Miller explained in his introduction, he did not intend *A View* as "another revelation of a pathetic victim" but a tragic story rooted in an ancient code, played out in the arena of the modern age.

The end of the play, like the endings of other Miller texts, has raised vigorous debate about the "tragic" implication of the play, as well as questions regarding the lack of choice and self-knowledge. The controversy mostly concerns the way Eddie dies and the effectiveness of Alfieri's final speech, which has generated as vigorous a debate as Linda's final speech in the requiem at the end of *Death of a Salesman*. In the original version, as Eddie transfers his passion from Catherine to Marco in a desperate attempt to recover his honor, Marco fatally wounds him, and he crawls across the stage to die in Catherine's arms, seemingly oblivious to the true nature of his relationship with his niece, and a mere victim of inexorable forces. In a version first performed in Paris (and later in the 1962 Sidney Lumet film), Eddie kills himself, seemingly moving the play closer to tragedy, suggesting in Eddie's act a moment of self-judgment reminiscent of the ending of *Othello*. Such an ending, like that in Shakespeare's play, borders between melodrama, in which case suicide is a last act of pathetic self-aggrandizement, and tragedy, in which case the protagonist truly judges himself and inflicts self-punishment for his "crime." But in the revised text for the London production directed by Peter Brook that Miller chose for the *Collected Plays*, Eddie struggles with Marco, is mortally wounded, and dies in Beatrice's arms calling out, "My B.!" (*VB*, 85). To Miller this ending moved Eddie's death closer to being a suicide, but it fails fully to resolve the question of whether or not Eddie acts in self-awareness. Although it hints at Eddie's reconciliation with Beatrice, it offers no testament of responsibility or self-analysis.[40] Donald Costello considers this ending a "brilliant stroke" combining murder and suicide—and one might add, a fusion of imperative and impulse. "It is thematically appropriate that both Eddie and Marco have their hands, together, on the knife that kills Eddie," Costello explains. "Eddie's own actions killed him, of course, but so did Marco, keeper of the codes."[41] Eddie's responsibility for his death, however, does not make the case that he acts in tragic knowledge. Alfieri had already said that "his eyes were like tunnels," devoid of light and understanding; and when just before his fight with Marco, Beatrice accuses him of wanting to possess Catherine, he is unable to believe himself capable of such offense. He is "shocked, horrified" (83), even to the end. Like Willy Loman, he lacks the capacity to comprehend his own potential for evil, utterly convinced that he has acted properly in protecting Catherine. Just as Willy never recognizes that the imperative that drives him is specious, Eddie never can understand the deviant impulse that compels him to act. As much his own executioner as Willy is, he apparently dies believing in the innocence that ironically seals his tragic fate despite his unacknowledged feelings of guilt. No more the victim of simple neurosis than Willy is, he, like Willy, acts in total commitment to a specious concept of his own innocence and worth. In reference to a recurrent theme in the early plays, Miller essentially characterizes Eddie Carbone as one who expresses "an aspiration to an innocence that when defeated or frustrated can turn quite murderous" (*Conv.*, 362). As Miller remarks in his introduction, "like Willy Loman [Eddie Carbone] . . . can be driven to what in the last analysis is a sacrifice of himself for his conception, however misguided, of right, dignity, and justice" (*TE*, 166).

Furthermore, just as Biff has to articulate the tragic awareness of *Death of a Salesman* because Willy lacks the ability to understand the tragic nature of his fate, Alfieri gives voice to the tragic import of Eddie's destiny in his controversial "alarm" speech at the conclusion of the play:

> Most of the time now we settle for half and I like it better. But the truth is holy, and even as I knew how wrong he was, and

> death useless, I tremble, for I confess that something perversely pure calls to me from his memory—not purely good, but himself purely, for he allowed himself to be wholly known and for that I think that I will love him more than all my sensible clients. And yet, it is better to settle for half, it must be! And so I mourn him—I admit it—with a certain … alarm. (*VB*, 86)

Although, as Nada Zeineddine warns us, Alfieri's claim that Eddie "allowed himself to be wholly known" should be taken "with reservation,"[42] especially given Eddie's sustained self-ignorance, Alfieri's speech draws tragic meaning from the protagonist's fate. Neither the product simply of social determinism nor of mere psychological imbalance, Eddie's violation of social and moral taboo assumes mythic proportion in its consuming force. It is of course ironic that, although allowing himself to be "wholly known," Eddie did not know himself. But in near-Euripidean power, he embodies the universal, mythic passion, "perversely pure," of human potential. In this he exposes the "sacred truth" to which Alfieri alludes, a truth nonetheless "natural" and destructive in its assertion. Eddie is a fully realized human being, at once lesser than others, and, as Alfieri concludes, more—so we "mourn him with a certain … alarm."

Comparing the earlier and later versions of the play, Miller argues that the revised text frees the "original, friezelike character" and moves the play "closer toward realism," while at the same time sustaining Eddie's mythic nature. Again, like Willy Loman, Eddie "possesses or exemplifies the wondrous and human fact that he too can be driven to what in the last analysis is a sacrifice of himself for his conception" (*TE*, 166). As Vincent Canby wrote in response to Anthony LaPaglia's Tony-winning performance as Eddie in the Roundabout's revival in 1998, Eddie Carbone "aggressively invites his doom and invites it with a desperation that only increases as an awful self-awareness becomes inevitable. … [This is] as close as the skeptical contemporary theater will ever get to a classical tragic hero."[43]

It is perhaps symptomatic of Miller's risky argument for his plays as tragedy that he has shifted the weight of critical discussion from the virtues of the plays themselves to a continuing debate about the viability of tragedy in the modern age. It is hardly surprising, then, that alongside Canby's high praise of *A View* we might place Edith Oliver's qualified response to Ulu Grosbard's successful 1965 off-Broadway revival: "If the play never attains the stature of classical tragedy, it is still an effective and exciting melodrama."[44] Like many responses to *All My Sons*, *Death of a Salesman*, and *The Crucible*, it seems faint praise indeed—good melodrama but short of tragic greatness. Yet the fact is that Miller's commentaries have enjoined the debate and largely determined the course of Miller criticism for good or ill.

A MEMORY OF TWO MONDAYS

Miller has called *A Memory of Two Mondays* "an exploration of a mood, the mood of the thirties and the pathos of people forever locked into a working day," a "pathetic comedy," and a "moral romance" in which "the warehouse is our world—a world where things are endlessly sent and endlessly received; only time never comes back" (*TE*, 260, 263, 65). Although the play has generated sparse criticism and has been seldom performed, in the introduction to the *Collected Plays* Miller declares that he wrote it "in part out of a desire to relive a sort of reality where necessity was open and bare," and he "hoped to define for [himself] the value of hope." Despite its limited recognition since its first production along with the one-act version of *A View*, Miller declares in the introduction to the *Collected Plays*, "Nothing in this book was written with greater love, and for myself, I have nothing printed here better than this play" (*TE*, 164). Although few would agree with Miller's assertion or with Albert Wertheim's assessment that it is "perhaps Miller's best . . . and most neglected play," nevertheless, as Robert Hogan asserts, it is "a considerable achievement . . . moving, technically adroit . . . one of the rare instances of a one-act tragicomedy."[45]

Miller began working at an auto parts warehouse when he was eighteen. He stayed until August 1934, when he had saved the five hundred dollars he needed to enroll at the University of Michigan in September. Fictionalized as Bert in the play written some twenty years later, Miller projects his experiences onto the stage, peopling it with the men and women he worked with for nearly two years and recreating the grim setting of the warehouse filled with "filthy windows" looking out onto "a newly installed five-story bordello" (*T*, 218).[46] Feeling very much an outsider, an ambitious Jewish boy among Irishmen trapped in their economic and social cage, Miller came to gain a deep affection for the characters he saw bound to "serve an industrial apparatus which feeds them in body and leaves them to find sustenance for their souls as they may" (*TE*, 65). The story's Marxian quality emphasizes pathos, as all the characters, except for Bert, fall prey to a socioeconomic imperative they cannot escape, doomed forever to live in a purgatory of endless repetition.

Miller later admitted that the play was something of a departure from his earlier work, despite its heavy Marxian elements: "I have since come to believe we have a lot more to do with our fate than that play implies. But at the time . . . there seemed no conceivable way of escaping it" (*Conv.*, 309). Yet the play is not a simplistic social melodrama. Despite "the endless, timeless, will-less environment a boy emerges who will not accept its defeat or its mood as final. . . . The play speaks not of obsession but of rent and hunger and the need for a little poetry in life" (*TE*, 164).

Raymond, the manager, twice sounds the central theme: "It's the same circus every Monday morning" (*MTM*, 10, 37), and the others repeat it. Gus laments, "Oh, boy. Oh, goddam boy. Monday morning. Ach" (10), and the proper Kenneth echoes, "Oh here's another grand Monday! ... It's the sight of Monday, that's all, is got me down" (31, 34). Monday represents the repetitious cycle of aimless existence in their sordid world that provokes Bert's poetic evocation at the end of the play as he is leaving:

Every morning and every morning,
And no end in sight.
That's the thing—there's no end!
Oh there ought to be a statue in the park—
"To All the Ones That Stay." (42–43)

Miller's sympathetic identification with the characters is obvious: Kenneth, the moralistic poet "fresh off the boat"; the gruff Gus, veteran of twenty-two years in servitude, who fails even to make it to his wife's funeral; Gus's drinking buddy Tommy Kelly, who manages to defeat his alcoholism by the time Bert leaves but remains trapped after sixteen years at the job; Larry, whose dream to buy an Auburn because he "loves the valves" shatters when familial demands force him to sell the car; and Agnes, the spinster in her late forties who always tries to ease the tension in the little community—all are portrayed with compassion and dignity, however flawed they may be. As a sort of central consciousness, Bert, like Alfieri in *A View from the Bridge*, gains an appreciation for their worthiness and leaves with a painful awareness of the fate that awaits them all. Not fully realized as a character, perhaps, and not tragic in any critical sense of the word, he nonetheless provides the critical focus into a community of the oppressed who somehow achieve a measure of victory in their stubborn survival.

Miller's adroit choreography of entrances and exits around the shipping table, juxtaposed with Kenneth's plaintive songs, Bert's poetic speeches, and the lyric laments of characters against the sounds of workers riffling through orders, the coarse sexual talk of Frank and Jerry and the truck drivers, and the cacophony of sounds in the "fiery furnace" (*MTM*, 13) interweave pathos and naturalistic detail. When Kenneth begins to quote "When lilacs last in the dooryard bloom'd," Gus asks pointedly, "What the hell you doin'?" Kenneth ironically replies, "Why, it's the poetry hour, Gus, don't you know that?" (12). Throughout the text, harsh realism and poetry surface in delicate equipoise.

In the setting we see "a place of dust" on the first stifling hot Monday, with long shadows cast across a vast, cavernous space marked with Kafkaesque alleys and bins. By the second Monday, when Bert is about to depart, the cold light of a winter day illuminates the sterile microcosm where "It's rainin' dust from the ceiling!" (*MTM*, 17). The first Monday ends when Kenneth and Bert wipe off one of the caked windows and let in the lurid light illuminating the reality of their subterranean home. All through the first Monday, Kenneth pleads that someone clean the windows to let in "God's light" (29). He asks Gus, "What do you suppose would happen, Gus, if a man took it in his head to wash these windows?" (13), and he proposes to Larry, "you suppose we could get these windows washed sometimes? I've often thought if we could see a bit of sky now and again it would help matters now and again" (20). Finally he convinces Bert to act when he queries, "How would you feel about washing these windows—you and I—once and for all?" (29). But the act ends ironically when they look on a five-story brothel out the window and the brutal light of reality floods the stage.

Despite their personal anguish and gruff nature, the characters remain loyal to each other. On the first Monday, even Raymond, the manager, tries desperately to save Tommy from being fired for drunkenness. Gus, Jim, Larry, Kenneth, Bert, and Agnes all provide cover for their drunken colleague. When Gus thinks Mr. Eagle, the boss, is going to fire Tommy, he vows to quit in protest. For all their resentments and their being symbolically impaled like the orders stuck on the large spindle on the back wall, they find this "little world a home to which, unbelievably perhaps, [they] like to come every Monday morning" (*MTM*, 6). Amid this communal setting, Bert sometimes stands off and speaks in soliloquy. Part of the circle, yet separate from it, at one point he stands to the side and thinks, "There's something so terrible here! There always was, and I don't know what," and he concludes:

> It's like a subway;
> Every day I see the same people getting on
> And the same people getting off,
> And all that happens is that they get older. God!
> Sometimes it scares me; like all of us in the world
> We're riding back and forth across a great big room,
> From wall to wall and back again, And no end ever!
> Just no end! (30–31)

At the end of his time at the warehouse, Bert has seen the debilitating effects of the life he observes around him. Kenneth succumbs to drink. Gus guiltily abandons his dying wife Lilly and even misses her funeral for a drunken binge with Jim. The brothel intrudes on the warehouse, setting the puritanical Kenneth against the "lot of sex maniacs" (*MTM*, 39) who leer out of the window. Larry sells his Auburn, recognizing "It's out of my class" (40). In a moment of high irony, Kenneth protests to Mr. Eagle, "There's got to be somethin' done" about the brothel, and Eagle replies, "Shouldn't have washed the windows, I guess" (41). Most dramatically, Gus, driven by guilt, wastes the money collected from insurance for his wife's death and dies in Dionysian abandon in the arms of a whore in a taxi, trying, as Jim says, to "do it right" (45). After their initial shock, the characters resume their work in another choreographed scene: Jim takes an order off the spindle, Raymond goes back to his office, men walk up and down with orders in their hands, Kenneth begins wrapping a part, and the truckers prepare to make a delivery to the Bronx. As the workers resume their meaningless lives in the purgatorial realm of the warehouse, Bert vainly tries to say his goodbyes, leaving with the promise, "So long as I live they'll never die, / And still I know that in a month or two / They'll forget my name" (43).[47]

Claiming to have written the play "to define for myself the value of hope" (*TE*, 164), Miller in fact offers relatively little hope, save for the stoic determination of the characters to survive in their grim world and Bert's unwillingness to "accept its defeat or its mood as final" (164). But Bert possesses a ticket out from the beginning, and his departure is less an earned victory over defeat than the completion of a predetermined end. Indeed, the play lacks a fully developed protagonist. Bert can scarcely serve as a divided hero who gains awareness as a result of choices he makes, and a strong argument can be made for Gus being the more central character. But of course Miller never thought of *A Memory of Two Mondays* as tragedy, which he did the other more famous one-act he offered Martin Ritt for the Cornet Theater productions. Never bound by the constraints of genre, he saw the play as a nostalgic panegyric to a community of oppressed workers struggling to survive the agony of the Depression, which has so strongly marked Miller's work. Miller's fondness for the play is understandable, given his long-standing commitments and compassion for the socially and economically deprived. It is no real surprise that he could write, "Is this, I wondered, why writing exists—as a proof against oblivion? And not only just for the writer himself but also for all the others who swim in the depths where the sun of the culture never penetrates?" (*T*, 222).

NOTES

1. Arthur Miller, "Ibsen's Warning," 74.

2. David Bronson, "*An Enemy of the People*: A Key to Arthur Miller's Art and Ethics," 238.

3. Arthur Miller, "Why I Wrote *The Crucible*: An Artist's Answer to Politics," 159. In the 1999 Massey Lecture at Harvard entitled "*The Crucible* in History," Miller adds that the anticommunist rage was "paralyzing a whole generation and in a short time was drying up the habits of trust and toleration in public discourse" (*E*, 274).

4. Herbert Lindenberger, *Historical Drama: The Relation of Literature and Reality*, x.

5. Miller, "Why I Wrote *The Crucible*," 165.

6. Niloufer Harben, Twentieth-Century English History Plays, 45; Lindenberger, *Historical Drama*, x. For varying assessments of Miller's use of historical texts, see especially David Levin, "Salem Witchcraft and Recent Fiction and Drama"; Henry Popkin, "Historical Analogy and *The Crucible*"; Robert Warshow, "The Liberal Conscience in *The Crucible*"; William J. McGill Jr., "*The Crucible* of History: Arthur Miller's John Proctor"; Robert Martin Jr., "Arthur Miller's *The Crucible*: Background and Sources"; Cushing Strout, "Analogical History: *The Crucible*"; and E. Miller Budick, "History and Other Spectres in Arthur Miller's *The Crucible*."

7. Kenneth Tynan complains that Bolt "looks at history solely through the eyes of his saintly hero," whereas Brecht "looks at Galileo through the eyes of history" (*Tynan Right and Left: Plays, Films, Places, and Events*, 163). See also his discussion of Bolt and Brecht in *A View of the English Stage, 1944–63*.

8. William J. Free, "Robert Bolt and the Marxist View of History," 53 (see also 51); Tynan, *View of the English Stage*, 289; Eric Bentley, "Miller's Innocence"; Driver, "Strength and Weakness"; Bigsby, *Critical Introduction*, 248. On Marxist criticism, see especially Driver's "Strength and Weakness," and Bentley's "Miller's Innocence." Far from being a "quasi-Marxist" play, Miller's work counters the basic socioeconomic determinism of Marxism with the force of self-will. Just how un-Marxian Miller's play is can best be seen by comparing it with Sartre's simplistic 1957 film adaptation, *Les Sorcières de Salem*, which makes it a heavy-handed polemical document.

9. For a discussion of Bolt's use of Chambers's biography, see Harben, *Twentieth-Century English History Plays*, 161–62.

10. Robert B. Heilman, "Tragedy and Melodrama: Speculations on Generic Form," 237. In *Iceman, Arsonist, and Troubled Agent*, Heilman labels *The Crucible* "superior melodrama," though "Miller hovers at the edge of tragedy." Although Miller "raises *The Crucible* in the melodramatic scale" over *Death of a Salesman*, he argues that "the basic pattern is that of a good man destroyed by forces of evil" (143–47). Other critics have complained that Proctor is "wholly good"; but although he, like most tragic heroes, possesses an elemental goodness, he also expresses a capacity for evil, pettiness, and cowardice that Miller goes out of his way to illuminate. And just as important, he bears the consequences of his own choices as well as the wrath of his oppressors.

11. Robert Bolt, *A Man for All Seasons*, xxii, 118.

12. Mel Gussow, "A Rock of the Modern Age, Arthur Miller Is Everywhere." Of course, critics debate whether or not Proctor is really guilty; some find his guilt unconvincing. See, for example, Bentley, "Miller's Innocence"; Herbert Blau, *The Impossible Theater: A Manifesto*; Popkin, "Historical Analogy"; and Stambusky, "Arthur Miller: Aristotelian Canons." However, in Arthur Ganz's reading, Proctor's "heroism is a comparatively easy matter" ("The Silence of Arthur Miller," 234). But Miller's defenders point out that the play depicts not only Proctor's past offenses but present ones as well. Marcel Aymé, who adapted the play for the 1954 French production *Les Sorcières de Salem*, notes that he not only violates an adolescent girl in the past of the play but attempts to redeem himself in the present by sacrificing her reputation to save his wife ("I Want to be Hanged Like a Witch"). As will be discussed, Proctor also continues to betray his own moral beliefs until the end of the drama.

13. Joseph Valente, "Rehearsing the Witch Trials: Gender Injustice in *The Crucible*," 134; Robert Lee Feldman, "Arthur Miller and the Theme of Evil: An Interview," 92.

14. Bolt, *Man for All Seasons*, xii.

15. Wendy Schissel, "Re(dis)covering the Witches in Arthur Miller's *The Crucible*: A Feminist Reading," 463. Schissel goes on to attack Miller's "existential mysticism" that projects "the paternalistic monotheism of the Puritans" (406). See also Valente's

attack on gender injustice in the play in "Rehearsing the Witch Trials"; he predictably shares Schissel's view, claiming that "*The Crucible* treats the figure of the Salem witch . . . as metonymic of the figure of woman, whose victimization/vilification marks the very genesis of Judeo-Christian culture" (124).

16. Schissel, "Re(dis)covering the Witches," 466; Jay Carr, "Crucible Bewitches." Several months after the New York opening of the play, Miller added a controversial scene between Abby and Proctor to the end of act 2 in an attempt to clarify their relationship. Most critics find it superfluous or damaging to the action, although it can be argued that the scene provides further evidence of Proctor's guilt in the affair. Miller dropped the scene from the collected works.

17. Bolt, *Man for All Seasons*, 126.

18. Budick, "History and Other Spectres," 547–48.

19. T. S. Eliot, *Murder in the Cathedral*, 44.

20. Bolt, *Man for All Seasons*, 141.

21. Bigsby, *Critical Introduction*, 197.

22. Michael J. O'Neal, "History, Myth, and Name Magic in Arthur Miller's *The Crucible*," 116.

23. Bolt, *Man for All Seasons*, 152. In an interview Miller concurred with Steven Centola's description of his central vision as "a kind of existential humanism—a vision that emphasizes self-determination and social responsibility and that is optimistic and affirms life by acknowledging man's possibility in the face of his limitations and even sometimes the dramatization of his failures" (*Conv.*, 343). Miller forgoes the realistic or Marxist drama with which he is too easily aligned to embrace tragic possibility, even though he moves the play more in the direction of existentialism than traditional tragedy. Proctor achieves a tragic dimension within the context of a world little able to affirm the presence of divine justice or retribution. Miller's work is tragic as much because of as despite his existential vision.

24. Bigsby, *Critical Introduction*, 197.

25. Eric Bentley, *The Life of the Drama*, 218.

26. Part of the inspiration for writing *A View* may have stemmed from Miller's collaboration with Elia Kazan on a film script concerning the Red Hook district, *The Hook*. The collaboration ended when Miller refused to make labor racketeers in his script into communists to satisfy the desires of Hollywood producers bent on pleasing politicians caught up in the anticommunist movement. Kazan went on to make *On the Waterfront*, which some contend may have triggered *A View* in response, though others disagree. See Gerald C. Weales, "Arthur Miller and the 1950s," 648–50.

27. For example, in addition to Gerald C. Weales, Sheila Huftel deems the original more "majestic in its simplicity" (*Arthur Miller: The Burning Glass*, 158), whereas Nelson sees the one-act version as implausible and too "rarefied . . . a neo-Grecian bubble machine" (Nelson, *Arthur Miller*, 211).

28. Heilman, *Iceman, Arsonist, and Troubled Agent*, 324, 150; John Orr, *Tragic Drama and Modern Society: Studies in the Social and Literary Theory of Drama from 1870 to the Present*, 229–30; Stambusky, "Arthur Miller: Aristotelian Canons," 408–9; J. L. Styan, "Why *A View from the Bridge* Went Down Well in London: A Story of a Revision," 148; Clinton W. Trowbridge, "Arthur Miller: Between Pathos and Tragedy," 229.

29. He remarks elsewhere, "I wanted to eliminate all the usual machinery. . . . so I introduced a narrator who would set up what I call the moral situation" (*AMC*, 111). In William Bolcom's successful 1999 operatic version of the play, premiered by the Lyric Opera of Chicago with Arnold Weinstein as colibrettist, a full Greek chorus serves the traditional functions of commenting on and interpreting the action.

30. Donald P. Costello, "Arthur Miller's Circles of Responsibility: *A View from the Bridge* and Beyond," 449.

31. Bigsby, *Critical Introduction*, 206.

32. Iska Alter, "Betrayal and Blessedness: Exploitation of Feminine Power in *The Crucible*, *A View from the Bridge*, and *After the Fall*," 133.

33. Albert Rothenberg and Eugene D. Shapiro, "The Defense of Psychoanalysis in Literature: *Long Day's Journey into Night* and *A View from the Bridge*," 66.

34. Henry Popkin calls Beatrice's speech "no more than a plea for pity" that divides responsibility for the tragedy ("Arthur Miller: The Strange Encounter," 44), but it is Eddie's guilt that ultimately concerns Miller.

35. Steven R. Centola, "Compromise as Bad Faith: Arthur Miller's *A View from the Bridge* and William Inge's *Come Back, Little Sheba*," 107.

36. Arthur D. Epstein (in "A Look at *A View from the Bridge*") and others note that it is highly possible that Eddie and others consider Rodolpho gay, especially in the macho world of Red Hook. Henry I. Schvey argues that Eddie in fact exposes his own "latent homosexuality" in his attention to Rodolpho ("Arthur Miller: Songs of Innocence and Experience," 78), a claim shared by Myles R. Hurd ("Angels and Anxieties in Miller's *A View from the Bridge*," 5–6). We might add that the Lord Chamberlain's office at first denied the British production because of Eddie's grabbing and kissing Rodolpho, so the play was performed at the Comedy Theater, a designated private theater club, to escape the prohibition.

37. Zeineddine notes Rodolpho's singing of "Paper Doll" and the longshoremen's taunting him with the name, but she relates Rodolpho's "paper doll" to Eddie. "Catherine is Eddie's paper doll. That the singer wants to buy a paper doll parallels Eddie's insistence on his right [as breadwinner] to claim Catherine's actions due to the fatherly sacrifices he has made to raise her" (*Because It Is My Name*, 186).

38. Stambusky, "Arthur Miller: Aristotelian Canons," 109.

39. Bigsby, *Critical Introduction*, 202, 204.

40. Murray claims that the ending's ironic depiction of a reconciliation between Eddie and Beatrice shows Eddie to be more "normal" than before, but it is difficult to draw such a conclusion when Eddie acts with such irrational passion (Arthur Miller, *Dramatist*, 109).

41. Costello, "Arthur Miller's Circles," 453.

42. Zeineddine, *Because It Is My Name*, 190.

43. Vincent Canby, "A Classically Riveting 'View from the Bridge.'" To the contrary, Driver, long a Miller critic, contends that in an age lacking "universal moral sanction," the theme of a man who destroys all his family because of jealousy has "no level of meaning, law, providence, or fate, upon which an action that transcends character can act" ("Strength and Weakness," 20). Driver echoes the sweeping contention of George Steiner and others that "the death of tragedy" occurred with the emergence of scientific determinism in the nineteenth century, a claim Miller has vigorously rejected.

44. Edith Oliver, "The Theatre: Off Broadway."

45. Albert Wertheim, "Arthur Miller: *After the Fall* and After," 24; Robert Hogan, *Arthur Miller*, 32.

46. In *Timebends*, Miller describes specific people at the warehouse who emerged as fictional characters in the play: Gus is modeled on the sixty-five-year-old packing boss at the warehouse; the new immigrant, Dennis MacMahon, appears as Kenneth; one of the three female bookkeepers, Dora, becomes Agnes; one of the stock clerks, Huey, surfaces as Larry; and the unnamed boss at the actual warehouse is fictionalized as Mr. Eagle in the drama.

47. Miller writes that when the other workers at the auto parts warehouse discovered he was going off to college, he, like Bert, felt alienation because "I was not only trying to escape their common fate but implicitly stating that I was better than they" (*T*, 218). He recalls that when he revisited the warehouse sometime later, he had indeed "vanished" from their minds even though "the whole crew . . . stayed fixed in mine" (222).

STUART MARLOW

Interrogating The Crucible:
Revisiting the Biographical, Historical and
Political Sources of Arthur Miller's Play

Arthur Miller's *The Crucible* is widely recognized as a thinly disguised attack on the tyranny of the HUAC (House Un-American Activities Committee) era. The dramatic intensity of the play is also driven by the playwright's struggle to develop a fictional framework, within which he could give voice to the on-going private conflicts he experienced, between the individual conscience, personal ambition, and the self-sacrifice required by collective action. However, some fundamental questions must be raised about some of the play's discursive implications, which at times reflect the fundamentalist reduction of the women in Judaic, Christian, and Islamic discourse, to either virtuous and maternal in essence or seductive and whore-like. In *The Crucible*, such prototypical reductions structurally reinforce rather than challenge the ideological notion of witches as agents of sexual corruption, whilst also tending to affirm the Old Testament legend of Adam's fall from grace as a result of Eve's actions. Similarly the cause of John Proctor's entrapment is directly linked to sexual jealousy and female intrigue. The youthful Abigail seduces him with her bewitching physical attraction. Elizabeth also contributes to his entrapment indirectly because she is frigid towards him, and directly in the defining moment of the courtroom scene where she lies to protect him. To complete Proctor's downfall, the servant girl Mary Warren caves in under pressure, denouncing him as a warlock. Thus Miller in attempting to focus on

From *Staging a Cultural Paradigm: The Political and the Personal in American Drama*, pp. 79–100. © 2002 by P.I.E.-Peter Lang.

the political exploitation of mass hysteria, wittingly or unwittingly ends up partially confirming rather than demystifying essentialist stereotypes.

The character of Proctor may be linked to the role generically blueprinted by the well-established conventions of self-doubt, residing in the narrative border-country between hero and anti-hero. However, the action in *The Crucible* falls into the same trap that had exposed Ken Russell's 1971 film *The Devils* to ridicule. The fallible hero, the vain but politically solid priest, Grandier, is rendered a true martyr as he falls victim to sexually driven female hysteria. In John Whiting's play as well as Ken Russell's film adaptation, sexual repression is a major agent in the process of political oppression. In exploring this causal link, fictionally as well as historically, there is the danger that writers and historians may end up iconographically colluding with the very orthodoxies they are ostensibly attacking. If Arthur Miller's Salem project was intended as a critical exploration of the mind set prevalent amongst the historical communities he is trying to represent, why did his own emplotment so uncritically adopt the simplistic martyr-like notions of virtue rewarded? *The Crucible* involves the portrayal of an essentially twentieth-century hero, who is plunged into martyrdom involuntarily through extraordinary circumstances thematically shifting the focus from broader historical processes onto the narrative conventions of heroism and martyrdom. John Proctor has many pre-modern role models, who have embodied the conventional oppositions, which struggle for the souls of the main protagonists. Accordingly, lust as opposed to propriety, personal as opposed to political loyalty, self-sacrifice as opposed to self-preservation, and rational thought as opposed to emotionality, have often tended to provide the morally discursive framework through which the main conflicts of the era were fictionally mediated. Intertextually therefore, John Proctor's predicament has many precedents in representations of seduction and betrayal. These range from Shakespeare's *Hamlet*, *Macbeth*, and *King Lear*, Marlowe's *Dr Faustus*, through to Hawthorne's *The Scarlet Letter*, and the central characters in Milton's and Bunyan's work.

On the other hand, one may well compare Miller's portraits of women with those which have emerged from the period of seventeenth-century Restoration Drama through to Ibsen and Strindberg, or George Bernard Shaw, Sean O'Casey, and Eugene O' Neill. The inherent essentialist flaws in the characterization of *Death of a Salesman*, *The Crucible*, *The Misfits* and *After the Fall* in particular have quite reactionary implications. Making allowances for the social climate and gender bias of the 1950s, it may still be asserted that Arthur Miller's women are often consigned uncritically to traditional roles. Perhaps one may be permitted to speculate that, if Miller had shaped Abigail in the manner of a more fundamentally iconoclastic play, he would have taken her contempt of Salem hypocrisy as a starting point, and developed her into a more plausible and challenging figure: "ABIGAIL, *in tears*: I look for John

Proctor that took me from my sleep and put knowledge in my heart! I never knew what pretense Salem was, I never knew the lying lessons I was taught by all these Christian women and their covenanted men! And now you bid me tear the light out of my eyes? I will not, I cannot!" (241).

In a recent radio interview for BBC Radio 4's arts program Front Row, Miller expressed the view that the only mode of representation he would now find suitable for the play were he to rewrite it, would be "sardonic humor." Only this mode of dramatic expression could adequately portray the absurdity of inconsistent and petty-minded provincial officials being vested with so much repressive power at a national level. Here the playwright also made reference, once again, to the offer he had received from HUAC Chairman Francis E. Walter of Pennsylvania in 1956 to have the hearing against him cancelled if Marilyn Monroe were to consent to being photographed with the politician. Clearly the forces of democratic integrity, including the American Constitution itself, had proved ineffective in preventing this almost farcically bogus authority from taking its toll on so many people. In an extended article for the *Guardian*, Arthur Miller stressed that it was the intense fear felt by those who had been under HUAC scrutiny, which determined and perhaps undermined the quality of so much writing in the early 1950s.

> But it is impossible to convey properly the fears that marked that period. Nobody was shot to be sure, although some were going to jail, where at least one, William Remington, was murdered by an inmate hoping to shorten his sentence by having killed a communist. Rather than physical fear, it was the sense of impotence which seemed to deepen with each week, of being unable to speak accurately of the very recent past when being left-wing in America and for that matter in Europe, was to be alive to the dilemmas of the day.

However, the interlinking contexts of historical and contemporary reference between 1692 and 1952 were so highly charged after the renewed 1951 HUAC onslaughts, that they indeed required a less decontextualized approach to the explosive thematic material, or at least the kind of emotional distance associated with Shaw and Brecht. But once having gone down the road of exploring the sexual ramifications of the Salem story, Miller subjected his material to the dangers of stereotyping and decontextualization. The element of sexually loaded and strictly pre-determined characterization, which reduces the interpretive scope of *The Crucible*, is evident in the stage directions where we first see Parris encounter his niece and are directly informed that she is glamorous and a compulsive liar: "He is bending to kneel again when his niece Abigail Williams, seventeen, enters—a strikingly beautiful girl, an orphan, with an endless capacity for dissembling. Now she is all worry and apprehension and propriety" (230).

Ignoring any autobiographical references to Marilyn Monroe for a moment, it is clear that Miller is representing Abigail as the central sex symbol and destabilizing element that, in *The Crucible*, drives the Salem crisis towards Proctor's arrest and execution. This in effect narrows the focus of *The Crucible*'s main project, which was to explore thematic links between the Salem witch-trials and the HUAC era. Arthur Miller made it clear that the sexual parallels between 1692 and 1952 were autobiographically inspired, but as such the material produced was always going to run the danger of becoming an allegorical non sequitur. The fundamental weakness of *The Crucible* lies within the conflict between biographical urgency of expression, and the play's claim to be at least partially historically representative.

In his eagerness to find a historical objective correlative for his own predicament, Arthur Miller, prior to his 1952 research mission to Salem, had readily embraced Marion Starkey's 1949 dramatized historical narrative *The Devil in Massachusetts* as the source of a potential historical parallel. Marion Starkey had indeed allowed herself plenty of room for the projection of fictionalized characters onto her own historical screen, but as popularization, the work remained well within its own parameters. Miller's project was, however, politically much larger and certainly more explosive given the timing of the opening performance. In the course of his research, Miller accepted the relatively well-known descriptive narrative of the Salem witch hunts, Charles W. Upham's sexually loaded nineteenth-century account *Salem Witchcraft*, as historical fact, rather than scrutinize the work to identify fictional or speculative narrative strategies within it. The playwright claimed to have found in Upham's account: "the hard evidence of what had become the play's center; the breakdown of the Proctor marriage and Abigail's determination to get Elizabeth so she could have John" (*Timebends* 337). As most of the hard evidence traced subsequently from documentary sources put Abigail at around age eleven, and Proctor as a sixty-year-old publican on his third marriage, one has to question the allegorical authenticity of Miller's project. How significant is it, for example, that Proctor's courtroom exclamations are based on the binary simplicity of the evil whore and the virtuous wife images? Once entrapped in the Salem courtroom, Proctor confesses his sexual intercourse with Abigail in the most puritanically censorious of terms:

PROCTOR, *his voice about to break, and his shame great*: In the proper place—where my beasts are bedded. On the last night of my joy, some eight months past. She used to serve me in my house, sir. *He has to clamp his jaw to keep from weeping.* A man may think that God sleeps, but God sees everything, I know it now. I beg you sir, I beg you—see her for what she is. My wife my dear good wife, took this girl soon after, sir, and put her out on the highroad. (304)

If the central role of the dramatic project is personal and political allegory, the defense of Proctor's attitudes to women in terms of representing the mentality of a seventeenth-century farmer, would appear to be somewhat tenuous. Both Abigail and Elizabeth had clearly been reduced to contrasting stereotypes. Representing Elizabeth Proctor's virtue in unambiguous opposition to Abigail's sinfulness therefore tends to disqualify the play from being able to meet the criteria of analytical sophistication to which any piece of serious fiction can be expected in one form or other to adhere.

Proctor first appears as the common-sense driven, rational pragmatist, but under pressure he lapses into the use of demonic, sexist terminology to condemn the court proceedings. This structure of imagery equates female sexual transgression with judicial corruption. In his short preface to *The Crucible*, "A Note on the Historical Accuracy of this Play," Miller claims on the one hand that the play does not represent documentary history in a way that would qualify it as history in the academic context. On the other hand, in the same paragraph, he goes on to make the ambitious statement that: "However, I believe that the reader will discover here the essential nature of one of the strangest and most awful chapters in human history. The fate of each character is exactly that of his historical model, and there is no one in the drama who did not play a similar—and in some cases exactly the same—role in history" (224). Was the playwright implying that the sexually-driven historical parallel the reader or spectator is supposed to discover the essential nature of is the McCarthy era and the influence the puritanical forces that operated both there and through the Hollywood performance code?

All this raises the fundamental question of criteria for the incorporation of documentary and historical sources as a fictional work's referential starting point. To some extent, any work of documentary or historically based fiction will owe a representational debt to its sources. If there are contemporary accounts available that place a different causal emphasis on the incidents of courtroom hysteria in Salem for example, how justified may one be in critically encroaching upon the playwright's artistic freedom to determine the balance between fiction and non-fiction? Why *The Crucible* should come under critical scrutiny is related to the political and historical significance Arthur Miller has attached to what has turned out to be his most performed play. As much of the Salem material has been researched and edited since 1953, could the playwright have been reasonably expected to re-examine his source material for the screenplay of the 1996 film of *The Crucible*? According to at least one clearly documented leading eye witness account of the 1692 Salem trials, the so-called "female hysteria" was orchestrated by at least one male member of the Putnam faction:

> Those wenches being present who plaid their juggling tricks, falling down, crying out, and staring in the Peoples Faces; the Magistrates demanded of them several times at one Captain Hill, there present, but spake nothing; the same Accuser had a man standing at her back to hold her up; he stooped down to her Ear, then she cried out, Aldin. Aldin afflicted her; one of the Magistrates asked her if she had ever seen Aldin, she answered no, he asked her how she knew it was Aldin? She said, the man told her so. (Boyer & Nissenbaum 102)

Despite contemporary observer Robert Calef's comprehensive attempt to attack, demystify, and expose the manipulative nature of the Salem trials, the emphasis in *The Crucible* tends to reinforce stereotypical notions of female hysteria being manipulated by Abigail, rather than make more profound reference to local political intervention as a driving force in the courtroom episode. This interpretive bias in *The Crucible* generally tends to reveal evidence of not only arbitrarily presented historical sources, but of a reductive thread, which reduces the conflict to a binary division between "goodies and baddies."

Looking through the Salem trial records and beyond to other documents of the time, it is clear that there were a whole number of relevant issues which would have, historically at least, thrown more light on the Salem tragedy. The unpopularity of Samuel Parris in 1692 was only the tip of the iceberg in terms of tension between the farming communities and the urban authorities. Magistrates, churchmen and high ranking officials were mostly orthodox figures with little or no pragmatic experience in the basic running of a farming and trading economy. Added to this was the fact that Parris, like so many second or third sons with relatively privileged and literate backgrounds, had been shunted conventionally into the church for lack of a better alternative.

Tensions with the native populations of New England were often exacerbated by the crude colonial orthodoxy of the founding fathers, as well as often insensitive and incompetent rule by England as the colonial power, whose interests in the New Colonies amounted to little more than exploitation and control. On the other hand, the farming communities often managed to live in some sort of working harmony with the indigenous peoples. The tensions in and around mid-seventeenth-century Boston mounted, as farmers were often not only obliged to pay for an essentially unproductive clergy and judiciary, but were subjected to a kind of military service, which meant having to abandon their farms for weeks or even months. This call-up involved sending able-bodied males to guard the towns against potential attack by Native Americans or colonial enemies such as the French. In the run-up to the Salem witch trials, this had become one of the farmers' major grievances, and a number of petitions of protest from tax-paying farmers were handed in against what many saw as a pointless exercise, which left many farms unattended and vulnerable.

New England was directly caught up in the violent ramifications of the English Civil War, the underlying conflicts of which already contained the seeds of the American War of Independence. In England, by 1650, many of the common people had lined up behind Oliver Cromwell to prevent the return of autocratic monarchical rule. One significant group made up of craftsmen, tradesmen, and smallholders, called themselves "The Levellers," with whom Miller's John Proctor may bear a clear affinity. This organized political movement represented one of the forerunners of social democracy. Also active during this period was a more radical anti-property group, "The Diggers," who in turn may be seen as the forerunners of communism. Both groups, along with various radical religious sects, had been initially fighting for democratic rights and the establishment of an English parliamentary republic. In fact, however, Cromwell turned out to be a puritanical patrician, who was fighting to maintain an oligarchic parliamentary system, and who in all probability would have preferred a constitutional monarchy to popular rule. Despite Cromwell's efficient Model Army, and his politically parliamentarian stance, the climate of orthodox puritan ethics enforced by his regime alienated many less orthodox sections of the English population. The puritan ethos was more closely associated with New England than it was with England itself.

This radical conflict of interests eventually spilled over into the American and French Revolutions after Cromwell's regime collapsed and monarchy made its comeback in the 1660s. The attempts to reestablish the English monarchy lurched from reactionary absolutism under James II, to the emergence of a constitutional monarchy under William and Mary of Orange in 1688 after yet another uprising. The effect of this political turmoil on New England was direct and profound. As a consequence of James II's attempt to return to absolutism, the Massachusetts Bay Charter that granted the colony the right to choose its own leaders was revoked. As unpopular as James himself in England proved to be, was the newly appointed Governor of New York and New England, Edmund Andros. Under Andros's rule, the population of New England was seen by the new rulers as a potentially rebellious majority, just as the authoritarian James in England feared the rebellious spirit that had toppled the crown in 1640. The broader political stage had been quite clearly set for the travesties of justice that befell Salem in 1692.

This major source of political tension, with its clear colonialist implications, finds no specific emphasis in *The Crucible*. This is indeed a fundamental omission, as in 1689 the New England colonies had rebelled against the 1684 suspension of their property-owning rights, which had been granted by James I back in 1623. Allowing the Salem witch hunts to get almost out of hand was one tactical measure aimed at letting community-driven colonial resistance weaken itself through internal division. Placing more emphasis on such cynical manipulation may provide a poignantly apt parallel to the HUAC persecution of the left by orthodox reactionaries. Another significant area of exploration relates to the role played by the regional colonial Governor Sir William Phips, who had left in 1691 to plead for the restoration of some of the 1623 privileges with the new constitutional parliament of William of Orange. Phips returned to find Salem in chaos. The area was beset with conflicts between settlers and Native Americans, as well as those that had been generated through the friction between French and English colonial ambitions. Nevertheless, his decision to squash the Salem proceedings and release the prisoners on condition that they pay for their own jail fees was perhaps as much aimed at appeasing the orthodox establishment, as it was at restoring justice.

The Salem trials, of course, were closely bound to the European witch hunts that had plagued the sixteenth and seventeenth centuries. There is in this context one particular link, which adds an element of chilling irony to the Salem episode. The way in which the New England purges were conducted had borne a particularly close resemblance to those in East Anglia in the 1640s, when England was drawn into the savage religious persecutions of seventeenth-century Europe. At that time, a minor East Anglian clergyman, Matthew Hopkins, grew to prominence in a climate of religious persecution and chaos after the Cromwellian parliament had executed the reactionary Catholic King Charles I. In some ways a potential McCarthy role model in his own right, witch-finder General Hopkins carried out widespread acts of persecution in pursuit of rigid orthodox power, property acquisition and personal ambition. His methods were very closely adhered to in Salem. In the East Anglian fishing port of Great Yarmouth, according to the Norfolk Record Office, two key personal fates within this historical link can be identified. This involves the family history of Rebecca Nurse and her sister Mary Easty, who were both executed in the Salem witch trials. As children, the sisters, then registered under their maiden names as Rebecca and Mary Towne, had emigrated together with their own family and many others from Great Yarmouth around 1645, when the town's governing body had requested the services of Matthew Hopkins to identify and prosecute witches. As a result of this purge, of the nine women and two men tried in Yarmouth Tollhouse, five women were executed (Norfolk Record Office). Like many emigrants, the Towne family had most likely been émigrés fleeing the prevailing climate of religious oppression.

The whole Hopkins episode serves also to embody the essential continuity of cultural and economic links between England and the New England American colonies. Danforth and Hathorne were closely set in the Hopkins mould. As the Massachusetts settlers were torn between incompetent orthodox hierarchies and destabilizing Colonial wars against both the French and the Native American peoples, East Anglia had been torn apart by the English Civil War. The war itself had been triggered by deep-seated conflicts involving Protestants and Catholics, as well as traditional monarchists opposing parliamentarians and republicans. Underpinning these ostensibly ideological confrontations was the threat of a proletarian uprising that, under the pressure of violent land acquisition by powerful groups and the legacy of oppressive feudalism, had represented a continuous source of potential rebellion. Within these contexts, the course and outcome of the English Civil War was to shape American history to such a degree that the total lack of any historical reference to these colonial links in *The Crucible* might once again point to a politically limited approach to contextualization and causality. Those underlying hierarchical continuities between the old and new worlds that contradict the populist, democratic, and libertarian principles, fuelling the myth of the American Dream, can underscore this. Those continuities, in terms of tensions between patrician elites and the majority immigrant populations, have dominated American history, through to more recent confrontations between corporate power and industrialized labor.

By the time that Arthur Miller adapted the script for the 1996 filming under Nicholas Hytner's direction, little had been done to redress the play's decontextualization or its reduction of broader issues down to the level of mass hysteria and poorly explained community tension. Winona Ryder's and Daniel Day Lewis's performances also tend to reinforce the use of gender stereotyping. One of the more scathing reviews of Miller's own 1996 film adaptation provides a provocative and irreverent view of those essential flaws. Theater critic Lloyd Rose, referring cynically to the whole project as a guilt trip, commented:

> Avoiding similar social calamities in the future is clearly quite simple—the good people (us) must simply find the evil people (them) and neutralize them.... The kitten with-a-whip villainess, the pseudo-poetic dialogue, the melodramatic division of good folk vs. evil—all these bring the script to the verge of the ludicrous. But Hytner treats it as if it were Shakespeare. He doesn't understand that what he's directed could be subtitled, "Blood-Crazed Teen Bimbos From Inner Space". (*Washington Post*, 32)

This may be a little harsh on Arthur Miller, but the critic's barbs can be aimed as much towards Miller's own script as they are towards Nicholas Hytner's direction. The film script sticks very closely to the play itself, which now being so far removed from the world of 1953, was always going to be in danger of inviting some added degree of mockery.

On a more serious note, employing elements of basically unchallenged colonialist assumptions in terms of ethnic privileging may well be added to the charge of gender stereotyping in *The Crucible*. The action, taking place when and where it does, is set in an era and in a location within which a significant number of native American communities were being so rapidly eradicated that an ethnic and demographic tragedy of major proportions had already taken place. Although Arthur Miller does go to some trouble to outline the violent expropriation, displacement, and cultural destruction of the indigenous American peoples in his introduction to the play, this is in no way reflected through the action. In fact, the link between the more broadly based introduction and the play can be seen in a number of ways. No work of dramatic art can afford to allow itself to become a lecture, and therefore it has to trim off those narrative elements, which may seriously impede the plot structure or undermine the dramatic tension. On the other hand, a play has to form a conceptual whole that should not depend too much on extraneous historical material to place the significance of the action in a broader context.

To what extent then should the historical information provided by Arthur Miller in the introduction form part of the action? This is a moot point, as the playwright altered much of the historical base of *The Crucible* in order to draw more personal parallels within the qualifying sphere of artistic license. Whether the playwright had deliberately changed Tituba's ethnicity to Caribbean from Native American, or had simply followed one line of interpretation in assuming that, as Parris had brought her from Barbados she must be Afro-Caribbean, the effect of this was to further erase any direct representation of Native Americans from the plot. In doing so this tended to marginalize Massachusetts' own ethnic heritage more effectively than the crudest Hollywood Western.

In 1953 *The Crucible*, of course, was compared to Arthur Miller's artistic achievement in *Death of a Salesman*. Miller's main character Willy Loman was represented as having been blinded by the central mirage, the simonizing iconography of the American Dream. But by the time the playwright had become involved in writing *The Crucible*, a difficult question arose; had Arthur Miller himself been enslaved by that central icon of the American Dream and Hollywood glamour in the figure of Marilyn Monroe, and in doing so lost a sense of critical distance? Miller's personal struggle with Monroe and McCarthy found moral and political expression in *The Crucible*. After its initial

Broadway staging at the Martin Beck in January 1953, critics like Kenneth Tynan, and *New York Times* critic Brooks Atkinson greeted the play with only muted or qualified approval. But it was the initial response of Eric Bentley both to the play itself and its inappropriate staging, that has troubled Arthur Miller ever since:

> There is a terrible inertness about the play, the individual characters, like the individual lines, lack fluidity and grace. There is an O'Neill-like striving after poetry and an eloquence that the author does not achieve. 'From Aeschylus to Arthur Miller,' say the textbooks. The world has made this author important before he has made himself great; perhaps the reversal of the natural order of things weighs heavily upon him. (24)

With more disturbing implications for the assumed relationship between the playwright, his material, and the audience of the day, the critic went on to remark: "At the moment when we are all being 'investigated' or imagining that we shall be, it is vastly disturbing to see indignant images of investigation on the other side of the footlights" (Bentley, quoted in Kauffmann). The uncanny silence in the Broadway auditorium in January 1953, within the context of Eric Bentley's much debated review cited here, points to an almost insoluble dilemma for the harassed intelligentsia of the time. Any profoundly critical work of art produced in the HUAC era was most likely to have been both produced under emotional pressure and branded subversive. Nor would it be too conspiratorial to assume that any members of the audience showing appreciation of *The Crucible*'s overt attack on the practice of "naming names" may well have had themselves identified as red sympathizers. Was the only alternative to keep quiet or create attacks on HUAC so subtle, as in Hitchcock's *North by Northwest*, that few but the initiated would get the message? In his review, Bentley was making too few allowances for the fact that HUAC had deprived America of much potentially brilliant art. Furthermore, Bentley's own political persuasions must be questioned, as he occasionally revealed himself to be seeing "reds under the bed," (26) where there were perhaps none: "In the McCarthyite 50s, Eric Bentley speculated that the disguised character of many Broadway plays was a communist" (Brustein). Typical of the manifestations of the hostile and threatening critical climate of early 1953 are the reactions of one of the more openly right wing critics, Richard Hayes, writing in the journal *Commonweal*, who had clearly misread vital personal elements of the play asserting that: "It is a critical commonplace that the communities of Mr. Miller's plays are ideological rather than personal, that he does not create a world so much in its simple humanity, or its perceptible reality, as in its intellectual alarms and excursions, *The Crucible* reinforces this tradition" (498).

From the opposite end of the ideological spectrum, arts critic David Walsh has dismissed the writing and production methods of Arthur Miller, Elia Kazan and Tennessee Williams of the early 1950s. "Most of their work suffers from a false 'depth;' a kind of cluttered psychologizing that covered up at least as much as it revealed" (12). The latter's orthodox Marxist view of the playwrights as revisionist, taken together with the schools of thought represented by Richard Hayes, emphasize once more the dilemma and isolation of the liberal left, which had been in many ways one of the main targets of the HUAC committees.

There is a central continuity in the conflict represented by attacks on *The Crucible* coming from both the left and the right. From an orthodox left wing position, Walsh is also attacking many of the central contradictions in the ideological position and development of the Group Theater in the 1930s. By 1939, the movement had indeed evolved away from the leftist collective spirit of thirty actors founded by Harold Clurman during the Depression. However, its collectivism, although rooted in the liberal left spirit of democratic socialism, had never been directly, at least officially, aligned to the communist left, or indeed ideologically well defined. Helen Krich Chinoy went into some detail, in her plenary lecture at the May 2000 Málaga Conference, on the rigorous and almost autocratic individual self-analysis promoted by Lee Strasberg and Elia Kazan. This in turn was to form the methodical base and underpinning philosophy of the Actor's Studio, which was founded jointly by the two men in 1947. The long-running conflict between this approach and that of Stella Adler, who saw Stanislawski's priorities as being more socially and artistically driven than by individual introspection, was highly significant in that it foreshadowed the later rifts between ideological commitment and personal betrayal which informed *The Crucible*. Lurking in the background was the notion that many of the Group Theater members were superficially embracing left-wing ideals in order to find a vehicle for their own personal and artistic ambitions.

Kazan, however, had been one of those group members who had also joined the Communist Party between 1934 and 1936. Although he objected to the authoritarian nature of the party, he maintained the trappings at least of ideological allegiance to the cause. Only when the full implications of what such affiliations could mean in career terms to someone who had now become a leading film director, did he decide to renounce all his links with communism, past and present, under HUAC pressure in 1952. The ostensibly collective allegiances of the Group Theater had indeed always been at odds with the individualism and automatic privileging of male interests exhibited by the behavior of its leading figures. Recognition in the wider world of performance had, by the end of the 1930s, begun to stroke the individual egos of both male and female members. Seeing things in more macro-economic terms, Harold

Clurman himself identified the central cause of the Group Theater's demise as the inability of an economically unstable idealistic venture to defend itself against the materialism of a society whose icons of success were Hollywood and Broadway: "There was an emotional tug of war constantly going on between the members of the group and forces outside it. The Group felt itself menaced by the wooing of the outside world as by its attacks; hence the fanatic, almost hysterical clinging to the ideal of Group unity and antagonism to every possible force that might threaten it" (Clurman 284). The final stage of this tug of war was to be played out in the HUAC era. Arthur Miller's response to the post 1951 rigor of the committee was in many ways driven by his own struggle between personal ambition and collective responsibility. Kazan's turning informer, as opposed to Lillian Hellman's solid stance against HUAC, formed the negative and positive poles, between which the electric current of personal anguish and moral soul searching was to flow.

It is difficult to say precisely how much of the liberal left distancing itself from the communist left had been HUAC induced, but such conflicts, however, had formed part of the much greater ideological rift, which had been splitting the core of the liberal left for some time. The divide between the orthodox and the more liberal left had also manifested itself in Freudian versus Marxist approaches to literature and performing art. The resulting conflicts between focusing socially explorative fiction narrowly down to Freudian self-analysis, as opposed to focusing more widely on the socioeconomic determinants of capitalist modes of production, hit writers like Arthur Miller, at a time when the broadsides unleashed by HUAC onto those individuals or movements considered left of center prevented any kind of more differentiated synthesis from developing: "My difficulties were surely personal, but I could not help suspecting that psychoanalysis was a form of alienation that was being used as a substitute not only for Marxism, but for social activism of any kind" (*Timebends* 310).

By 1952, Arthur Miller's life was being defined by the interlocking conflicts associated with the intensity of the HUAC witch hunts and his growing infatuation for Marilyn Monroe who, in the early 1950s, was having an affair with Arthur Miller's friend and role model, Elia Kazan. Like Miller, Kazan was married with a wife back East, but whereas many involved in film and theater felt free to explore extra-marital liaisons, the more hesitant Arthur Miller was struggling to hold onto his own more conventional integrity. Initially, Arthur Miller broke with Kazan over the latter's betrayal of the left, but a deep residual bond plagued the conscience of the playwright. The resulting complex feelings of envy, disgust, and deep affection towards both Kazan and Monroe, created a thematic template that informed much of Miller's later work. The conflict is clearly present in *A View from the Bridge*, John Huston's film *The Misfits*, and *After the Fall*, directed in 1964 by Kazan himself. However, the fact that the play presented a harsh portrait of the recently deceased and much pitied Marilyn did not win the playwright many friends. The conscience of the central male character, Arthur Miller's alter ego figure Quentin, like that of John Proctor, is portrayed as being tortured by female instability. But perhaps the uneven script of *The Misfits* represents the most sexist reduction. A mentally sick and drug dependent Marilyn Monroe was pressured into performing a sanitized and quite blatantly sexist parody of herself in the character of Roslyn Taber. The perhaps unwittingly parodic elements were induced by the clearly autobiographical nature of the script, in which the Hollywood icon found herself having to play the role of a rather feeble if not "dumb" blonde, against three romantically anachronistic machos. The male protagonists are presented, at times quite powerfully, as dislocated victims of greater socio-historical forces. The main female role however, seems to reside somewhere between that of a sex-hormone stimulant and a clichéd agent of feminine sensitivity who tempers the boys' rough behavior. Marilyn Monroe was also partially re-enacting Arthur Miller's subjective fictionalization of events, which bore a distorted resemblance to incidents in her real life.

The playwright's interpersonal relationship with the real Marilyn Monroe had been determined from the start by the signification of her public image as a cultural product. Iconic film divas form signification patterns, which paradigmatically fuel not only Hollywood's symbolic order, but also that of the American Dream itself. Arthur Miller's association with Marilyn ensured him a prominent place within the hierarchical registers of cultural relevance. The schizoid situation, in which the interpersonal reality of any given figure clashes with the intersubjective and highly mystified public perception of that figure, was also reflected in the ideological dilemma of the liberal left. Allowing oneself to be caught up in the iconic identification process may be totally at odds with the purported aims of socially critical fiction, which are to identify and demystify false social values. In this context, one may well ask if Miller's preoccupation with the fact that the HUAC chairman wanted to be photographed with Marilyn, was triggered by the awareness that both Senator Walter and he himself were essentially locked into the same status game? This central paradox was therefore ideological as well as deeply personal. Media analysts John Fiske and John Hartley, amongst others, have emphasized that analyzing the socio-cultural aspect of image making at all levels involves far more than examining individual instances, from which one may draw morally or politically critical conclusions: "The myths which operate as organizing structures within this area of cultural inter-subjectivity cannot themselves be discreet and unorganized, for that would negate their prime function (which is to organize meaning): they are themselves organized into a coherence we might call a mythology or an ideology" (46).

Since the 1930s the American entertainment industry, with Hollywood at its forefront, has been largely responsible for the cultural production of images and patterns of signification, which create and reinforce various collective notions of American identity. Awareness of the potency of these mechanisms, of course, was the rationale behind the HUAC purges of the Hollywood left. In 1947 HUAC chair J. Parnell Thomas, who ironically was later to be convicted of fraud on unrelated charges and jailed alongside some of his blacklisted political victims, chaired the committee that condemned the famous Hollywood Ten to being barred from employment or jailed for Contempt of Congress. Insisting on the right to silence as in the First Amendment, or on the right not to incriminate oneself as in the Fifth Amendment, was suddenly seen as an act of treason. Washington was putting pressure on the banks, who were in turn putting pressure on Hollywood film producers, to exclude any writers, directors, actors, or trade union leaders, who refused to be publicly purged of any leftist associations. Hollywood was further weakened by the shift away from cinema into television, at the same time being intimidated by a highly inflated mainstream political assumption that communist infiltration was being channeled through Hollywood scriptwriters. Boycotting the work of blacklisted or grey-listed (those suspected of having sympathy with suspected subversives) artists was no mere political ploy. The Soviet development of the atomic bomb, Stalin's European territorial aggression and the Korean War, exacerbated widely felt Cold-War fears of a communist take-over. Nationwide fear of 'reds under the bed' led to the formation of many local anti-red initiative groups, that would regularly demonstrate outside cinemas wherever they suspected a left-of-center scriptwriter, director, or actor to be featured in any particular movie.

Behind the scenes, however, Hollywood contradicted but never subverted its own mythologies. Studio and stage door gossip was as popular as the star-studded world it fed on, but the public by and large tended to disconnect personal from fictional systems of signification. However, for those working in the theater and film industry, this basic separation was much more difficult to maintain. Hollywood career making was associated with the kind of orgiastic opportunism both Kazan and Miller had fallen victim to, whilst clinging onto the skeletal structures of not only conventional family life, but to their self-appointed function as socially critical writers, whose purpose was, ostensibly at least, to work for a more just society. It may well be speculated that Miller's initially unquestioning adulation of Kazan's notions actually reflects an underlying matrix of competitive and sexist attitudes, which ultimately enslaved him not only to the Marilyn Monroe icon but cut right across his own ideological stance as a writer associated with the left: "What I did feel was a love for this man (Kazan) in his insatiable rooting out of the least weakness. You knew you were on the first team and that the idea was to win, and that no margin of safety was too great. The audience was an enemy that had to be overwhelmed and dominated like a woman and only then loved" (Leaming 48). In embracing this competitive male mythology, was Arthur Miller eventually espousing a whole value system that would render him no more than a house radical?

The playwright's marriage problems with his first wife Mary had surfaced at a time when his own ambition and quest for wider acclaim as a left-wing socially critical writer were getting him into political trouble. Marilyn Monroe embodied something key that may have appealed not only to Miller's ambition, but also to his whole sense of self-worth. It is possible therefore, that the integrity of his morally correct and conventional wife Mary not only stood between himself and the heady world of artistic renown, but also reminded him of how his pursuit of that elusive artistic success was vital in shaping the self-image of most American writers, performers, and artists. All this became a source of guilt association, which was perhaps decisive in the creation of the three dimensional portrayal of John Proctor. The triangular intensity between Abigail, Elizabeth and Proctor clearly gives voice to many underlying autobiographical conflicts. Might one go as far as to speculate that, had Miller focused *The Crucible* more narrowly and critically on this area of conflict, rather than trying to interweave the issues into an ambitious political allegory, the play would have gained, at least thematically, greater depth and consistency? Barbara Leaming, in her 1998 biography of Marilyn Monroe, seemed in little doubt:

> Poring over old court records, he imagined there might have been an affair between John Proctor and a young servant girl named Abigail Williams, who went on to accuse Proctor's wife Elizabeth, of witchcraft. In this story Miller discovered an armature for the adultery play he wanted to write ... and the adultery theme invigorated the political witch-hunt material with a deeply felt conflict of his own. ... Miller, in his notebook, dug more deeply into the sources of Proctor's guilt than he dared in the finished play. Early on Miller contemplated allowing Proctor to realize that he actually wants his wife dead. It would appall a principled man to discover that about himself. Unfortunately, ideas like that did not find their way into *The Crucible*. If they had, if Miller had permitted John Proctor to be darker, edgier, and more complex, he might have written a better play. (78)

The popular image of the 1950s is a stark contrast to the shadows thrown by HUAC onto the American public. Under this shadow, Miller worked on an autobiographical play involving his alter ego Quentin, who took center stage in the playwright's personal notebook-cum-diary. Quentin was drawn as a guilt ridden married man quite clearly creating an Abigail figure to deal with the inner conflict of a Hollywood film diva's lure. The reduction of sex to an act of opportunist career-making disturbed Miller, who saw Marilyn Monroe both as an icon of the unattainable, and as somebody hardened to the expediency of using sex to further personal ambitions. This contradiction mirrored the conflicts that posed a threat to the order of his own moral universe. The tenor of Budd Schulberg's portrayal of Hollywood directors and producers in *What Makes Sammy Run?* is classically summed up in the phrase he used to describe the general attitude to young actresses, "unpacking a new crate of virgins" (56). Miller's highly charged character John Proctor exists in stark contrast to Sam Glick, Schulberg's Hollywood cynical opportunist anti-hero. Schulberg turned informer to save his career, and ended up writing the script for *On the Waterfront*, a sanitized, anti-communist version of Miller's own project on the exploitation of dockworkers, *The Hook*. As Kazan and Schulberg went on to shoot *On the Waterfront* with the rising star Marion Brando, the two-fold betrayal drove Miller to come up with a powerfully emotional hero that functioned as an objective correlative for his personal dilemma.

Undoubtedly the playwright had found enough intense moral outrage and personal anguish in Hollywood to project onto his historical sources. *The Crucible*'s dramatic intensity therefore resides in the inseparability of the personal and the political in times of harsh repression. It was just after being hit by the shock-waves of Kazan's revelation that he would co-operate fully with HUAC by more than simply naming names and relinquishing any left wing associations he had had, that Miller had driven to Salem, Massachusetts, on his urgent mission to create an allegorical and highly personal account of the machinations and effects of the American equivalent of the Stalinist purges. Of course, the parallels between HUAC and the Stalinist show trials were deeply ironic, considering that the Western alliance had been basing its whole political and military raison d'etre on fierce opposition to state communism, and the dictatorial power associated with Stalin himself. Purges against the left had been there in waiting since the 1920s, beginning in earnest with the establishment of the Dies Committee in 1938. The Hollywood studio system had become increasingly political in that it claimed to be un-political. Its restrictive and often puritanical 1930s Hollywood Code thus blazed the trail for political censorship under HUAC. By 1954, the committee had removed 212 Hollywood workers from all levels of production. This figure does not include those who simply left rather than stay and face an almost impossible predicament. Of those that had been blacklisted, only around ten percent ever returned. In a broad sense, Sam Goldwyn's famous comment on films and the notion of thematic depth, "if you want to send a message use Western Union" (quoted in Jahiel), reflected the tight control exerted by the producers and studio bosses, which was to be so crucial to the workings of HUAC. Films that did manage to carry overtly politically critical messages were few and far between.

In his critique of the 1991 film *Guilty by Suspicion* that revisited the effect of HUAC on Hollywood in the early 1950s, Edwin Jahiel reminds us that taking a biographical approach can obscure the fundamentally historical nature of the HUAC era: "The blacklisting did not spring out—like Athena from the head of Zeus—of America's political system, ready-made and fully armed. It was but a tragic link in a long chain of American attitudes and reactions to what could generically (and vaguely) be called 'the Left.' Those attitudes can easily be traced back to the end of the nineteenth century." Irwin Winkler's broadly biographical portrayal of the Hollywood HUAC conflict, with its strong focus on how individual lives were affected, is somewhat harshly dealt with in this critique. But Jahiel's reaction against subjectivity and emotionality further reflects the potential pitfalls of focusing on individual fates when characterizing the effects and ramifications of broader political developments.

After 1945, America, still largely pervaded at home by a legacy of puritan ethics, stood poised to become the world's greatest superpower. A glance at the military hardware on display in the early post-war Washington parades graphically illustrates the vastness of the project. Military expansionism at all costs was to provide the weaponry for an unprecedented era of cultural domination. It was unfortunate that the reactionary forces that were in the driving seat outweighed the material and political benefits of this. Eventually tens of millions were to have been investigated if not interrogated by HUAC and the Congressional committees linked to it. Most of these names were locked away for 50 years in 1976 when the recently formed House Internal Security Committee put the files under lock and key.

The sword of a right-wing Damocles had been descending on Hollywood after the initial purges of the House Un-American Activities Committee; prominent victims included Bertolt Brecht and the famous Hollywood Ten. As the Cold-War intensified in the early 1950s, another arch right-winger John S. Wood was put in charge of the committee and Miller and Kazan were directly in the firing line. Despite a broad understanding of those under pressure, there was shock and disgust over Kazan's sudden pro-active support for the myth of a communist conspiracy. Shortly after his HUAC denunciation session he went so far as to publish a full-page advertisement in the *New York Times* underlining the fact that he felt himself to be duty bound to name members of the Communist Party. This virulent volte-face involved the unnecessary exposure of the Theater Union as a communist unit. Both actions clearly went beyond the level of collaboration needed to appease HUAC, and were linked to a general assumption that Kazan would have been big enough to challenge the strength of HUAC, and even disrupt the blacklisting procedure. Given the enormous power of the HUAC however, this assertion may be seriously doubted. It may, on the other hand, be asserted that Kazan had not necessarily been artistically if not ideologically inconsistent. Both Miller and Kazan had been, at least in part, driven by the assumption that writers and artists tend to enjoy privileged status within the cultural codes of western societies. The ideological rift between the two men may be qualified by the assumption that both understood each other's motives, but Miller had opted to salvage his integrity. Miller's stand, which he never saw as heroic, cost him a conviction for Contempt of Congress and huge lawyer's fees. On the other hand Kazan was immediately restored to the position of a well-paid leading director after his ritual about-face in 1952. However his politically sanitized film work such as *On the Waterfront* and *Rebel Without a Cause* suffered considerable thematic unevenness, and Kazan's work also lost the respect of most people he respected and admired.

John Proctor's reaction and eventual refusal to fully co-operate with the 1692 court, predicts and reflects Miller's own refusal to co-operate with HUAC in 1956. Lillian Hellman's famous words before the Committee in 1952, "I cannot and will not cut my conscience to fit this year's fashion" (quoted in Horn 98), indeed influenced Arthur Miller's voicing of John Proctor's pre-execution response in *The Crucible* and in turn the playwright's own conduct at his HUAC hearing in 1956. Ironically, Miller's subpoena was largely triggered by the play's obvious challenge to and disapproval of HUAC. Thus the prosecutors saw the play as communist inspired, and as such, likely to weaken America's so-called just pursuit of its enemies by "naming names." It is quite remarkable that in creating the fictional Proctor, Miller had not only created a fiction-to-fact, self-fulfilling prophesy, but in doing so had also committed himself to his own eventual mode of response when summoned to appear before the committee. Partially at least, Arthur Miller's strategic difficulties with the committee hearing were due to the fact that he had been unprofessionally equipped to deal with the interrogations, and for the distorted versions of his responses in press reports, which the committee had clearly manipulated. There was however speculation at that time that his decision to announce his intention of marrying Marilyn Monroe in the middle of the HUAC interrogation had involved at least some strategic thinking on the playwright's part.

> Marilyn, in tight beige toreador pants, heard the news of Miller's wedding announcement and later called Norman and Hedda Rosten in Brooklyn Heights. "He announced it before the whole world!" Marilyn exulted. "He told the whole world he was marrying Marilyn Monroe. Me! Can you believe it?" The Rostens,

for their part, wondered whether Arthur wasn't simply using Marilyn "to get off the hook." (Leaming 234)

Be that as it may, Arthur Miller eventually managed to escape the full force of a sentence for Contempt, largely because the most intense phase of HUAC's harassment of those broadly associated with the liberal left, had already run its course. At the dawn of a somewhat more liberal era, or at least more relaxed socio-cultural climate, both the body politic and the judiciary were beginning to distance themselves from the worst abuses of the McCarthy era. Furthermore the suspicion had always been there amongst many observers, that Joseph McCarthy had been used as a tool. By 1954, he had already become the necessary evil, from which more moderate right-wingers could distance themselves, once the purges had flushed out most communists and the New Dealers along with them, from the decks of the ship of state:

> After Eisenhower's election, the Republican Party had no more use for McCarthy who the party leadership tended to view as a loose cannon on deck; useful in stirring up trouble when it suited them but just as likely to make trouble for them when it didn't. McCarthy did not understand, of course, that his real value was not uncovering spy rings (which he had certainly not been doing) but as a partisan ploy, allowing worthier men to keep their hands clean. It was clear from the outset that Eisenhower was not happy with McCarthy's wild accusations, but like a genie, once he had been loosed, there was almost no stopping him. (Trescott 2)

The continuing reverberations of that 1950s anti-liberal crusade are however very much still with us. The extent of Elia Kazan's perceived betrayal has never been forgotten, and there was renewed controversy when he was given the Motion Picture Association of America Academy Award in 1999. Many artists objected to the retrospective recognition for someone who they saw as having betrayed the course of the liberal conscience, and ruined the careers of others in the process. Ian Hartman-O'Connell noted in the *Hoya* magazine in March 1999: "One of the most fascinating things to watch during the presentation was who refused to clap as Kazan accepted his award. The camera flashed to Ed Harris who starred in 'The Truman Show' and Steven Spielberg. Both sat on their hands" (2).

The Crucible also fails as serious dramatic art however, as the thematic reduction to the core binary conflict between good and evil outlined above also deprives us of any deeper representation of those who bowed to pressure, as well as failing to provide an adequate frame of reference for the broader political forces that were behind the acts of individual betrayal in both eras. Parris and Hale are as near as we get, but they remain essentially decontextualized. Proctor's property and that lost by most of Putnam's rivals would have originally been acquired through colonial expropriation, as was the opportunist acquisition of their property in turn, by the lobby behind the witch-hunting officials.

An interesting rider to this debate is the favorable portrayal of the Reverend Hale as the naive establishment figure, who realizes too late that the Salem proceedings have nothing to do with justice and public morality, and consequently makes a desperate plea for clemency and a deeper sense of justice. One of the cruelest moments of dramatic irony in *The Crucible* occurs in the courtroom when Elizabeth Proctor suppresses her knowledge of Abigail's sexual transgression to protect her husband, and thus unwittingly condemns him. Hale's realization of this is expressed in pleas which also carry quite obvious allusions to the miscarriages of justice practiced by the HUAC hearings: "HALE: Excellency, it is a natural lie to tell; I beg you, stop now before another is condemned! I may shut my conscience to it no more, private vengeance is working through this testimony. From the beginning this man has struck me true. By my oath to Heaven, I believe him now, and I pray you call back his wife" (87). Much hinges on whether Miller meant Hale to be read as a naive but liberal voice of decency, who had himself fallen victim to the cynical abuses of power represented by the witch hunts as some kind of freak phenomenon. In this case, the allegorical reference to the McCarthy era would be rather misleading, as HUAC's most blatant abuses had emerged as part of a long-term process that many liberals themselves had either ignored, or had tacitly supported. Was it Hale as a character or Miller as the author, who failed to make this connection? After all, neither Salem's Hathorne and Danforth nor Wisconsin's Senator McCarthy had been sudden aberrations. There is a strong body of historical opinion, which sees the HUAC reign of terror as the inevitable outcome of a longer-term political process, which had its roots in the establishment of oligarchic hierarchies in the early colonial period, and reached its peak in the superpower rivalry of the early post-war years. "With spokesmen for the Truman Administration calling for a holy war against Communism, it is hardly surprising that McCarthyism flourished during the early 1950s, or that McCarthyite congressmen effectively attacked the Administration for failing to act in accordance with its own alarmist and conspiratorial rhetoric" (Theoharis 8).

WORKS CITED

Bentley, Eric. "Arthur Miller's *The Crucible* Review." *New Republic*. 24 January 1953.
Boyer, Paul & Nissenbaum, Steven. *Salem Village Witchcraft*. Boston: Northern University Press, 1993.

Brustein, Robert. "On Theater. A Question of Identity." *New Republic Web Archives*. (30 August 1999). Online. Internet. <http//www.thenewrepublic.com/archive/1999/Brustein>

Chinoy, Helen Krich. "Premature Feminists and the 'Boys' in the Group Theatre. Plenary Lecture given at the First University of Málaga Conference on American Theater. 22 May 2000.

Clurman, Harold. *The Fervent Years: The Group Theatre & the 30's*. New York: Da Capo Press, 1962.

Fiske, John & Hartley John. *Reading Television*. London: Routledge. 1989.

Hartman-O'Connell, Ian. "Kazan's Award: Art and Politics a Controversial Mix." *The Hoya*. Online. Internet. (26 March 1999): <http://mviv.thehoya.com/guide/032699>

Hayes, Richard. "Hysteria and Ideology in *The Crucible*." *Commonweal* 57. (February 1953): 498.

Jahiel, Edwin. "Guilty by Suspicion." *Movie reviews by Edwin Jahiel-Kino*. Online. Internet. 28 February 1998. <http//www.prairinet.org/ejahiel/guiltyby.html>

Kauffmann, Stanley. "Latter Day Look." *New Republic*. Online. Internet. 16 December 1996: <http//www.thenewrepublic.com/archive/1996/Kauffmann>

Leaming, Barbara. *Marilyn Monroe*. London: Weidenfeld & Nicholson, 1998.

Horn, Barbara Lee. *Lillian Hellman*. Westport, CT: Greenwood Publishing Group, 1998.

Miller. Arthur. "In Conversation with Arthur Miller." *Front Row*. BBC Radio 4, London. 16 August 2000.

———. Are You Now Or Were You Ever." *The Guardian Unlimited*. Online. Internet. 17 June 2000. <www.guardian.co.uk>

———. *The Crucible*. London: Methuen, 1988.

———. *Timebends*. New York: Methuen. 1987.

Rose, Lloyd. "Reviewing Hytner's Crucible." *The Washington Post*. 20 December 1996.

Schulberg, Budd. *What Makes Sammy Run?* New York: Vintage Reissue, 1993.

Theoharis, Athan. *The Politics of Scholarship: Liberals, Anti-Communism, and McCarthyism*. Online. Internet. <http//www.English.upenn.edu/~afilreis/50stheoharis/html>

Trescott, Andrew. "McCarthy and Murrow." *20th Century History*. Online. Internet. 3 January 1998. <http//www.history1900s.about.com/education/his>

Walsh, David. "Hollywood Honors Elia Kazan Film Maker and Informer." *WSWS Arts Review*. Online. Internet. February 1999. <http//www.wsws.org/articles>

STEPHEN A. MARINO

Poetry and Politics in *The* Crucible

*T*he Crucible has long been considered one of Arthur Miller's more social—if not overly political—plays. As a result, much critical examination has focused on connections between the Salem Witch Trials and the so-called Communist Witch Hunts of the 1950s. However, few studies explore how the poetic language of the play supports Miller's social and political concerns.

In *The Crucible*, Arthur Miller uses figurative language—images, symbols, metaphors—indigenous to the society of the play's characters. The language of the Salemites is steeped in the biblical and religious allusions of their theocratic society. Moreover, the poetic language of the text is distinguished by the use of opposites, which illustrate the extreme conflicts that polarize the Salem community. In this expression of opposites, Miller effectively connects the parlous times of Salem village in the 1690s to the similar state of America in the 1950s.

In an interview given a few months after the premiere of *The Crucible*, Miller discussed how what he termed "diabolism"—the fear and hatred of opposites—is one of the central themes of the play:

> "When tensions exist," he explained, "This fear is organized. In Salem, these people regarded themselves as holders of a light. If this light were extinguished, they believed the world would end.

From *A Language Study of Arthur Miller's Plays: The Poetic in the Colloquial*, pp. 55–80. © 2002 by the Edwin Mellen Press. Reprinted in *The Critical Response to Arthur Miller*, pp. 468–486. © 2006 by Steven R. Centola and Michelle Cirulli.

When you have an ideology which feels itself so pure, it implies
an extreme view of the world. Because they are white, opposition
is completely black." (Grim 26)

As this chapter shows, Miller's use of images, symbols and metaphors in a
series of opposites indicates the Salemites' view of a world totally of extremes;
heat and cold, white and black, light and dark, soft and hard, lightness and
weight signify the existence of the ultimate opposites: good and evil. In the
same interview, Miller pointed to his belief that the diabolism at work in
Salem also existed in the 1950s in America: "We have come to a time when
it seems there must be two sides, and we look back to the ideal state of being
when there is no conflict. Our idea is that conflict can be wiped out in the
world" (26). In *The Crucible*, Miller's poetic language illustrates how opposing
sides of the conflicts wish to wipe each other out.

A few studies of *The Crucible* examine how the language supports the
themes. In "Setting, Language and the Force of Evil in *The Crucible*," Penelope
Curtis maintains that the language of the play is marked by what she calls
"half-metaphor," which Miller employs to suggest the themes. For example,
she examines the interplay of language between Elizabeth and Abigail which
indicates reputation, such as "something soiled," "entirely white," "no blush
about my name." John Prudhoe in "Arthur Miller and the Tradition of Tragedy"
notes how the characters use Biblical imagery in their language because "a
large context of traditional beliefs gives meaning to their words." However,
Stephen Fender in "Precision and Pseudo-Precision in *The Crucible*" argues that
the language of the Salemites actually reveals "the speech of a society totally
without moral referents." Among the articles which discuss the importance of
"name" in the language of the play are Ruby Cohn in *Dialogue in American
Drama*, Gerald Weales in "Arthur Miller: Man and His Image," and Michael
J. O'Neal in "History, Myth and Name Magic in Arthur Miller's *The Crucible*."
Edward Murray traces word repetition in the play. In *Arthur Miller, Dramatist*,
he examines how in *The Crucible*, Miller "in a very subtle manner, uses key words
to knit together the texture of action and theme." He notes, for example, the
recurrent use of the word "soft" in the text. Robert Wilcox has pointed out that
although the word "crucible" is not used in the play, "images of heat and its
opposite, cold, appear with some frequency" (341).

In *The Crucible*, the images, symbols, and metaphors in patterns of
opposites rely heavily on the interplay between the literal and figurative
meanings of words. In an article, "Why I Wrote *The Crucible*," which appeared
in *The New Yorker* a few weeks before the November 1996 premiere of the film,
Miller explained that he was drawn into writing the play by the chance it gave
him to use the seventeenth-century language of New England: "That plain,
craggy English was liberating in a strangely sensuous way, with its swings

from an almost legalistic precision to a wonderful metaphoric richness" (164). In the play, Miller uses the sense of opposites to re-create "the swing" of the seventeenth-century language with its denotative and connotative meanings. Moreover, the swing of language effectively depicts how polarized society became in Salem in 1692 and America in the 1950s. Each side became deeply entrenched in opposition so that there was no middle ground; the extremes denied the moderation necessary for political, personal, emotional, and rational compromise.

The opposition of heat and cold provides one of the more dramatic tensions of the play. Images of heat and cold define the emotional relationships between John and Elizabeth Proctor and between John Proctor and Abigail Williams. These images also buttress Miller's religious and political concerns. Cold evokes the judgment of God. Heat contains its obvious religious connection to the fire of hell, but Miller significantly applies the metaphor of fire to the political and court activities of Danforth. Miller also juxtaposes the metaphoric meanings of heat and cold with the literal heat and cold of the Massachusetts wilderness.

The language of heat and cold signifies the complicated emotional relationship among Elizabeth and John Proctor and Abigail Williams quite early in the play. In act 1, sc. 1, when Abigail is questioned by her uncle, Reverend Parris, why she has been dismissed from Elizabeth Proctor's service, Abigail responds, "It's a bitter woman, a lying, cold, sniveling woman" (12). Although describing someone as emotionally "cold" is a common rhetorical device, Miller assigns great metaphoric significance to this. When John and Abigail are left alone in Betty Parris's room, we learn for the first time about their previous sexual relationship. Abigail speaks of their attraction in images of heat and cold: "I have a sense for heat, John, and yours has drawn me to my window, and I have seen you looking up, burning in your loneliness" (23). In these lines, Abigail and John's sense for heat—the euphemism for their sexual passion—directly opposes them to Elizabeth's coldness. Abigail significantly repeats and reinforces this coldness to Proctor a few lines later. "She is a cold, lying sniveling woman" (24). Moreover, the sexual heat which both John and Abigail possess is expressed in an opposite image. She describes him as "no wintry man" (23), ironically using the deep literal cold of the season to describe the heat of John's desire.

Miller clearly establishes heat and cold as metaphoric opposites since their usage recurs throughout the play. At the beginning of act 2, John has arrived home from a day of planting, hoping for "a fair summer," confident that: "We'll see green fields soon. It's warm as blood beneath the clods" (50). Although these lines literally indicate Proctor's satisfaction at completing the seeding of the farm, the images of warmth and summer signify the sense of opposites, for they echo the heat and cold imagery that has been established in act 1. The sense of opposites clearly is reinforced when John contrasts the literal warmth of late spring and early summer outside the farm with the figurative coldness inside of the farmhouse. He says to Elizabeth: "It's winter in here yet" (50). Of course, the implied winter here is the emotional coldness of Elizabeth, which the reader sees as quite evident by the way she acts toward John. John shudders at the winter in the house and in Elizabeth. However, he is "no wintry man;" his attraction to summer, heat, and passion is clearly evident at this point in the play. The imagery vivifies John's conflict as an attraction to opposites—the heat of Abigail and the coldness of Elizabeth.

Elizabeth's coldness is heightened later in the scene, when she and John speak of Abigail's part in the witchcraft investigations and John's adultery with her. Their dialogue employs another significant metaphor of the play—judging—which merges with the language of heat and cold. While judgment literally is the obvious mechanism of the entire play, Miller uses the language of judgment in its figurative context with particular sophistication. The most pervasive use of the metaphor of judging occurs not in act 3, the courtroom scene, but during this conversation between John and Elizabeth in act 2. John declares his anger at Elizabeth's treatment of him in the seven months since she discovered his adultery: ". . . I cannot speak but I am doubted, every moment judged for lies, as though I come into a court when I come into this house" (54–55). In fact, Miller creates an intriguing inversion of house, church, and prison in the entire play, where each structure is used not for its original purpose, but rather as a court. The Proctor farmhouse is turned into a court by Elizabeth and Hale in act 2; the vestry room of the Salem meetinghouse is used as a court by the magistrates in act 4; the jail is turned into a court in act 4. In a play so heavily immersed in the principles of a theocracy, no scenes occur in an actual church or courtroom; even the minister's house is turned into a court of inquiry in act 1. Perhaps Parris's conclusion that his own household is "the very center of some obscene practice" (11) best characterizes the inversion that occurs in religion, law, state, and emotional relationships in the play.

Proctor indicates the inversion of his emotional relationship with Elizabeth when the metaphor of judging combines with the imagery of coldness in his conversation with Elizabeth:

> PROCTOR. Some dream I had must have mistaken you for God that day. But you're not, you're not, and let you remember it. Let you look sometimes for the goodness in me, and judge me not.
> ELIZABETH. I do not judge. The magistrate sits in your heart that judges you. I never thought you but a good man, John—*with a smile*—only somewhat bewildered.
> PROCTOR, *laughing bitterly*. Oh, Elizabeth, your justice would freeze beer. (55)

Proctor has inverted his perception of Elizabeth because he believes she judges him like God. Yet, John seeks forgiveness from Elizabeth as a wife, not as a God-like judge. He desires emotion from her, perhaps the same heat and passion he found in Abigail. Most importantly, John associates Elizabeth's justice with the coldness Abigail has previously applied to her, because it "would freeze beer." The addition of judgment as a metaphor significantly expands the heat and cold imagery from the emotional level to the religious and political levels of the play. As a result the tension increases between the opposites of heat and cold. Moreover, judgment—because it decides right or wrong—significantly contributes to the polarizing effect of the conflicts.

Proctor's use of "freeze" to describe Elizabeth's justice significantly resembles his description of God's justice at the end of act 2. After Hale's arrival and examination of the Proctors and Elizabeth's subsequent arrest, John urges Mary Warren to testify in court against Abigail. After Mary reveals her knowledge of his lechery, Proctor grasps her, declaring:

> Peace. It is a providence, and no great change; we are only what we always were, but naked now. *He walks as though toward a great horror, facing the open sky.* Aye, naked! And the wind, God's icy wind, will blow! (81)

Proctor's description of the wind as "icy"—presumably God's justice—obviously connects to the freezing imagery of Elizabeth's justice. Here Miller effectively highlights the tension between the opposite images of heat and cold. If God is associated with an icy cold wind, then John, whose sin and passion have been associated with heat, cannot have God as a magistrate in his heart (55). John ultimately becomes his own judge since Elizabeth insists that she does not judge him and that he must judge himself. Yet, Proctor does not judge himself until the end of the play, when John and Elizabeth's next private conversation occurs. In the intervening dramatic time, Miller establishes the ultimate opposites of good and evil as the thematic focus of the play.

The political and religious forces intervene with John and Elizabeth's emotional reconciliation until the last act. They do not meet again until three months later in act 4, after their enforced separation and imprisonment, when Elizabeth agrees to speak with John to ask if he will confess. The language indicates how tightly Miller has constructed the poetic language of the text. Images of heat, cold, and judging again define the Proctors' emotional relationship and support the tension between good and evil. Although Proctor seeks Elizabeth's forgiveness in this scene, she now realizes that she cannot be John's judge since she shares in the adultery with "sins of my own to count" (137). Her realization is couched in the coldness metaphor of the play, for as she admits, "It needs a cold wife to prompt lechery" (137). She reinforces the metaphor even further by her expression, "It were a cold house I kept" (137), a line which echoes Proctor's remark, "It is winter in here yet" in act 2. However, the language of the play suggests that John and Elizabeth's reconciliation is not only emotional but also theological. For rather than encourage him to confess falsely at the evil bidding of the magistrates, she leaves the decision to him alone, telling him to "Do as you will, do as you will" (138). When Proctor asks if she would give the prosecutors such a lie, he realizes, "You would not; if tongs of fire were singeing you you would not!" (138). Proctor ultimately comes to realize that Elizabeth's coldness constitutes her essential religious goodness. He knows that even "tongs of fire"—clearly the evil of hell and political persecution—could not threaten her sanctity. However, at this moment of crisis in the play for Proctor—as a man, as a Christian, as a husband, and as a citizen—he perceives himself as the opposite: "It is evil. Good, then—it is evil, and I do it" (138). Therefore, he associates himself with the fires of damnation.

The Crucible contains many images of heat with its obvious religious association with hell. However, throughout his canon, Miller quite effectively assigns new meaning to familiar metaphors. The most intriguing images of burning and fire in *The Crucible* refer not to burning in hell, but burning on earth, which Miller clearly uses for political implications. The first reference in this context occurs in act 2 when Giles Corey and Francis Nurse arrive at the Proctor farmhouse and announce the arrest of their wives. Nurse asks Reverend Hale what he should do, and Hale responds: "Believe me, Mr. Nurse, if Rebecca Nurse be tainted, then nothing's left to stop the whole green world from burning" (71). Hale's use of burning expands the figurative meaning of fire. The poetic language connects the burning to the political and religious fever which infects Salem and accuses innocent people of witchcraft. Of course, when *The Crucible* is read as an analogy of the witch-hunts of the 1950s, this language accurately depicts how the Communist threat was perceived to the western world. For example, Senator Joseph McCarthy, the central figure of the Senate hearings, referred to the "fires of communism that are sweeping across Europe and Asia and flickering on the shores of America" (Weales 407). He also described the fight against Communism using opposites: "The struggle between light and darkness, between good and evil, between life and death" (406–07).

In act 3, Judge Danforth, who is the personification of theocratic power in the play, significantly reinforces the imagery of burning on earth. When John Proctor requests that Danforth hear Mary Warren's deposition about Abigail's lies, Danforth warns him: "Now, Mr. Proctor, before I decide whether I shall hear you or not, it is my duty to tell you this. We burn a hot fire here; it melts down all concealment" (89). Danforth's admonition holds particular weight, for in his role as chief magistrate, he decides the guilt and innocence of the accused. However, Danforth's fire does not burn under a crucible of truth and religious purity, but rather for the political punishment of innocent people unwilling to bend to the will of the state. More importantly, in the sense of opposites with which Miller constructs the poetic language of the play, Danforth's control of the hot fire of the witchcraft hysteria suggests that his judgment is the antithesis of God's justice, which Proctor earlier has associated with icy wind at the end of act 2. Thus, Danforth's hot fire is evil.

At the end of act 3, Proctor himself evokes fire imagery to signal Danforth's evil. After Elizabeth does not substantiate Proctor's adultery and Mary Warren accuses him of being the devil's man, he declares that God is dead, exclaiming: "A fire, a fire is burning! I hear the boot of Lucifer, I see his filthy face! And it is my face, and yours Danforth . . . God damns our kind especially, and we will burn, we will burn together!" (119–20). Although these lines ostensibly refer to the fire of hell, a close reading reveals that Proctor's language also places this fire on earth. The "boot" of Lucifer implies that he and his fire have traveled to Salem village, not in the evil of the accused, but rather in the accusers and those judges who inflame their accusations. For the hot fire that Danforth burns in the previous act, now is equated with Lucifer's fires come into the world since Proctor sees the image of Lucifer's fiery face in Danforth's. Arthur Miller wrote in the Introduction to *Collected Plays* that if he had to write *The Crucible* again, he would alter Danforth's character. Miller believes he was wrong in mitigating the evil of Danforth and the judges he represents. He wrote: "I would perfect his evil to its utmost and make an open issue, a thematic consideration of it in the play . . . There are people dedicated to evil in the world; that without their perverse example we should not know the good" (158). Miller implies that the evil of Danforth is necessary in order to understand its opposite—the goodness of John Proctor. Yet, at this crucial moment in the play, Proctor also sees his own face in Lucifer's, for John believes his evil—his adultery, his fraudulent life, his failure to negate Abigail's lies—has permeated the world as well. Thus, he declares "We will burn together" (158).

However, John Proctor ultimately finds his goodness. Arthur Miller maintains that the driving force behind *The Crucible* is connections he made between the social and political climate of the early 1950s and the historical events in Salem in 1692. Miller wished to create a play "which would show that the sin of public terror is that it divests man of conscience, of himself" (Introduction 155). Significantly, in act 4, John's conscience turns out to be the magistrate who sits in his heart. Elizabeth urges him, "But let none be your judge. There is no higher judge under heaven than Proctor is" (137). Proctor wonders, "Then who will judge me?" (138). Ultimately John judges himself, consequently finding the goodness of individual conscience which defeats its opposite: the evil of state-sponsored fanaticism.

The language of heat and cold implies this defeat. Act 4 occurs in the fall, months after the initial crying out. In the subtle interplay of opposites that Miller uses in the play, the literal coldness of the season indicates the subsiding of the heat of the trials. At the beginning of the act, Danforth and Hathorne come to Salem jail to inquire about Reverend Hale's activity among the prisoners. When Danforth asks Herrick if he is drunk, Herrick responds, "No sir; it is a bitter night, and I have no fire here" (124). At this point in the play, the figurative importance of fire is established, for the fervor of the trials clearly has cooled We see Danforth and Parris's fear at the impending executions of John Proctor and Rebecca Nurse, the disappearance of Abigail, the dagger left on Parris's doorstep, and the rebellion in Andover. In fact, the language indicates quite strongly that individual conscience is indeed prevailing. Hale warns Danforth about possible rebellion.

> DANFORTH. You have heard rebellion spoken in the town?
> HALE. Excellency, there are orphans wandering from house to house; abandoned cattle bellow on the highroads, the stink of rotting crops hangs everywhere, and no man knows when the harlot's cry will end his life—and you wonder how they do not burn your province! (130)

Thus, the most important fire in the play ultimately is threatened not by theocratic authority, but rather a populace whose consciences finally burn in revolt against injustice.

Robert Wilcox has examined some of the other metaphors, symbols, and images in *The Crucible* which are used in opposites. His examination of cleanliness and dirt includes other diametrics like black and white, and soiled and cleansed in their association with reputation. He maintains that:

> The imagery of the dirty versus the clean, with its clearly defined opposites, expresses the determination of the people of Salem to hold to firm standards of right and wrong and of good and evil in the face of a world that seems increasingly to be slipping toward a chaos in which all traditional standards for making judgments are lost. (349)

Wilcox also notes the frequent use of the opposites of light and dark, especially to distinguish between right and wrong. Wilcox judges that Proctor's salvation at the end of the play depends upon finding his white "shred of goodness," an image which "links the imagery of light and dark with the imagery of cleanliness and dirt in one encompassing image of the conflicting forces of good and evil" (352).

In *The Crucible*, the images of light and darkness signify not only the tension between good and evil, but also the private vengeance which fuels the witchcraft accusations. The first reference in the play to darkness occurs early in act 1 when Ann Putnam reveals that she sent her daughter Betty to Tituba to conjure up Ann's dead babies:

> PARRIS. Goody Ann, it is a formidable sin to conjure up the dead!
> MRS. PUTNAM. I take it on my soul, but who else may surely tell us what person murdered my babies?
> PARRIS, *horrified.* Woman!
> MRS. PUTNAM. They were murdered, Mr. Parris! And mark this proof! Mark it! Last night my Ruth were ever so close to their little spirits; I know it, air. For how else is she struck dumb now except some power of darkness would stop her mouth? It is a marvelous sign, Mr. Parris! (16)

In the religious context of Salem's theocratic society, Ann obviously equates the power of darkness with the evil force of Satan and his human agent. However, "darkness" clearly takes on other metaphoric meanings in the play: ignorance and fear. For the darkness that overtakes the Salemites is their fear of the unknown: their inability, their unwillingness, and their ignorance to look beyond demonic explanation for the girls' illness. The power of her own ignorance has caused Ann Putnam to send her daughter to Tituba. Clearly, Betty Parris and Ruth Putnam's inability to speak are caused by their ignorance and fear of punishment for their misdeeds in the forest. Thus, the real darkness of the play has less to do with witchcraft, and more with the darkness of the human spirit, a spirit which invokes private vengeance.

Ann's husband, Thomas Putnam, reinforces the figurative meaning of darkness when he remarks: "Don't you understand it sir? There is a murdering witch among us, bound to keep herself in the dark" (16). Putnam's lines again reveal the sophistication with which Miller uses figurative language in the play. For although Putnam ostensibly means the same Satanic darkness that his wife means, the line also contains another, more significant figurative context. For Ann Putnam is actually an agent of evil in the play, a "murdering witch" who has put the hysteria into motion by bidding her daughter to go to Tituba. The reader ultimately comes to understand that Ann Putnam is bound to keep herself in the darkness of her own ignorance and fear. Moreover, later in the act, when Reverend Hale examines Abigail and he reveals that Tituba made her drink blood, Ann Putnam cries out, "My baby's blood?" (43), a significant catalyst to the later accusations against Goody Osburn and Rebecca Nurse. In addition, Thomas Putnam himself actually suggests the names of Sarah Good and Goody Osburn (46) during Hale's interrogation of Tituba. When Tituba calls out these women, Ann secures their damnation when she exclaims, "I knew it! Goody Osburn were midwife to me three times" (47). Thus, the imagery suggests that personal vengeance is the actual darkness which is unleashed in Salem village.

Giles Corey also uses the imagery of darkness to describe the community squabbles which feed the vengeance. In act 1, when Proctor argues with Reverend Parris about his salary, the deed to his house, and his firewood, Giles is impressed with the "iron" in Reverend Parris. In a reflective speech which clearly refers to the past arguments in Salem society, Giles says:

> It suggests to the mind what the trouble be among us all these years. *To all*: Think on it. Wherefore is everybody suing everybody else? Think on it, it's a deep thing, and dark as a pit. (31)

In these lines, Giles compares litigation—the legal manifestation of social rancor in the community—to a "deep thing, and dark as a pit," a significant comparison given the earlier association of darkness. For indeed, the dark trouble among the Salemites explodes under the guise of Satan's darkness. The role of the Putnams as instigators of these dark troubles is heightened immediately after Giles's speech, when Putnam accuses Proctor of cutting lumber down from his tract of land. This charge, of course, foreshadows Giles's accusation of Thomas Putnam reaching out for land, an accusation which leads to Giles's own arrest. Thus, Salem falls into a dark evil pit of personal vengeance masked as the goodness of witchcraft accusation.

Reverend Hale also uses darkness imagery in a metaphoric context. In act 2, during his examination of John and Elizabeth at their farmhouse, he informs the Proctors of the accusation against Rebecca Nurse:

> ELIZABETH, *shocked*. Rebecca's charged!
> HALE. God forbid such a one be charged. She is, however, mentioned somewhat.
> ELIZABETH, *with an attempt at a laugh*. You will never believe, I hope, that Rebecca trafficked with the Devil.
> HALE. Woman, it is possible.
> PROCTOR, *taken aback*. Surely you cannot think so.
> HALE. This is a strange time, Mister. No man may longer doubt the powers of the dark are gathered in monstrous attack upon this village. There is too much evidence now to deny it. You will agree, sir? (64)

Hale, as an expert on demonic arts, clearly believes that the dark powers of Satan are attacking Salem village. However, Hale's language strongly supports the figurative meaning of darkness which has been established. For the accusations against both Elizabeth and Rebecca Nurse are the visible evidence of the private vengeance at work under the guise of the dark power of evil. The vengeance of the Putnams has fueled the accusation against Rebecca; the vengeance of Abigail has manipulated the charge against Elizabeth; the vengeance of Parris has partially instigated Hale's examination of John. In fact, the language even implies that Parris is part of the powers of darkness since Proctor tells Hale his son is not baptized because he sees "no light of God" (65) in Parris. In addition, Hale, too, is associated with the darkness. For despite his idealism as an expert in the demonic arts, in acts 1 and 2 Hale also resides in the darkness of his own ignorance regarding the real motivation behind the witchcraft hysteria.

Yet, Hale's significance as a character is that he gradually comes to understand the light of truth behind the accusations. Moreover, it is not through his expertise that he comes to this judgment, but rather through his conscience. In act 3, after Elizabeth Proctor lies to protect John's reputation, Hale entreats Danforth: "I beg you stop now before another is condemned! I may shut my conscience to it no more—private vengeance is working through this testimony" (114). In act 4, when Hale returns to Salem after quitting the court, the reader understands the significance of Hale's realization. When he asks Elizabeth Proctor to encourage John to lie and to confess so that he may live, Hale's language suggests the depth of his realization:

> Let me not mistake your duty as I mistook my own. I came into this village like a bridegroom to his beloved, bearing gifts of high religion; the very crowns of holy law I brought, and what I touched with my bright confidence, it died; and where I turned the eye of my great faith, blood flowed up. (132)

Hale's description of his "bright" confidence in religion and the "eye" of his great faith recalls the light imagery of the play, especially Abigail's lines in act 1 to "tear the light out of my eyes." This connection is crucial since Abigail has associated her light with the lying and hypocrisy of the covenanted men and women of Salem village. Hale, too, realizes the hypocrisy of Salem society, but his realization is on a much greater level than Abigail's. He realizes he has been part of an entire religious system which destroys life. Moreover, in his role as a minister who is now counseling men to lie, he realizes his damnation will be "doubled" for doing so (132).

Robert Wilcox also has pointed out Abigail's association with images of light and dark. He notes how in act 1 she threatens the other girls with vengeance "in the black of some terrible night" (349). Wilcox also explains that Abigail's sexuality is evoked in images of night that have awakened her to its opposite—light: "I look for John Proctor that took me from my sleep and put knowledge in my heart!" Wilcox maintains that Abigail expresses that knowledge in an image of light: "And now you bid me tear the light out of my eyes? I will not, I cannot!" However, when her actions in the forest are uncovered, she uses the image "with the same hypocrisy she claims to despise in the pious people of Salem: 'I want the light of God!'" (350). However, Abigail is not infused with the light of God, for her private vengeance on Elizabeth allies her with all the levels of darkness in the play. Perhaps Abigail's connection to darkness as both private vengeance and Satanic evil power is best expressed in her threat to Danforth in act 3 when he questions her accusations: "Let you beware, Mr. Danforth. Think you to be so mighty that the power of Hell may not turn your wits? Beware of it!" (108). Here the power of hell contains all its imagistic associations, for Abigail becomes a dark power of hell in the play.

In *Arthur Miller, Dramatist,* Edward Murray discusses the recurrent use of the word "soft" in *The Crucible.* He notes its use as a metaphor for Abigail and John's passion (John thinking of Abigail "softly") and proof of religious devotion (Hale noting the "softness" of John's church attendance). However, other uses of "soft," and its opposite "hard," are scattered throughout the text. In act 4, "soften" is used as a euphemism for the "weakening" of John Proctor and Rebecca Nurse's resolve in their refusal to confess. When Parris informs Danforth that Hale sits among the prisoners urging them to confess, Danforth replies, "Why—this is indeed a providence. And they soften, they soften?" (125). Danforth later inquires of Parris if Elizabeth Proctor's presence may "soften" Proctor (130). The application of "soften" to the condemned holds great resonance, since it implies the opposite—their "hard" position in refusing to confess. Ironically, the pervasive use of "hard" until this point in the play has been applied to the court activity and the political pressure put upon the innocent: Mary Warren describing the proof against Sarah Good as "hard proof, hard as a rock" (59); Cheever saying the needle in the poppet "go hard" with Elizabeth Proctor (73); Hale begging Danforth to hear the "hard evidence" Proctor claims for Elizabeth (86); Danforth threatening Abigail with "hard questioning" (103). However, by act 4 the witchcraft hysteria has subsided, and there is growing opposition to the court. The only image of "hard" in the act is Danforth's warning to Herrick to, "Beware hard drink, Marshal" (124), an indication of how the hysteria has changed into stupor. The hardness of John Proctor and Rebecca Nurse's convictions do not soften.

Of images connected to hardness, "weight" possesses some of the more significant metaphoric meanings in the play.[1] One of the more intriguing historical events Arthur Miller included in *The Crucible* was the last words of

Giles Corey who refused to answer his indictment for witchcraft in order to preserve his land for his sons' inheritance. In punishment, Corey was pressed with great stones, still refusing to confess to witchery. Corey died, still in defiance, uttering the words, "More Weight." Miller assigns great significance to Corey's words for he uses them in act 4 at a decisive moment for his protagonist, John Proctor. In hearing about Giles' death, Proctor repeats Corey's words, as if to consider their meaning for himself. In fact, Miller intimately connects the word "weight" to the theme of the play by employing it ten times throughout the four acts. Tracing the repetition of "weight" in *The Crucible* reveals how the word supports one of the play's crucial themes: how an individual's struggle for truth often conflicts with society.

Certainly the struggle for truth is at the center of the play's conflicts. Jean Selz believes "the avatars of truth" are the most important of the underlying themes: "We see truth—at first forceful and sure of itself—get enmeshed in the ways of uncertainty, falter and grow pale and transform itself little by little into a mean and sorry thing . . . whom everyone refuses to accept." Selz analyzes that truth is at odds with the very people, the judges and ministers, who are supposed to discern it. "Those impostors who call themselves judges," Selz thinks, are particularly indictable because they force truth to become the "invisible heroine" of the play. Similarly, Miller's thematic use of weight is intimately connected to the conflicts that occur when an individual's struggle to know truth opposes society's understanding of it. For the dramatic tension of the play is based on the clashes of truth between those characters who allege to speak it, those who profess it, those who live it and those who die for it.

Miller's initial use of "weight" in the first scene immediately connects it with truth. Reverend Parris, trying to discover the cause of his daughter Betty's unnatural sleeping fit, pleads with, and then threatens, his niece Abigail:

> Now tell me true, Abigail. And I pray you feel the weight of truth upon you, for now my ministry's at stake, my ministry and perhaps your cousin's life. (11)

The "weight of truth" Parris implores Abigail to consider operates on a number of levels both in this scene and in the rest of the play. Obviously, Parris wants to discover the literal truth about the abominations that Abigail, Betty, and the other girls, led by Tituba, are alleged to have performed in the forest. However, the "weight of truth" which Parris begs Abigail to consider more importantly encompasses all of its figurative meanings: seriousness, heaviness, gravity, importance, burden, pressure, influence—all of which are connected to religion and law, the foundations upon which the theocracy of Salem village is built. For clearly *The Crucible* questions the meaning of truth in this theocratic society and the weight that truth bears on an individual and on the society itself.

Thus, Parris beseeching Abigail with the "weight of truth" contains many thematic implications. On one level, Parris's use of weight as "importance" or "serious" appeals to Abigail on a personal level since her uncle's ministry and her cousin's life are at stake. On another level, because Parris invokes his ministry in connection with the "weight of truth," the religious connotation is clear. If Abigail felt the weight of religious truth, she would confess to Parris about the abominations performed in the forest, thereby releasing her from the heaviness of falsehood, sin, guilt, and the power of Satan. On another level, Miller clearly establishes negative connotations of the "weight of truth." For there is no doubt that Parris threatens Abigail with all the heaviness of his ministry, and the severe power of theocracy it represents for Abigail and the inhabitants of Salem village—a power whose weight and truth which we see unleashed in the play.

When Reverend Hale enters, Miller expands the thematic implications with the second use of "weight." Hale carries half a dozen heavy books:

> HALE. Pray you, someone take these!
> PARRIS, *delighted*. Mr. Hale! Oh! It's good to see you again!
> *Taking some books*: My they're heavy.
> HALE, *setting down his books*. They must be; they are weighted with authority. (36)

In these lines Miller significantly connects the literal heaviness of the texts to their figurative meaning, something even Hale as a character is aware of. For later in the scene, Hale explains their significance as the authoritative texts on witchcraft:

> Here is all the invisible world, caught, defined, and calculated. In these books the Devil stands stripped of all his brute disguises. Here are all your familiar spirits—your incubi and succubi; your witches that go by land, by air, and by sea; your wizards of the night and of the day. (39)

Hale's mission is to use these texts to discover the truth of the alleged witchcraft in Salem village. Thus, his mission is equally connected to the same religious "weight of truth" as Parris's.

However, Hale's mission is not the same as Parris's. What marks Hale's mission and his importance as a character is that he truly believes in the books' authority. The textual notes explain at length Hale's serious devotion to his grave tasks. Hale comes to Salem village as an outside observer, an examiner with not only the expertise but the objectivity to discover the truth. Thus, his eventual judgment that private vengeance fuels much of the witchcraft accusations illustrates the difference between the truth of religion and truth of law. Hale and his texts, weighted so heavily with the authority of religion, become at odds with the civil authority of the law, an irony in this theocracy where Church and State law are intertwined.

On this level, the reader and audience certainly perceive the growing conflict between Church and State in the play. For the modern audiences, the religious authority of incubi and succubi, with which Hale believes his books are weighted, clearly does not exist. We see the hypocrisy of a religious system which bases the truth on nothing but the words of young girls. We see that actual authority and weight lie in the secular laws that these religious texts are going to put in motion to crush innocent people. Thus, the first two uses of "weight" in the play significantly intertwine the "weight of truth" and the "weight of authority." For the "crying out" is about to begin, and the audience already knows the "sport" (11) that the witchcraft rumors are based on, as Abigail has told both John and Parris. Furthermore, the audience has already witnessed the personal squabbles of the Salem villagers over land, meetinghouse and minister, and the personal intimacies between Abigail and John. The weight and authority of religious truth that Hale so reverences quickly turns into the weight and authority of law.

The third reference to weight does not occur until act 2, sc. 2, and it significantly connects the word to the law. Elizabeth Proctor relates to John how their servant girl, Mary Warren, is now a witness to the court that has been convened:

> PROCTOR. Court! What court?
> ELIZABETH. Aye, it is a proper court they have now. They've sent four judges out of Boston, she says, weighty magistrates of the General Court, and at the head sits the Deputy Governor of the Province. (52)

With this line, Miller intertwines the religious connotations that "weight" had in Parris's and Hale's lines with the disposition of that religious law in Massachusetts Bay Colony. Indeed, the weighty power of the magistrates' civil law is based on the truth of religious dogma. This connection between law and religion is reinforced by Mary Warren herself a few lines later when she comes home after spending a long day at the court proceedings:

> PROCTOR. You will not go to court again, Mary Warren.
> MARY WARREN. I must tell you, sir, I will be gone every day now. I am amazed you do not see what weighty work we do. (58)

In this line, "weighty" possesses all of the figurative connotations of both law and religion. Clearly, the exposure of witches to the community is the work of God and religion, but it is equally the work of the community in its legal entity to dispose of such witchcraft. Thus, the "weight of truth" that Parris uses in all its ramifications and the "weight of authority" that Hale so reverences are all dispensed by the weight of the law.

Ironically, in the entire play the word "weight" never directly describes the law. In act 2, sc. 4, after Hale's examination of the Proctors, Ezekiel Cheever comes to arrest Elizabeth, a significant scene in Hale's realization that the weight of the court and law is now outweighing the weight of his authority. Cheever says:

> Now believe me, Proctor, how heavy be the law, all its tonnage I
> do carry on my back tonight. I have a warrant for your wife. (72)

What is implied that "heavy" and "tonnage," instead of "weight," are employed in this line? Perhaps it shows how the law is now operating on its own, without the benefit of the religious "weight of truth" or "weight of authority." The arrest of Elizabeth and others does occur without Hale's authority and knowledge. Perhaps it also suggests that in a theocracy there must be the balance between law and religion or the results will be tragic. Certainly, Hale, as the outside observer, ultimately discovers the truth about Proctor's character and the falseness of Abigail's. Thus, describing the law as "heavy," as opposed to "weighty," removes the religious association and endows it with the power to suppress, pressure, and crush whomever opposes it, accurately foreshadowing the action to Giles Corey, Rebecca Nurse, and John Proctor. At this point in the play, we understand that the "tonnage" that Cheever carries will ultimately break the backs of the lives of the characters and the back of theocracy in Massachusetts.

The character who best signifies the power of the law is Judge Danforth. In act 3, sc. 2, when Proctor and Francis Nurse are attempting to prove the falseness of the accusations against their wives, Nurse remarks to Danforth: "I never thought to say it to such a weighty judge, but you are deceived" (87). Nurse's description of Danforth as a "weighty" judge occurs at a crucial moment in the play in terms of Miller's use of it. For Danforth, in his role as Deputy Governor, represents the height of power in Massachusetts. Francis's words exhibit how Danforth should be the arbiter of religious and civil truth, discerning between the accusations and defenses that are made. However, this scene illustrates how tenuous is the relationship between law and religion, and how the law has superseded religion. At this crucial point in the play the audience perceives the hypocrisy of the religious and legal truth. Danforth uses the weight and power of the law to crush dissent, as when he declares Corey in contempt, proclaims court in session, and calls for the arrest and examination of those people who have signed depositions as character witnesses for Martha Corey, Rebecca Nurse, and Elizabeth Proctor. Ironically, after Danforth spouts the "invisible crime" speech (100), the audience perceives how this "weighty judge" is indeed deceived.

We see how the "weight of truth" has changed from its initial association with religion. Danforth, as the personification of the law, is in marked contrast to Reverend Hale. Hale and Danforth best represent the tension between the truth as discerned by law and the truth as discerned by religion. The conflict between Hale as a "minister of the Lord" and Danforth as the "arbiter of justice" reaches a climax in this scene since Hale has increasingly come to doubt the truth of the girls' claims. This scene culminates with Hale's realization that the civil law is out of control, and he denounces the proceedings after the examination and arrest of Proctor by Danforth.

Interestingly, Hale's plea to Danforth to let a lawyer argue on behalf of John includes "weight":

> HALE. Excellency, a moment. I think this goes to the heart of the matter.
> DANFORTH. It surely does.
> HALE. I cannot say he is an honest man; I know him little. But in all justice, sir, a claim so weighty cannot be argued by a farmer. In God's name, sir, stop here; send him home and let him come again with a lawyer—
> DANFORTH. Now look you, Mr. Hale—
> HALE. Excellency, I have signed seventy-two death warrants; I am a minister of the Lord, and I dare not take a life without there be a proof so immaculate no slightest qualm of conscience may doubt it.
> DANFORTH. Mr. Hale, you surely do not doubt my justice. (99)

Hale's application of "weighty" to Proctor's claim indicates a crucial and marked shift of the word's use in the play. David Levin in "Salem Witchcraft in Recent Fiction and Drama" discusses how Miller uses the Salem Witch Trials to show how people are blinded to the truth. Levin maintains that Miller "has his characters turn the truth upside down" (251). He cites as examples the change in Hale from his belief in truth in the beginning of the play to his remorseful plea to the innocent victims to confess falsely. Levin also points out the irony of how Abigail's lies are taken as the truth, and how Proctor's truths are taken as lies. Miller uses a similar movement in the play to shift the meaning of weight. The first five references associate weight to the religion and law of the Salem theocracy whose truth, power, and authority the audience perceives as false, unjust and hypocritical for destroying innocent people. However, Hale's reference to Proctor's claim as "weighty" shifts the application of the word—from the state and religion to those innocent characters who are accused, and then destroyed, by the false weight and authority of religious and civil truth: Proctor, Giles, Rebecca. Thus, "weight" can be traced as it moves from theological truth, to legal truth and finally to the truth of individual conscience.

How ironic that Parris, who first gives the word its thematic significance, also indicates the shift in its usage. In act 4, sc. 2, he exhibits his fear at the impending executions of Proctor and Rebecca Nurse:

> Judge Hawthorne—it were another sort that hanged till now. Rebecca Nurse is not Bridget that lived three year with Bishop before she married him. John Proctor is not Isaac Ward that drank his family to ruin. *To Danforth*: I would to God it were not so, Excellency, but these people have great weight yet in the town. Let Rebecca stand upon the gibbet and send up some righteous prayer, and I fear she'll wake a vengeance on you. (127)

On one level, the weight that Parris refers to is the influence that Proctor and Nurse have because of their social status in the community. On another level, their weight connotes the religious weight of truth that Parris earlier has invoked. The irony lies in the "righteous prayer" he fears Rebecca could send. For the audience now understands the falseness of Parris's weight of truth, and that Rebecca and John have been empowered with their own weight of truth and righteousness. Parris fears Rebecca's weight will carry some vengeance, but the audience understands that vengeance is only the tactic of those preaching and administering falseness. The weight of Rebecca and John becomes the threat to Parris.

The most historically accurate use of "weight"[2] occurs in act 4, sc. 3, a scene which is significant for Proctor's connection to the theme of truth. Confronted with his pending execution, he is tempted to confess falsely in order to save his life. Elizabeth relays to John the details of Giles Corey's death:

> ELIZABETH. Great stones they lay upon his chest until he plead aye or nay. *With a tender smile for the old man*: They say he give them but two words. "More weight," he says. And died.
> PROCTOR, *numbed—a thread to weave into his agony*. "More Weight."
> ELIZABETH. It were a fearsome man, Giles Corey. (135)

In Giles's last words, "weight" connects with both its literal and figurative meanings, as it did with Hale's books. Obviously, the great weight of the stones literally crushed Giles to death. However, the literal and figurative are intimately intertwined here. For even if Giles used the words only to end his torture, in the context of the play the symbolic importance of Corey's words and the weight which pressed him to death are crucial. Those great stones represent the power, heaviness, seriousness, and gravity of a Massachusetts theocracy which crushed the life out of Giles. Despite this power, Corey refused to answer his indictment so that his sons could inherit his property. Thus, the words "More weight" liberate the individual conscience of the defiant Corey from the law of society. They become the weight of truth that he, Nurse, and Proctor possess.

In this scene, the same weight is about to crush John Proctor as well. In his repetition of Corey's words he seems to understand their significance for Giles, yet struggles to understand their significance for himself. Proctor's personal struggle in the play is at a crisis in this scene. Because of his affair with Abigail and its effect on his relationship with Elizabeth, his Christian character, his soul and his conscience, he does not consider himself the fearsome man like Corey or the saint like Rebecca. He is willing to confess because he does not think he possesses the great weight they have.

Ultimately, John discovers the "shred of goodness" (144) in himself: the weight of truth of his name and character. Significantly, Parris applies the word "weight" to Proctor's name after John has confessed.

> It is a great service, sir. It is a weighty name; it will strike the
> village that Proctor confess. I beg you, let him sign it . . . (140)

Proctor comes to understand not the weightiness of his name for the village, but the weightiness of it for himself. His unwillingness to have his confession signed for posting on the church door is connected to his name. His name is the only truth that Proctor knows; it is the only item he knows still bears weight, as Parris has indicated. Yet the weight that Parris assigns to Proctor's name is not the same that he assigns. For Proctor, a man's name represents the weight of his existence in the world. A name is not connected to his religiosity or his spirituality. For Proctor, a man cannot live without the weight of his name; he cannot teach his sons to be men without it. "How may I live without my name. I have given you my soul; leave me my name" (143). Thus, he dies with the goodness and weight of his name. Note that his last words to Elizabeth connect to the power of weight: "Show honor now, show a stony heart and sink them with it" (144). The weight of truth sets Proctor, Elizabeth, and Massachusetts free.

After *The Crucible* opened on Broadway, Arthur Miller wrote an extra scene which was added before the production closed. Act 2, sc. 2 is a forest scene where John tells Abigail his intentions to prove false her accusations against Elizabeth. Although its theatrical purpose has been the subject of much debate, Abigail's longest speech in the scene contains an intriguing combination of the images of heat and cold, cleanliness and dirt, and black and white:

> PROCTOR. . . . How am I good?
> ABIGAIL. Why you taught me goodness, therefore you are good. It were a fire you walked me through, and all my ignorance was burned away. It were a fire, John, we lay in fire. And from that night no woman dare call me wicked and more but I knew my answer. I used to weep for my sins when the wind lifted up my skirts; and blushed for shame because some old Rebecca called me loose. And then you burned my ignorance away. As bare as some December tree I saw them all—walking like saints to church, running to feed the sick, and hypocrites in their hearts! And God gave me the strength to call them liars, and God made men to listen to me, and by God I will scrub the world clean for the love of Him! Oh, John, I will make you such a wife when the world is white again! *She kisses his hand.* You will be amazed to see me every day, a light of heaven in your house, a—*He rises, backs away amazed.* Why are you cold? (150)

With utmost poetic precision, Miller compacts most of the significant images of the play into this one speech. His sophistication as a verse stylist is evident because the language operates almost wholly on the metaphoric level. The "fire" through which John walked Abigail clearly is their sexual passion. Abigail's language also echoes the imagery she uses when alone with John in act 1 when she declares he "put knowledge" in her heart. But in this scene, she evokes an opposite image, and combining it with the significant burning imagery, declares Proctor "burned her ignorance away" which, she claims, enables her to understand the hypocrisy of Salem village. In her declaration that, "By God I will scrub the world clean," Abigail also implies that the fire is also a cleansing fire, which evokes the unstated crucible imagery of the play.

However, Abigail's language suggests that the fire has cleansed neither her nor the world. For her hope that she will make John a wife "when the world is white again" implies that its opposite exists—the darkness of the hysteria, evil and ignorance which has gripped Salem. Moreover, Abigail's statement that "no woman dare call me wicked any more" carries the threat of her vengeance, not her purity. In addition, she perceives the change in passion between her and John because she asks him, "Why are you cold?" Perhaps her sense for his heat, which she was drawn to in act 1, already perceives the justice of "God's icy wind" which Proctor has evoked at the end of the previous act.

Finally, the language of *The Crucible* indicates how the composition of the world itself was in tension for the Puritans. For the dominant images, symbols, and metaphors of the play express the substances of air, earth, fire, and water which these eighteenth century people believed composed the physical world. For the Salemites, the wilderness and darkness of a physical universe which surrounded them in the new world of Massachusetts could only be tamed by its opposite: the light of their religious, political, and personal beliefs. These were an elemental people who used the language of the visible world, which surrounded them, to express the power of its opposite: an invisible universe which existed in their minds, hearts, and souls.

NOTES

1. The following discussion of "weight" appeared in *Modern Drama* 38 (1995): 488–95.

2. The historical accuracy of Corey's last words has been the subject of some debate. Fred L. Standley in "An Echo of Milton in *The Crucible*," suggests that Miller borrowed this line from an identical passage in Milton's poem, "Another on the Same." Oliver H. Ferris defends Miller's research on the Salem Witch Trials asserting the tradition that ascribes these words to Corey.

WORKS CITED

Cohn, Ruby. *Dialogue in American Drama*. Bloomington: Indiana UP, 1971.

Curtis, Penelope. "Setting, Language and the Force of Evil in *The Crucible*." In *Twentieth Century Interpretations of The Crucible*. Ed. John H. Ferres. Englewood Cliffs: Prentice Hall, 1972.

Fender, Stephen. "Precision and Pseudo Precision in *The Crucible*." *Journal of American Studies* 1 (1967): 87–98.

Ferris, Oliver H.P. "An Echo of Milton in *The Crucible*." *Notes and Queries* n.s. 16 (1969): 268.

Griffin, John and Alice. "Arthur Miller Discusses *The Crucible*." *Conversations With Arthur Miller*. Ed. Matthew C. Roudané. Jackson and London: UP of Mississippi, 1987.

Levin, David. "Salem Witchcraft in Recent Fiction and Drama." *Arthur Miller's The Crucible, Text and Criticism*. Ed. Gerald Weales. New York: Penguin Books, 1986.

Miller, Arthur. *Arthur Miller's The Crucible, Text and Criticism*. Ed. Gerald Weales. New York: Penguin Books, 1971.

———. Introduction to the *Collected Plays: The Theatre Essays of Arthur Miller*. Ed. Robert A. Martin. New York: Viking, 1978.

———. "Why I Wrote *The Crucible*." *New Yorker* 28 October 1996: 158+.

Murray, Edward. *Arthur Miller, Dramatist*. New York: Frederick Ungar, 1967.

O'Neal, Michael J. "History, Myth, and Name Magic in Arthur Miller's *The Crucible*." *Clio* 12 (1983): 111–22.

Prudhoe, John. "Arthur Miller and the Tradition of Tragedy." *English Studies* 43 (1963): 430–39.

Selz, Jean. "Raymond Rouleau Among the Witches" in *Arthur Miller's The Crucible, Text and Criticism*. Ed. Gerald Weales. New York: Penguin Books, 1986.

Standley, Fred L. "An Echo of Milton in *The Crucible*." *Notes and Queries* n.s. 15 (1968): 303.

Weales, Gerald. "Arthur Miller: Man and His Image." *Tulane Drama Review* 7 (1962): 165–80.

———. *The Crucible, Text and Criticism*. New York: Penguin Books, 1971.

Wilcox, Robert Harland. *The Poetry of Realistic Drama*. Diss. U of Wisconsin, 1982. Ann Arbor: UMI, 19821. 18215972.

CHRISTOPHER BIGSBY

'The Crucible'

Salem in 1692 was in turmoil. The Royal Charter had been revoked. Original land titles had been cancelled and others not yet secured. Neighbour accordingly looked on neighbour with some suspicion for fear their land might be reassigned. It was also a community riven with schisms which centred on the person of the Reverend Parris, whose materialism and self-concern was more than many could stomach, including a landowner and innkeeper called John Proctor.

As Miller observed in his notebook: 'It is Shakespearean. Parties and counter-parties. There must be a counter-party. Proctor and others.'[1] John Proctor quickly emerged as the centre of the story Miller wished to tell, though not of the trials where he was one among many. But to Miller, as he wrote in the notebook: '*It has got to be basically Proctor's story.* The important thing—the process whereby a man, feeling guilt for A, sees himself as guilty of B and thus belies himself—accommodates his credo to believe in what he knows is not true.' Before this could become a tragedy for the community it had to be a tragedy for an individual: 'A difficulty. This hanging must be "tragic"—i.e. must [be] result of an opportunity not grasped when it should have been, due to "flaw."'

That flaw, as so often in Miller's work, was to be sexual, not least because there seemed a sexual flavour to the language of those who confessed to possession by the Devil and who were accused of dancing naked, in a

From *Arthur Miller: A Critical Study*, pp. 147–171, 495–496. © 2005 by Christopher Bigsby.

community in which both dancing and nakedness were themselves seen as signs of corruption. But that hardly seemed possible when Abigail Williams and John Proctor, who were to become the central characters in his drama, were eleven and sixty respectively. Accordingly, at Miller's bidding she becomes seventeen and he thirty-five and so they begin to move towards one another, the gap narrowing until a sexual flame is lit.

Where the girls were, in the historical record, reported as dancing in the woods, Miller has them dancing naked, in part, as he explained, to make it easier for the audience to relate the Puritans' horror at such a thing to their own. But in part he made the change in order to introduce the sexual motif at the very beginning of a play in which sexuality is both the source of Proctor's disabling guilt and, in some way, at the heart both of the hysteria of the accusing girls and of the frisson that made witchcraft simultaneously an abomination and a seductive idea.

Elizabeth Proctor, who had managed an inn, now becomes a solitary farmer's wife, cut off from communion not only with her errant husband, who has strayed from her side, but also in some degree from the society of Salem, a woman whose sexual coldness is both a motivating force in her husband's sin and a quality that lifts her above the frenzy of bad faith which surrounds and eventually engulfs her.

Other changes are made. Giles Corey, a cantankerous old man who carelessly damns his wife by commenting on her fondness for books, was not killed, pressed to death by stones, until 19 September, a month after Proctor's death. Miller brings that death forward so that it can prove exemplary. By the same token John Hale's growing conversion to scepticism did not come to its climax with Proctor's death but only later when his own wife was accused. The event is advanced in order to keep Proctor as the focus.

At the same time the playwright resisted another aspect of the story that would have damaged the parallel to fifties America, though it would have struck a chord with those in many other countries who were later to seize on *The Crucible* as an account of their own situation. For the fact is that John Proctor's son was tortured. As Proctor wrote in a Petition: 'My son William Proctor, when he was examin'd, because he would not confess that he was Guilty, when he was Innocent, they tied him Neck and Heels till the Blood gushed out of his Nose.' The effect on the play of including this detail would have been to transform Proctor's motivation and diminish the significance of the sexual guilt that disables him.

Historically, John Proctor did not immediately intervene on learning of the trials and does not do so in the play. The historical account offers no explanation. In the notebooks Miller searched for one: 'Proctor—guilt stays his hand (against what action?)'. The guilt derives from his adultery; the action becomes his decision to expose Abigail.

In his original plan Miller toyed with making Proctor a leader of the anti-Parris faction, who backtracks on that role and equivocates in his dealings with Hale. He entertained, too, the notion that Proctor should half wish his wife dead. He abandoned both ideas. If Proctor emerges as a leader it is inadvertently as he fights to defend the wife he has wronged and whose life he has placed in jeopardy because of his affair with Abigail.

What is at stake in *The Crucible* is the survival of Salem, which is to say the survival of a sense of community. On a literal level the village ceased to operate. The trials took precedence over all other activities. They took the farmer from his field and his wife from the milk shed. In an early draft of the screenplay for the film version Miller has the camera observe the depredations of the countryside: unharvested crops, untended animals, houses in disrepair. But, more fundamentally than this, Miller is concerned with the breaking of that social contract which binds a community together, as love and mutual respect bind individuals.

What took him to Salem was not, finally, an obsession with McCarthyism nor even a concern with a bizarre and, at the time, obscure historical incident, but a fascination with 'the most common experience of humanity, the shifts of interest that turned loving husbands and wives into stony enemies, loving parents into indifferent supervisors or even exploiters of their children . . . what they called the breaking of charity with one another'. There was evidence for all of these in seventeenth-century Salem but, as Miller implies, the breaking of charity was scarcely restricted to a small New England settlement in a time distant from our own. For him the parallel between Salem in 1692 and America in 1953 was clear:

> people were being torn apart, their loyalty to one another crushed and . . . common human decency was going down the drain. It's indescribable, really, because you'd get the feeling that nothing was going to be sacred any more. The situations were so exact it was quite amazing. The ritual was the same. What they were demanding of Proctor was that he expose this conspiracy of witches whose aim was to bring down the rule of the Church, of Christianity. If he gave them a couple of names he could go home. And if he didn't he was going to hang for it. It was quite the same excepting we weren't hanged, but the ritual was exactly the same. You told them anyone you knew had been a left-winger or a Communist and you went home. But I wasn't going to do that.[2]

Neither was John Proctor.

One dictionary definition of a crucible is that it is a place of extreme heat, 'a severe test'. John Proctor and those others summoned before a court in

Salem discovered the meaning of that. Yet such tests, less formal, less judicial, less public, are the small change of daily life. Betrayal, denial, rash judgement, self-justification, are remote neither in time nor place.

The Crucible, then, is not merely concerned with reanimating history or implying contemporary analogies for past crimes. It is Arthur Miller's most frequently produced play not because it addresses affairs of state nor even because it offers us the tragic sight of a man who dies to save his conception of himself and the world, but because audiences understand all too well that the breaking of charity is no less a contemporary fact because it is presented in the context of a re-examined history.

There is, then, more than one mystery here. Beyond the question of witchcraft lies the more fundamental question of a human nature for which betrayal seems an ever-present possibility. *The Crucible* reminds us how fragile is our grasp on those shared values that are the foundation of any society. It is a play written not only at a time when America seemed to sanction the abandonment of the normal decencies and legalities of civilised life but in the shadow of a still greater darkness, for the Holocaust was in Miller's mind, as it had been in the mind of Marion Starkey, whose book on the trials had stirred his imagination.[3]

What replaces this sense of natural community in *The Crucible*, as perhaps in Nazi Germany (a parallel of which he was conscious) and, on a different scale, fifties America, is a sense of participating in a ritual, of conformity to a ruling orthodoxy and hence a shared hostility to those who threaten it. The purity of one's religious principles is confirmed by collaborating, at least by proxy, in the punishment of those who reject them. Racial identity is reinforced by eliminating those who might 'contaminate' it, as one's Americanness is underscored by the identification of those who could be said to be Un-American. In the film version of his play, Miller, free now to expand and deepen the social context of the drama, chooses, in an early draft, to emphasise this illusory sense of community: 'The CROWD's urging rises to angry crescendo. HANGMAN pulls a crude lever and the trap drops and the two fall. THE CROWD is delirious with joyful, gratifying unity.'

If it was Alexis de Tocqueville who identified the pressure towards conformity even in the early years of the Republic, it was a pressure acknowledged equally by Hawthorne, Melville, Emerson and Thoreau. When Sinclair Lewis's Babbitt abandons his momentary rebellion to return to his conformist society he is described as being 'almost tearful with joy'. Miller's alarm, then, is not his alone, nor his sense of the potentially tyrannical power of shared myths which appear to offer absolution to those who accept them. If his faith in individual conscience as a corrective is also not unique, it was, perhaps, harder to sustain in the second half of a century which had seen collective myths exercising a coercive power, in America and Europe.

Beyond anything else, *The Crucible* is a study in power and the mechanisms by which power is sustained, challenged and lost. Perhaps that is one reason why, as Miller has noted, productions of the play seem to precede and follow revolutions and why what can be seen as a revolt of the young against the old should, on the play's production in Communist China, have been seen as a comment on the Cultural Revolution of the 1960s in which the young Red Guards humiliated, tortured and even killed those who had previously been in authority over them: parents, teachers, members of the cultural elite.

On the one hand stands the Church, which provides the defining language within which all social, political and moral debate is conducted. On the other stand those usually deprived of power—the black slave Tituba and the young children—who suddenly gain access to an authority as absolute as that which had previously subordinated them. Those ignored by history become its motor force. Those socially marginalised move to the very centre of social action. Those whose opinions and perceptions carried neither personal nor political weight suddenly acquire an authority so absolute that they come to feel they can challenge even the representatives of the state. Tituba has a power she has never known in her life.

To be a young girl in Salem was to have no role but obedience, no function but unquestioning faith, no freedom except a willingness to submit to those with power over their lives. Sexuality was proscribed, the imagination distrusted, emotions focused solely on the stirring of the spirit. Rebellion, when it came, was thus likely to take as its target firstly those with least access to power, then those for whom virtue alone was insufficient protection. Next would come those who were themselves regarded as politically vulnerable and finally those who possessed real power. Predictably it was at this final stage that the conspiracy collapsed, just as Senator McCarthy was to thrive on those who possessed no real purchase on the political system and to lose his credibility when he chose to challenge the US Army. The first three witches named were a slave, a labourer's wife, who had become little more than a tramp, and a woman who had absented herself from church and reportedly lived in sin.

The Crucible is a play about the seductive nature of power and for pubescent girls that seductiveness is perhaps not unconnected with a confused sexuality. These were people who chose not to enquire into their own motives. They submitted to the irrational with a kind of perverse pleasure, a pleasure not entirely drained of sexual content. They dealt, after all, with exposure, with stripping souls bare, with provoking and hearing confessions of an erotic forthrightness which no other occasion or circumstance would permit. The judges saw young women cry out in a kind of orgasmic ecstasy. They witnessed men and women, of position, intelligence and property rendered into their power by the confessions of those who recalled abuses and assaults revealed to them only in a religiously and therapeutically charged atmosphere.

These were the 'recovered memories' of Puritan New England and the irrational nature of the accusations, their sexual frisson, the lack of any proof beyond 'spectral evidence' (the dreams and visions of the accusers) was a part of their attraction. When Mary Warren accuses Elizabeth Proctor she says, 'I never knew it before ... and all at once I remembered everything she done to me!'[4] In our own time we are not so remote from this phenomenon as to render it wholly strange. Men and women with no previous memory of assaults, which were apparently barbaric and even demonic, suddenly recall such abuse, more especially when assisted to do so by therapists, social workers or religionists who offer themselves as experts in the spectral world of suppressed memories. Such abuse, recalled in later life, is impossible to verify but the accusations alone have sufficed to destroy entire families. To deny reality to such abuse is itself seen as a dangerous perversion, just as to deny witchcraft was seen as diabolic in Puritan New England.

Did the young girls in Salem, then, see no witches? Were they motivated solely by self-concern or, in Abigail's case, a blend of vengeance and desire? *The Crucible* is not concerned to arbitrate. Tituba plainly does dabble in the black arts, while Mrs Putnam is quite prepared to do so. Abigail seems a more straightforward case. Jealous of Elizabeth Proctor, she sees a way of removing her and marrying John. In the original version of Miller's screenplay, however, in a scene subsequently cut, Abigail does have a vision of Elizabeth's spirit visiting her in her bedroom:

> Int. Night Abigail bedroom
> *She is asleep in bed. She stirs, then suddenly sits up and sees, seated in a nearby chair, a* WOMAN *with her back to her.* ABIGAIL *slides out of bed and approaches the woman, comes around to see her face—it is* ELIZABETH PROCTOR.
>
> ABIGAIL   Elizabeth? I am with God! In Jesus name begone back to Hell!
>
> ELIZABETH'S FACE *is transformed into that of a* HAWK, *its beak opening.* ABIGAIL *steps back in terror.*[5]

Whatever her motives, she plainly sees this phantom even though it is conjured not from the Devil but from guilt and desire, which in Puritan New England were anyway seen as synonymous. In the early screen version Proctor is described as 'Certain now that she's mad'. This takes us beyond the portrait we are offered by the play where she is presented as more clearly calculating, but the essential point is not the nature of her motivation nor even the substantiality or otherwise of witches, but the nature of the real and the manner in which it is determined. Proctor and the others find themselves in court because they deny a reality to which others subscribe and in which, whatever their motives, they in part believe, until, slowly, scepticism begins to infect them with the virus of another reality.

Six months after the play had opened, when Miller restaged it prior to a national tour (the New York run ended on 11 July), he interpolated a new scene to be added to the second act. The *Playbill* for 1 June lists it as Act 1, scene 1. However, since Act 1 was then nominated as the Prologue it appeared in the acting edition as Act 2, scene 2. It features an encounter between Proctor and Abigail, the night before his wife is to appear in court. They meet in the forest, that antinomian world, the place where the whole drama had begun and where the play was originally to have opened had construction costs not led to the elimination of the scene.

Proctor comes to save the life of his wife. He warns Abigail what he intends to do. He has, he explains, documentary proof that she knew that the poppet discovered in their house had no connection with Elizabeth. For her part, Abigail, dressed, significantly, in a nightgown, still hopes that their relationship will flare up again. Why else, after all, has he thrown pebbles against her bedroom window? Most significantly, however, this Abigail has convinced herself that she does indeed do the Lord's work. Accused by Proctor of hypocrisy, she defends herself and it seems not without some inner conviction.

As in the deleted film scenes, she appears to have an imperfect grasp on reality. Her outrage that the victims should be permitted to pray seems genuine enough. She is, we are told, 'Astonished, outraged'. Equally clear, however, is her state of mind. As Proctor talks to her, a stage direction indicates that he sees 'her madness now'. He feels 'uneasiness', as though before an unearthly thing, detects 'a wildness in her'.[6] She looks at him as if he were out of his mind, as he warns her that he will confess to adultery if necessary, but the real fear is that she is out of hers. He accuses her of being a 'murderous bitch!' but she responds by accusing him of hypocrisy, the real terror being that she seems to believe it.

The additional scene does throw light on their relationship. Miller also uses it to underscore the extent to which Abigail has gained notoriety and a kind of sexual allure which accompanies her fame. However, it blunts the force of the court scene and, like the rejected film scenes, risks turning Abigail into a pathological case, less evil than herself deluded.

It is the essence of power that it accrues to those with the ability to determine the nature of the real. They authorise the language, the grammar, the vocabulary within which others must live their lives. As Miller observed in his notebook: 'Very important. To say "There be no witches" is to invite

charge of trying to conceal the conspiracy and to discredit the highest
authorities who alone can save the community!' Proctor and his wife try to
step outside the authorised text. They will acknowledge only those things
of which they have immediate knowledge. 'I have wondered if there be
witches in the world', observes John Proctor incautiously, adding, 'I have no
knowledge of it', as his wife, too, insists that 'I cannot believe it' (66). When
Proctor asserts his right to freedom of thought and speech—'I may speak
my heart, I think'—he is reminded that this had been the sin of the Quakers
and Quakers, of course, had learned the limits of free speech and faith at the
end of a hangman's noose on Boston Common.

There is a court which John and Elizabeth Proctor fear. It is one,
moreover, which, if it has no power to sentence them to death, does nonetheless
command their lives. As Proctor says to his wife: 'I come into a court when I
come into this house!' Elizabeth, significantly, replies: 'The magistrate sits in
your heart that judges you' (55). Court and magistrate are simply synonyms for
guilt. The challenge for John Proctor is to transform guilt into conscience and
hence into responsibility. Guilt renders him powerless, as it had Willy Loman
in *Death of a Salesman*; individual conscience restores personal integrity and
identity and places him at the centre of social action.

Despite the suspicions of his judges, though, Proctor does not offer
himself as social rebel. If he seeks to overthrow the court it is, apparently, for
one reason only: to save his wife. But behind that there is another motive:
to save not himself but his sense of himself. In common with so many other
Miller protagonists he is forced to ask the meaning of his own life. As Tom
Wilkinson, who played the part of Proctor in a National Theatre production,
has said, 'it is rare for people to be asked the question which puts them squarely
in front of themselves'.[7] But that is the question which is asked of John Proctor
and which, incidentally, was asked of Miller in writing the play and later in
appearing before the House Un-American Activities Committee.

Jean-Paul Sartre objected to the French production of the play, which
opened at the Théâtre Sarah Bernhardt on 16 December 1954, translated by
Marcel Aymé. For Sartre, the play was essentially a battle for possession of
the land between the old and the new settlers. He thus found the ending as
smacking of what he called a 'disconcerting idealism'.[8] Proctor's death, and the
death of his fellow accused, would 'have had meaning if they were shown as
an act of revolt based in social conflict'. He blamed the production in which,
he said, the social conflict had become 'incomprehensible' and the death of
Proctor 'a purely ethical attitude, not like a free act which he commits to
unleash the shame, effectively to deny his position, like the only thing he can
still do'. The result was that the play became 'insipid' and 'castrated' because
'the political ideas and social bases of the witch-hunt phenomenon do not
appear clearly here'.[9]

The argument is presented as though it were a debate with the translator but actually he is arguing with the original text, which he approaches as a Marxist and finds unsatisfactory precisely because it lacks a Marxist perspective. The fact is that Miller did not see the witch-hunts as emerging from a battle between old and new money, there being precious little new money in a colony quite as young. There were, to be sure, arguments over property, and such arguments often lay not too far below the surface as complainants came forward to point the finger, but this is not where the essence of the play lies. Miller is, indeed, careful to expose these to the audience. But, in a time of flux, property rights had been thrown into some disarray and authority was uncertain.

Power, certainly, is an issue in *The Crucible* but it is not in the hands of the rich landowners. It is in the hands of young girls who contest the order of the world. It is in the hands of those offered a sudden sanction for their fears and prejudices. Indeed, it begins to contaminate the agencies and procedures of the state and hence of God's order. It is not, then, the politics of the affair that is Miller's primary concern but precisely Proctor's free act, his ethical attitude. He does not die for the landless, for social justice, but for his sense of himself. It is, strangely, given Sartre's engagement with the play, an existential act and, as Sartre was to say, and as Miller certainly believed, individual decisions do have social consequences. That is the connection between the private world, in which a man decides whether to sign his signature to a lie, and the public world, in which conformity is demanded in the name of an ideal. Sartre, however, looked for some more tangible and external evidence of the social dynamics he assumed to lie beneath the events in Salem.

It is not that Miller wished to focus on the dilemma of a single man. Quite the contrary. In fact in an article to mark the 1958 Off-Broadway production, which was to run for 653 performances and, incidentally, to employ a narrator called 'The Reader' to set the scenes and convey the historical background, he expressed his regret at the narrowing focus of much drama. He now believed, he said, that it was no longer possible to contain the truth of the human situation 'within a single man's guts'. The documentation of 'man's loneliness', he insisted, 'is not in and of itself ultimate wisdom'.[10]

In *The Crucible*, he explained, he wished to explore the tension between a man's actions and his concept of himself, and the question of whether conscience is an organic part of the human sensibility. He wished to examine the consequences of the handing over of that conscience to others. Aware of the degree to which conscience may be a social construct, as of the degree to which public forms and procedures are a product of willed choices, he set himself to stage the dilemma of the individual who comes to acknowledge a responsibility beyond the self.

Proctor begins the play as a man who believes it possible to remain aloof. The betrayal that obsesses him is born out of a private action and instills a private guilt. He debates with himself as history gathers momentum. He finally steps into the courtroom to defend something more than his threatened wife and dies for an idea of community no less than of personal integrity. Asked to concede a lie—not simply the lie of his own supposed actions but the lie of the state which seeks to define the real and consolidate an abstract authority—he declines. It is simultaneously a private and a public act and it is this that Sartre seemed not to understand or, if understand, accept.

When, later, Sartre wrote his own adaptation of the play for a film version, *Les Sorcières de Salem*, he injected those very qualities he found lacking, concluding not with the sound of drums rattling 'like bones in the morning air', but with the beginnings of revolt. Miller was not amused.

Nor was this the end of Miller's argument with Sartre. In a discussion of Judge Danforth, he confessed he should have made him more irremediably evil. Danforth, he explained, was something more than an arbiter of the law in this frontier community. He was the rule-bearer. He patrolled the boundary. He, in Miller's phrase, 'is man's limit'. He stands between men and knowledge. Sartre, as it seemed to Miller, 'reduced him to an almost economic policeman'.[11] Sartre's Danforth never comes to the point at which he realises that he has appropriated his faith to serve the interests of the state and consolidate his own power. Miller conceded that he had himself been remiss in this respect, failing clearly to demarcate the moment at which, knowing, finally, the deceptions being practised, Danforth nonetheless decides to proceed. This, as he suggests, is the obverse of Proctor's final decision that he cannot sign his name to a lie. Danforth can. Sartre's version, however, lacks even the ambivalent awareness that is a mark of Miller's text.

To Miller, therefore, Sartre's conception 'lacks a moral dimension' because it precludes 'a certain aspect of will'.[12] In his version, Danforth remains the same throughout. Lacking self-awareness, he never confronts and rejects the possibility of being other than he is. He is implacable, but the nature of that implacability is different. There is no kinetic morality, no momentary doubt and therefore no decision. He is a representative of unyielding power but his evil is less conscious, seemingly, than a product of historic process. He is a member of a ruling elite, of an unquestioning ideology. He is, in other words, a significant marker in the kind of drama that Sartre preferred to construct from *The Crucible* rather than the figure Miller created, whatever the playwright's subsequent regrets at his failure to sharpen the issues at stake.

Not that Marcel Aymé, translator-adapter of the first French production, seems to have been any more in tune with Miller's intentions. Having offered something of a travesty of the plot, complete with historical inaccuracies, he observes that 'the sympathy of the American spectator belongs to the seducer' because he is a rugged pioneer and one of a breed of 'New England plowmen who carry in their Puritan round heads the shining promises of the age of skyscrapers and the atom bomb'. The farmer, he concluded, 'is an indisputable hero from the outset. He has only to step on a Broadway stage. It's as if he were wrapped in a Star-Spangled Banner, and the public, its heart swollen with tenderness and pride, eat him up.' This, he suggests, is inadmissible for a Frenchman. No doubt it would be, but the interpretation has a certain ring to it, as does his further suggestion that Abigail is presented as 'little more than a little slut come to sully the glorious dawn of the USA'.[13]

Such, of course, is liable to be the fate of writers who offer their work for translation, as cultural values do not so much clash as annihilate one another. So, with John Proctor cast as the wilful seducer, nonetheless perversely embraced by the American psyche, Abigail becomes the ruined girl to be celebrated by the French translator. Aymé then asks, not unreasonably perhaps, why, in his remorse for his sin, Proctor assumes so little responsibility for the girl he has ruined. For, as Aymé insists, 'he shows no regrets regarding his gravest shortcoming, that of having led astray a little soul who had been entrusted to him, an orphan, to boot', he points out. After all, 'In the eyes of the American today, a Puritan family in Massachusetts in 1690 [sic] is one of those good biblical families in which the master of the house exercises prudent thrift in conjugal patience by screwing the servant girls with God's permission.' This delightful travesty has the virtue of misreading the play, theology and social history simultaneously and within a single sentence. To Aymé, John Proctor is a 'petticoat-rumpler' who 'dreams only of restoring peace in his household'.

So, where Sartre sought to redress the political balance of the play, Aymé set himself to rebalance the scales between seducer and seducee: 'It seemed to me necessary', he explained,

> to bring the pair of lovers back into balance, that is, to blacken the victim and give her a Machiavellianism that she does not have in the Arthur Miller play, in which, in order to save her life and in the sway of group hysteria, she is led to unleash a witch hunt. I wanted to give her full consciousness of the evil in her. Doubtless, in doing that, I greatly falsified the author, and I sincerely regret it.[14]

The regret did not, however, extend much further than resisting too complete a falsification. 'I am far from taking all the liberties with his text that seemed desirable to me', he insisted, as if this were sufficient by way of moral virtue to purge such alterations as he did make. He would, however, he insisted, abjure from any further adaptations. He did not. In 1958 he adapted *A View from the Bridge*.

Miller seems to have written *The Crucible* in a kind of white heat. The enthusiasm and speed with which he went to Salem underlines the urgency with which he regarded the project, as did his later comment, on returning from Salem, that he felt a kind of social responsibility to see it through to production. His achievement was to control and contain that anger without denying it. Linguistically, he achieved that by writing the play, in part, first in verse. Dramatically, he accomplished it by using the structured formality of the court hearings, albeit hearings penetrated by the partly hysterical, partly calculated interventions of the accusing girls.

Much of the achievement of *The Crucible* lies in his creation of a language that makes the seventeenth century both distant and close, that enables his characters to discover within the limiting vocabulary and grammar of faith-turned-dogma a means to express their own lives. For British dramatist John Arden, who first encountered the play at a time when his own attempts at historical writing had, in his own words, proved 'embarrassingly bad', it 'showed me how it could be done'. In particular, 'it was not just the monosyllabic Anglo-Saxon strength of the words chosen so much as the rhythms that impregnated the speeches', that and 'the sounds of the seventeenth century, not tediously imitated, but . . . imaginatively reconstructed to shake hands with the sounds and speech patterns of the twentieth'.[15] The language of *The Crucible* is not authentic, in the sense of reproducing archaisms or reconstructing a seventeenth-century lexis. It is authentic in that it makes fully believable the words of those who speak out of a different time and place but whose human dilemmas are recognisably our own.

Proctor and his judges were articulate people, even if they were fluent in different languages: he, in that of a common-sense practicality, they in that of a bureaucratic theocracy. He believed what he saw and finally accepted responsibility for his actions. They believed in a shadow world in which visions were substantial and the observable world no more than a delusion, seeing themselves as the agents of an abstract justice and hence freed of personal responsibility. These figures speak to each other across an unbridgeable divide and that gulf is the flaw which fractures their community.

But there is never any sense that those involved in this social and psychological dance of death are rhetoricians, pushing words forward in place of emotions. There may have come a time when the judges ceased defending the faith and began defending themselves, but there is a passion behind their calculation, albeit the passion of those who sacrifice humanity for what they see as an ideal. In that they hardly differ from any other zealot whose hold on the truth depends on a belief that truth must be singular.

These are people, Miller has insisted, who 'regarded themselves as holders of a light. If this light were extinguished, they believed, the world would end.' The effect of this, however, was that if 'you have an ideology which feels itself so pure, it implies an extreme view of the world. Because they are white, opposition is completely black.'

This was the world of Puritan New England but it was also the world of 1950s America and, beyond that, a defining characteristic, perhaps, of the human psyche. 'We have come to a time', he insisted, 'when it seems there must be two sides, and we look back to an ideal state of being, when there was no conflict. Our idea is that conflict can be wiped out of the world. But until man arrives at a point where he realizes that conflict is the essence of life, he will end up knocking himself out.' The crucible is designed to drive out impurities, but impurities are definitional. At the same time a messianic impulse is potentially deadly. What gave a special force to the world of Salem was that he was dealing with people who were very conscious of their ideology, 'special people' who 'could voice the things that were buried deep in them'.[16]

The Crucible is both an intense psychological drama and a play of epic proportions. Its cast is larger than that of almost any of Miller's plays until The American Clock (1980) because this is a drama about an entire community betrayed by a Dionysian surrender to the irrational. Some scenes, therefore, people the stage with characters. It is also, however, a play about the redemption of an individual and through the individual of a society. Some scenes, therefore, show the individual confronted by little more than his own conscience. That oscillation between the public and the private is a part of the structural pattern of the play.

It is a play in which language is a weapon but it is also a physical play, never more so than in Richard Eyre's 2002 Broadway production in which actors sweated in the heat of the day and Proctor, the farmer, enters from the fields and throws water on himself. These are people who seize one another in anger, hope, despair as if they could shake the truth free. Imprisonment leaves Proctor scarred and wrecked. The set itself becomes an actor as an attic room becomes a vaulting courtroom reaching up into an indefinite space, wooden beams swinging ominously up and then down again to compress those committed to jail, their options run out. The play ends, in this production, as abstract shapes seemingly fixed to vertical beams cascade down while Proctor goes to his death, the force which held this community together collapses and we hear the sound of a society crack apart.

Miller was not unaware of the danger of offering the public such a play in 1953 and thereby writing himself into the wilderness, politically and personally. Three years later, he knew that his refusal to name names would be to invite charges of being unpatriotic. Indeed, appearing before the House Un-American Activities Committee he was stung into insisting on his patriotism while defending his right to challenge the direction of American policy and thought.

In the end, though, the House Un-American Activities Committee lost all credibility, the Red Scare passed, and if the accusers did not stand in a church, as Anne Putnam did in 1706, and listen as the minister read out her public apology and confession ('as I was the instrument of accusing Goodwife Nurse and her two sisters, I desire to lie in the dust and be humbled for it . . . I desire to . . . earnestly beg forgiveness of all those unto whom I have given just cause of sorrow and offence, whose relations were taken away and accused'),[17] they quickly lost their power and influence.

Today, compilers of programme notes feel as great a need to explain the history of Senator McCarthy and the House Un-American Activities Committee as they do the events of seventeenth-century Salem. In fact, the play's success now owes little to the political and social context in which it was written. It stands, instead, as a study of the debilitating nature of guilt, the seductions of power, the flawed nature of the individual and of the society to which the individual owes allegiance. It stands as a testimony to the ease with which we betray those very values essential to our survival but also to the courage with which some men and women can challenge what seems to be a ruling orthodoxy.

In Salem, Massachusetts, there was to be a single text, a single language, a single reality. Authority invoked demons from whose grasp it offered to liberate its citizens if they would only surrender their consciences to others and acquiesce in the silencing of those who appeared to threaten order. But *The Crucible* is full of other texts. At great danger to themselves men and women put their names to depositions, signed testimonials, wrote appeals. There was, it appeared, another language, less absolute, more compassionate. There were those who proposed a reality which differed from that offered to them by the state nor would these signatories deny themselves by denying their fellow citizens. There have been many more such since the 1690s, many more, too, since the 1950s, who have done no less. But *The Crucible* is not to be taken as merely a celebration of the resister, of the individual who refuses incorporation, for John Proctor had denied himself and others long before Tituba and a group of young girls ventured into the forest which fringed the village of Salem.

Like so many of Miller's other plays it is a study of a man who wishes, above all, to believe that he has invested his life with meaning, but cannot do so if he betrays himself through betraying others. It is the study of a society which believes in its unique virtues and seeks to sustain that dream of perfection by denying all possibility of its imperfection. Evil can only be external, for theirs is a City on a Hill. John Proctor's flaw is his failure, until the last moment, to distinguish guilt from responsibility. America's flaw is to believe that it is at the same time both guilty and without flaw.

In 1991, at Salem, Arthur Miller unveiled the winning design for a monument to those who had died. It was dedicated the following year by the

Nobel laureate Elie Wiesel, thus forging a connection, no matter how fragile or disproportionate, between those who died in Salem in 1692 and those in Europe, in the 1940s, who had been victims of irrationality solemnised as rational process. Speaking of the dead of Salem, Miller said that he had written of them out of 'a strong desire to raise them out of historic dust'.[18] Wiesel had done likewise for the Jews of the camps.

Three hundred years had passed. The final act, it seemed, had been concluded. However, not only do witches still die, in more than one country in the world, but groundless accusations are still granted credence, hysteria still claims its victims, persecution still masquerades as virtue and prejudice as piety. Nor has the need to resist coercive myths, or to assert moral truths, passed with such a final act of absolution. The witchfinder is ever vigilant and who would not rather direct his attention to others than stand, in the heat of the day, and challenge his authority?

Writing more than forty-five years after *The Crucible*, Miller explained that part of the attraction of the play for him lay in the chance it offered for him to write in a new language, 'one that would require new muscles'.[19] One of the interests in reading the notebooks he kept at the time he was writing the play, indeed, is to see him tensing those muscles, not only choosing the story he wishes to tell, forging the historical record into a dramatic shape, but exploring a language that can simultaneously convey the linguistic rhythms of the age and the heightened prose of a work accommodating itself to a tragic sensibility.

He was responding to a phenomenon which, in the seventeenth century and the contemporary world alike, was not only 'paralyzing a whole generation' but was 'drying up the habits of trust and toleration in public discourse'.[20] Language, indeed, was in part the battleground. God and the Devil, capitalism and communism, constituted the ideological site for a conflict in essence about power but also, therefore, about which legitimising language would prevail. Within America, it was not a true debate since in neither time frame were there any who spoke out either for evil or a diabolic communism. Victory was to be declared over those whose cunning made them foreswear themselves or invoke ambiguity at a time of absolutes. Yet those who exercised power felt insecure in their possession of it.

The victory of righteousness in seventeenth-century Massachusetts seemed threatened by internal and external powers while, in the twentieth century, the Soviet possession of nuclear weapons and the 'loss' of China to communism made the United States seem physically vulnerable and ideologically insecure. To be an un-American was to move outside a set of presumptions about national values and also outside of a language. Suddenly, the issue was loyalty. In whose book had you signed your name, God's or the

Devil's? And the signing of names became an iconic gesture, again in both periods. If *The Crucible* is full of petitions, warrants, confessions, then before the House Un-American Activities Committee individuals were confronted with their signatures on petitions, Party membership forms, published articles, invoked now as evidence of collusive and public subversion. Miller himself, during his own appearance before the Committee, was repeatedly asked to confirm his signature, the listing of his name on declarations, statements, calls for social justice.

Nor was this only a product of the right. Miller has spoken of the linguistic contortions exercised by left-wing critics desperate to follow a shifting Party line and consequently exchanging one language for another as a work was hailed as progressive one week only to be condemned as reactionary the next, or vice versa. Language was unstable. It was no longer a precise agent of communication, fully transitive. It was a weapon, blunt, coercive, and frequently opaque. It was like a spell, pronounced over those who appeared the source of threat. Open discourse gave way to slogans, jargon, a pseudo-scientific mock precision.

His sense of being trapped in an Escher drawing perfectly reflected the paradox of a Puritan state or modern American society in which confession of guilt resulted in absolution while declarations of innocence were seen as the ultimate proof of guilt. His sense of inhabiting an art form, a metaphor, a system of signs whose meanings were the province of a select priesthood, simultaneously left him with a profound sense of unreality and a determination to capture that feeling in an art of his own, equally arbitrary but a means of laying bare the mechanisms of unreality.

Informing was presented as a duty in the 1950s, professors on students, students on professors, as neighbour was encouraged to inform on neighbour in seventeenth-century Salem. What both societies felt in the face of such sanctioned betrayal was a form of impotence. It was a world in which 'the outrageous had so suddenly become the norm'. And impotence, or, more precisely, paralysis, became a familiar Miller trope as he witnessed and dramatised individuals and societies seemingly in thrall to the idea of their own powerlessness. Proctor stays his hand when he should have intervened but learns that there is no separate peace. The price of living is involvement. His sense of guilt with respect to Abigail momentarily freezes his will to act, as guilt clouds the mind of a number of Miller's other protagonists. The problem, as he saw it, was that 'we had grown detached from any hard reality I knew about. It had become a world of symbols, gestures, loaded symbolic words, and of rites and of rituals.' What was at stake was ideas, by their nature invisible, and a supposed conspiracy aimed at the overthrow of established powers. His problem, as he saw it, was how to 'deal with this mirage world'.[21]

At issue, after all, was not simply a vision of the moral world but a definition of reality in a culture in which those in power sanctioned belief in spirits, embraced a paranoid version of social behaviour. The real was what such people held it to be. In one sense, then, the fictions of art were to be pitched against those of the state as, in another sense, history was to be invoked to redress the balance, though a history seen not from the perspective of those who presumed themselves its primary agencies.

For Miller, one of the curiosities of the Committee hearings was that few if any of the accused chose to stand their ground and defend their supposed faith, instead deploying legalities and appeals to constitutional guarantees. There was, in other words, an absence at the heart of the whole affair. The irony in Salem, in 1692, centred on another absence, that of the witches whom an investigating body sought and was obliged to identify in order to justify its own actions. Indeed, with every new victim it became necessary for its members to announce their belief with ever greater assurance or confront not only responsibility for injustice but a vision of the world that would leave them adrift, with no moral structure to embrace save one which would leave them profoundly culpable.

In the end, he said, the more he worked on *The Crucible* the less concerned he became with analogy, despite the cogency of such: 'More than a political metaphor, more than a moral tale, *The Crucible*, as it developed for me over the period of more than a year, became the awesome evidence of the power of the human imagination inflamed, the poetry of suggestion, and finally the tragedy of heroic resistance to a society possessed to the point of ruin'.[22] The choice of words is instructive. It is as if he saw in the events that took place in Salem the elaboration of a human drama that seemed already to have shaped itself into theatre because it drew on the same resources. The witch trials were produced, performed, staged because it is the essence of life seen under pressure to take on the appearance and substance of art. How else to engage it, then, except through the homeopathic agency of the theatre?

What drew him finally, though, as he researched his drama, was less the parallel between the investigation of supposed conspiracies than the rituals developed, rituals by which confession was seen as validating accusation, betrayal was seen as the route to redemption while proof lay in reiterated suspicion rather than in anything so banal as concrete and testable fact. The accusation was that the witches, the communists, the fellow-travellers, had chosen to inhabit another narrative, to perform roles in an alternative drama.

The existence of godless communists necessitated and justified the existence of those who identified, exposed and punished them. So, too, in Puritan New England, with a neat piece of inverted logic, the existence of investigators implied the existence of those they were appointed to investigate.

It is not that Miller himself was free of illusion, or that self-righteous vigour that comes with certainty no matter how shallow the soil in which it sinks its roots. Perhaps something of the force of *The Crucible*, indeed, comes less from the cant of his own subsequent accusers—not, in truth, like many of those who set themselves to track down modern witches, genuine ideologues— than from his own youthful dedication to the fantasies of a Marxism that required no evidence, no reliable witnesses, to validate its assumptions.

His own rejection of those who failed to endorse the orthodoxies of his new faith was no less peremptory, surely, than that of those 'Puritan judges who believed they saw evidence of unbelief or association with the forces of darkness'. In retrospect, his own commitment to Soviet ideals which turned out to be no more than cover for rapacity and ambition could not have seemed so remote from the delusions embraced with such evident enthusiasm by Puritans and fifties conservatives alike.

At stake, he realised, was a language, so easily accommodated to the purposes of power, whether in seventeenth-century Salem or 1950s Washington. In both periods people were ensnared with words, forced to present themselves and interpret their actions in terms of an idiolect precisely designed to create a new ontological matrix. McCarthy's America found itself not only at the interface of two ideologies, with their supporting linguistic systems, but at a moment in American history when New Deal politics, and the utopianism of thirties and wartime America, shattered on the ambition of those who rode a new conservatism, as it did on the paranoia they fostered.

It was the very insecurity of authority that made it implacable, as though it could stabilise a disturbingly fluid world by fiat. Language was policed, inspected for its hidden subversion, revealing nuances. The word 'socialist', Miller recalls, was less a word describing a particular ideology than a marker for the foreign and the menacing.

To speak of 'right' or 'justice', to lay claim to freedom of speech or assembly was to identify yourself as a non-player in the American game, a dissenter from that aggressive conformity that passed for patriotism. Why, after all, would you need to lay claim to American freedoms if you were not using them to conceal subversion? What was needed was confession and there was, as Miller has suggested, a religious tone to the period. Confession was required; absolution was available. The thing was to be in a state of grace. Sinners who repented were welcomed to the fold, especially if, as in seventeenth-century Salem, they traded in a few fellow sinners. In both cases, confession plus informing was the formula for personal security. By the same token, the sanction of excommunication was available, excommunication from the true church that is America. No wonder Miller felt convinced of the authenticity of the parallel between fifties America and the Salem of 1692.

There was, and seemingly not incidentally, the same distrust of intellectuals in both periods. One of the Salem accusers—like so many of them, young girls—denounced an older woman because she was seen to read books. Giles Corey directed a similar accusation at his wife, with fatal results. Only the Bible and the authorised texts of witchfinders are legitimate. McCarthy, himself scarcely an intellectual, made a point of going after and humiliating Ivy Leaguers, New Dealers, writers and teachers. Books were, indeed, banned. A deputation visited American embassies around the world, weeding out subversive publications, including Miller's, while American intelligence agencies were doing their best to infiltrate and influence the cultural and intellectual lives of their allies, secretly funding foundations, student organisations and publications.

In the end, *The Crucible* is perhaps about the tendency—never fully resisted—to condemn difference. We are, after all, constantly reminded—from Salem to the former Yugoslavia—that neighbour can swiftly turn informer, betrayer, accuser and even assassin. When the Stasi files were opened in Germany, after the fall of the Berlin Wall, husbands were found to have informed on wives and vice versa. In the pages that fluttered down from the looted building were the devastating truths of lifelong betrayals. The same was true in Rumania. In 1690s Salem, Sarah Good was doomed when her three-year-old daughter claimed that her mother had three familiars—'three birds, one black, one yellow, and that these birds hurt the children and afflicted persons'—while her husband confessed that he thought her a witch.[23]

It is as much that mystery as any that Miller's play explores. As he explained, writing in 1999,

> Salem village, that pious devout settlement at the very edge of white civilization, had taught me—three centuries before the Russo-American rivalry and the issues that it raised—that a kind of built-in pestilence was nestled in the human mind, a fatality forever awaiting the right conditions for its always unique, forever unprecedented outbreak of alarm, suspicion and murder. And to people wherever the play is performed on any of the five continents, there is always a certain amazement that the same terror that had happened to them had happened before to others.[24]

He has observed that there are times when he wishes he had chosen to write an absurd comedy rather than *The Crucible*, this being closer to his sense of a world in which rational principles were in abeyance. Indeed, he recalls the fate of two young men from Boston who were arrested when they responded to one of the more egregious idiocies of the Salem trial by laughing.

These two figures, indeed, appear in an early draft of the film script in a scene subsequently deleted.

In the notebooks Miller tried out a number of possible titles for his play: *The Devil's Handyman*, *The Spectral Experience*, *That Invisible World*, *The Easiest Room in Hell*, *Delusion*. He even copyrighted an earlier version under the title *Those Familiar Spirits*, which has unfortunate overtones of Noel Coward. In the end, however, *The Crucible* had the advantage of applying to all the characters, not excluding John Proctor, and the society itself. For this is a play about a testing time, about a moment, repeated throughout history, in which the true metal of individuals, and the society they have collaborated in creating, is finally exposed.

That few people seemed to know what a crucible might be was less important when the play opened than the cold alarm he felt move through the audience as they began to sense that they were becoming confederate with an attack on the ruling political orthodoxy. A securely remote historical work had transmuted in front of their eyes and confronted them with the passions of their own times. Half a century later, *The Crucible* still has the power to disturb. It may have been generated by a particular alignment of circumstances, but the dilemma at its heart, its concern with betrayal, self-interest, power, a coercive language, personal and public responsibility, abusive authority, injustice, corrosive myths, remains of central significance, as does its awareness of the individual's struggle to locate and define him or herself in the face of forces that seem to leave so little space for a moral being.

In 1703 the General Court of Massachusetts ruled spectral evidence inadmissible. In 1704 the Reverend Michael Wigglesworth wrote to Increase Mather suggesting that the failure to atone for the killing of the innocent meant that it was necessary for those who had been 'actors' in that calamity to acknowledge their guilt. The word was a telling one. For all Puritan hostility to theatre, few were as aware of life as drama. Miller, then, was not the first to recognise the nature of the inner procedures and central trope of that time. In his study of the witch-hunts, Charles Upham, in 1867, remarked of the young girls who brought so many to their deaths that they were better actors than were to be seen in the theatre and clearly there was a drama played out in Salem that was liable to fire the imagination of a playwright.

When, in 1706, Ann Putnam, still living in Salem Village, and now fourteen years older than the young girl who had named twenty-six people as witches, stood as the Reverend Green read her confession, it was less than a fulsome apology. She was, she insists, 'deluded by Satan'. Senator Joseph McCarthy, however, made no such an apology. He, after all, was deluded by nobody and nothing but his own inadequacies and ambition, a self-authenticated witch-hunter in search of significance. For Arthur Miller, such responsibility lay at the heart of *The Crucible*. John Proctor found himself at the intersecting point of private and public meaning. His decision, in fact and fiction, to confront those who offered him life at the price of capitulation played its role in ending the witch-hunt of 1692, as it simultaneously demonstrated the ability of the individual to challenge power and the language with which it seeks to legitimate itself.

In October 1710, the General Court finally agreed to reverse the convictions and attainders of a number of those who had suffered. Among these was John Proctor, now eighteen years dead. John Hale, meanwhile, stricken with guilt at having collaborated with the general frenzy, declared that the disaster had been a product of 'the darkness of that day' when 'we walked in the clouds, and could not see our way'.[25] The darkness, he implied, had now lifted. The evidence for that, however, as the centuries have passed and other witch-hunts, other acts of betrayal, have been committed, has been far from conclusive. The innocent are still destroyed by those who seek their own immunity or self-interest, by those so certain of their own convictions that they make others the proof of their righteousness, evidence of a faith that requires sacrifices to legitimate its central tenets. How else can you be sure that you live in the City on the Hill unless you can look down on those who thus confirm your own elevation?

In writing *The Crucible*, Miller saw himself as resisting what seemed to him to be a reductive tendency in modern playwriting and modern thought. As he remarked, 'Today's writers describe man's helplessness and eventual defeat'. In Salem, he conceded, 'you have the story of a defeat because these people were destroyed, and this makes it real to us today because we believe in defeat'. However, he insisted, these were people who 'understood at the same time what was happening to them. They knew why they struggled . . . they did not die helplessly'.[26] It was, he said, 'the moral size of these people' that drew him. They did not 'whimper'. In terms reminiscent of William Faulkner's Nobel Prize address, he insisted that 'we should be tired by now of merely documenting the defeat of man'. This play, he asserted, 'is a step toward an assertion of a positive kind of value in contemporary plays'.[27]

Somewhat surprisingly, he chose to suggest that since 1920 American drama had been 'a steady, year-by-year documentation of the frustration of man', asserting that 'I do not believe in this . . . this is not our fate'. He was thinking, perhaps, of O'Neill but also of those writers who had chosen to document the oppressive details of social life. 'It is not enough', he insisted, 'to tell what is happening; the newspapers do that.'[28] Even so, his observation that 'in our drama the man with convictions has in the past been a figure of comic fun' seems curiously at odds with a decade of committed drama in which the man with convictions had been the central protagonist of plays which presumed the immediate possibility of transforming society. Meanwhile, his assertion that 'he fits in our drama more now' and that he was 'trying to find a way, a form, a method of depicting people who do think' was a statement of intent which, beyond *The Crucible*, would not find its fulfilment until *After the Fall*.

Miller has always had an aversion to films. For him, they are incorrigibly trivial, favouring action over ideas and language. The role of the writer in the cinema is that of a hired man who does not own the product of his labour and who is subordinate to those who wield the real power: producer, director, actor. It is a world in which spectacle can replace thought, a world of Dolby Surround Sound, hugely magnified images, a made object, unyielding, unchanging. The theatre, by contrast, deals in danger and vulnerability. Actor confronts audience, words become a primary means of communication. The adaptation of play to film seemed to him necessarily a reductive process, one which rarely benefits either medium.

With *The Crucible*, however, he was forced to revise a number of these assumptions. Suddenly, it became possible to constitute the community of Salem more directly. He recalled his research, four decades earlier, in which the testimonies of those involved had 'created a marvellously varied tapestry of that seventeenth-century America still in the earliest stages of defining itself', and found that 'once I had begun thinking about it as a film it became obvious that I had in fact always seen it as a flow of images which had had to be evoked through language for the stage'.[29]

What was previously reported could now be shown, from the sexually charged scene in the forest, as repressions are momentarily abandoned, the disciplined code of the community secretly rejected, to the physical location of that community, clinging to the edge of the continent and slowly subordinating the land to human will in the service of divine intent. Suddenly the wild anarchy of the meeting house, breaking through the carapace of rational process, could be presented in its disturbing reality, as itself a product of a deepening hysteria rooted in private no less than public anxieties and fears.

The fact remained, however, that *The Crucible* was made from language, that much of the notebook he kept when writing it is concerned with capturing a tone, with creating what he has called 'a kind of sculpted language',[30] generating precise rhythms. These, to some degree, would have to take second place to images if it was not to become 'a static photographed play', which was all too often the fate of adapted works.

The script, he has explained, was rejected by at least a dozen directors before it fell into the hands of Nicholas Hytner, whose background at the Royal Shakespeare Company gave him a sympathy both for Miller's dedication to language and the challenge of creating a film based, as he understood, on that 'insistence on the inseparable link between communal chaos and personal trauma'[31] which lies at the heart of *The Crucible* and, indeed, most of Miller's work. Hytner felt, he has explained, 'the ancient stirrings of pity and terror'[32] as he read the screenplay, itself an indication that the director of Shakespearean tragedy registered Miller's intention in a work that had originally been crafted as a modern tragedy. Hytner's account of his approach to the making of *The Crucible* is, in fact, and unsurprisingly, a highly intelligent analysis of the play as well as of the screenplay that emerged in the course of filming.

For him, the essence of theatre is that, in film terms, it 'operates in permanent medium shot', while a film can 'contain a whole society and move in close enough to see into a girl's heart'. In truth, so can a play which, after all, its conventions once accepted, can have a fluidity and shifting perspective capable of matching that of a film. For Hytner, however, the energy that comes from cutting between shots, 'so that the violence of the mob becomes both the consequence and the source of pain and confusion behind the eyes of the girl in the close-up',[33] is different in kind from that produced in the theatre. The cascade of images, each one causally plausible, becomes a correlative for that seemingly unstoppable momentum created out of 'individual betrayals' and 'collective panic'. Certainly one of the achievements of the film version lies in this pulsing between private and public, cause and effect.

What it was not was a work that required the historical context of the 1950s to appreciate. The parallels were closer to hand and Hytner, and those involved, felt their pressure as they prepared to shoot the film: 'it spoke directly about the bigotry of religious fundamentalists across the globe, about communities torn apart by accusations of child abuse, about the rigid intellectual orthodoxies of college campuses'.[34] Nonetheless, as Hymer recognised, its power as paradigm depended on the very specificity of location, the details of a life simultaneously lived symbolically, and with a tangible facticity.

He was also concerned to capture another aspect of the play and, incidentally, one of Miller's own thematic concerns throughout his career. Salem was a utopia whose own utopian presumptions opened the way for corruption. In Hytner's words, 'The light gives birth to the dark'.[35] This, after all, was to be a new Eden and it became necessary to patrol its boundaries to prevent evil entering and to extirpate it should it appear. Violence, in other words, was imminent, a kinetic force ready to discharge itself in action. The location of his Salem, then, with the sea to one side and the forest to another, was to create a kind of *cordon sanitaire*. In both directions lay risks: the religious corruptions they had fled in Europe and the antinomian world of the frontier. That double threat left the community and the human heart open for the Devil's work. Hytner, accordingly, chose an idyllic setting, a paradise on the edge of the ocean whose equivocal location, whose tenuous hold on the continent, was in part an explanation for the hysteria which could fan from a spark to a fire.

In fact, as Hytner acknowledges, Salem is more than a mile inland, a harbour town, but for his purposes he wanted the sea in vision, as a reminder of their exposed location, of the world from which they had fled. In particular, he wanted to play the final scene here, on the edge of a continent, to dramatise the fact that the fate of a continent, as well as that of a single man, was at stake. In this he had Miller's support, as he did in his requests for amendments to the script that would adjust to new possibilities and new visual ideas, though much of the original dialogue remained. Interestingly, every one of the scenes quoted earlier from the original screenplay was excised as part of this process.

The first two acts, as Hytner has explained, were substantially revised. The camera was able to move swiftly around the community with news of Betty's sickness, not merely thereby establishing the extent of the town and its interconnecting relationships, but recreating the process whereby stories, rumours, insinuations, accusations were to move around the same social space, gathering momentum as they went, heightening tension, creating an emotional vortex. This swirl of movement, meanwhile, was to be played against the static, withdrawn, contained world of John Proctor whose 'passivity is matched by the camera's'.[36]

This is that paralysis that lies at the heart of *The Golden Years* and *Broken Glass*, a failure of will that is ultimately a failure of morality and individual responsibility. Through guilt, Proctor hesitates to involve himself and thereby becomes culpable. Not to act, therefore, is to become guilty. Not to speak is to become complicit, which is perhaps why *The Crucible* exists, why Miller did not withdraw from so public a confrontation with powers whose authority was growing daily.

For Hytner, the camera was to be an agent, an active player, static when observing moral stasis, swooping down as an embodiment of imagined evils, racing through the town as time accelerates and emotions run ahead of thought. It observes and participates in the sensuality of the opening sequence. This is no longer a report of the young girls' dancing in the forest but their actual and hesitant performance, their shedding of inhibitions and, indeed, clothes, their playful abandonment of repressions which anticipates the more lethal abandonment of repressions that follows and which makes the girls offer evidence of supposed depravities that will lead to the execution of their elders. Miller had, in fact, anticipated such a scene in his early notebook in which, in free-verse form, he has Abigail seek a genuine potion to render Proctor into her hands:

O Tituba. I can't wait.
I am of age, my blood, my blood.
My blood is thrashing in my hips,
My skin revels at every breeze
I never sleep but dreams come itching
Up my back like little cats
With silky tails! You promised
When I came of age you'd work a charm
No man can break outside my love

Then let's pretend; let's believe
I do, but that he never touches me
Like some I've heard don't touch a wife
But once a year. My husband's there,
Tituba, inside that tree. Now what
Shall I do to bring him out?
What shall I do to turn his face to me?

Miller's original film script had begun with a collage of shots, including fishermen returning with their catch, a blacksmith shoeing a horse, two men sawing a log, a house being raised, its beams tennoned and pegged, a man squaring a log with an axe, the normality, in other words, to be disturbed by the events that will follow. This segues into a further series of shots which introduce some of the principal characters, from the Putnams to Martha and Giles Corey to the Proctors. These scenes were to have their parallel at the end of the film as we see the fields in a state of decay and revisit fishermen, blacksmith and sawyer in order to register the general collapse of social order provoked by the witch-hunters. Looters are at large. This framing was abandoned in favour of entering the film through the young girls who leave their houses for the rendezvous in the forest which will provoke what follows, and leaving it through the climactic death of John Proctor.

The film ends with the intoning of the Lord's Prayer by one of those about to be hanged, a supposedly impossible feat for witches. In fact, when the historical John Proctor was killed, Sheriff Corwin hurried to his home and, in a reminder of the suspect motives of the witchfinders, illegally seized his property:

The sheriff come to his house and seized all the goods, provisions, and cattle that he could come at, and sold some of the cattle at half price, and killed others, and put them up for the West Indies; threw out the beer out of a barrel, and carried away the barrel; emptied a pot of broth, and took away the pot, and left nothing in the house for the support of the children.[37]

It was one last cruel action, one last evidence of tainted motives, of the fact that a campaign to defend the good requires its defining victims.

John Proctor was not the only one to lose his life and his property, but in Miller's hands he became the crucial figure. It was, after all, as he had reminded himself in his notebook that it should be, 'basically Proctor's story'. There is, indeed, a causal link between his affair with Abigail and the death of his neighbours. Her revels in the forest were her attempt to lure him back into a relationship to which he had once committed himself. His sense of guilt does stay his hand when he might have intervened. In an early version of the film script, as Abigail visits Proctor in his prison cell to urge him to escape with her, and the Rev Hale tries to salve his own conscience by convincing him to confess to untruth, Miller indicates that 'PROCTOR looks into HALE's eyes and understands his guilt. Now he looks to this 'whore', who bears the same message as the Minister. The guilt is now upon all of them, and it creates a kind of communion for this moment'. 'A strange matter, isn't it' he says, 'that you ... and she ... and I ... be all of us guilty?'

For the first time in his career, Miller was happy with the film version of one of his plays. Perhaps, in part, this was because his son Robert was its producer, and anxious to protect his father's work. But it was also because in Hytner he found someone, trained in theatre, with a respect for language but who brought to the production a strong sense of how film could be used to relate the private to the public. It seemed to him that film could add depth to certain aspects of the drama and the camera move through the community whose tragedy this ultimately was. The film also had one other long-lasting effect. It was while it was being shot that Miller's daughter Rebecca met Daniel Day Lewis whom she was to marry. In 1953, though, this lay well over forty years in the future.

NOTES

1. *The Crucible* notebook held at the Harry Ransom Center, University of Texas at Austin.

2. Christopher Bigsby, ed., *Arthur Miller and Company* (London, 1990), p. 81.

3. Marion L. Starkey, *The Devil in Massachusetts: A Modern Enquiry into the Salem Witch Trials* (New York, 1969).

4. Arthur Miller, *The Crucible* (Harmondsworth, 2000), p. 57. Further page references appear in parenthesis in the text.

5. All quotations from the original screenplay are from a typescript in the author's possession.

6. John and Alice Griffin, 'Arthur Miller Discusses *The Crucible*', *Theatre Arts*, vol. 37, October 1953, pp. 53–4.

7. Bigsby, ed., *Arthur Miller and Company*, p. 95.

8. Gerald Weales, ed., *The Crucible: Text and Criticism* (New York, 1971), p. 422.

9. *Ibid.*

10. Arthur Miller, 'Brewed in the *Crucible*', *New York Times*, 9 March 1958, ɪɪ, p. 3.

11. Sheila Huftel, *The Burning Glass* (New York, 1965), p. 146.

12. *Ibid.*, p. 147.

13. Weales, ed., *The Crucible*: Text and Criticism, p. 240.

14. *Ibid.*, p. 241.

15. Bigsby, ed., *Arthur Miller and Company*, pp. 90–92.

16. Griffin and Griffin, 'Arthur Miller Discusses *The Crucible*', pp. 33–4.

17. Starkey, *The Devil in Massachusetts*, p. 227.

18. Henry Hewes, 'Arthur Miller and How He Went to the Devil', *Saturday Review*, 36, 31 January 1953, p. 225.

19. Arthur Miller, *'The Crucible in History' and Other Essays* (London, 2000), p. 3.

20. *Ibid.*

21. *Ibid.*, pp. 26–8.

22. *Ibid.*, pp. 34–5.

23. Larry Gregg, *The Salem Witch Crisis* (Westgate, 1992), p. 50.

24. Miller, *'The Crucible* in History', p. 55.

25. Starkey, *The Devil in Massachusetts*, p. 230.

26. Griffin and Griffin, 'Arthur Miller Discusses *The Crucible*', p. 33.

27. *Ibid.*, pp. 33–4.

28. *Ibid.*, p. 34.

29. Arthur Miller, 'Author's Note', *The Crucible: A Screenplay* (London, 1996), p. vii.

30. *Ibid.*

31. 'Director's Foreword', *The Crucible: A Screenplay*, p. ix.

32. *Ibid.*, p. x.

33. *Ibid.*, p. ix.

34. *Ibid.*, p. x.

35. *Ibid.*, p. xi.

36. *Ibid.*, p. xiii.

37. Gregg, *The Salem Witch Crisis*, p. 129.

Chronology

<table>
<tr><td>1915</td><td>Arthur Miller is born on October 17 in Harlem, New York City, the second son of Isadore Miller, a manufacturer of women's clothing, and August Barnett Miller. Characters in several of Miller's plays would be modeled on his older brother, Kermit.</td></tr>
<tr><td>1921</td><td>Joan Miller is born. She will become an actress with the stage name Joan Copeland.</td></tr>
<tr><td>1928</td><td>Father's business fails and family moves to Brooklyn. Attends James Madison High School; injury received playing football later keeps him from military service.</td></tr>
<tr><td>1930</td><td>Transfers to Abraham Lincoln High School.</td></tr>
<tr><td>1933</td><td>Graduates from high school and becomes interested in literature after reading Dostoyevsky's *The Brothers Karamzov*. Refused admission to University of Michigan because of poor grades; works for his father in family's new garment business. Writes a short story, never published, "In Memoriam," about the difficult life of a salesman.</td></tr>
<tr><td>1934</td><td>Admitted to University of Michigan after writing persuasive letter to the dean. Meets Mary Grace Slattery, who will be his first wife. Studies playwriting.</td></tr>
<tr><td>1936</td><td>*No Villain* wins Avery Hopwood Award.</td></tr>
<tr><td>1937</td><td>*Honors at Dawn* wins Avery Hopwood Award.</td></tr>
</table>

1938	*They Too Arise* (a revision of *No Villain*, revised again that year as "The Grass Still Grows") wins the Theater Guild National Award and a cash prize of $1,250. Miller graduates from the University of Michigan with a bachelor's degree in English.
1939	Returns to New York and participates in the New York Federal Theater Project; coauthors *Listen My Children* with Norman Rosten.
1940	Federal Theater Project ends, and Miller goes on relief; completes *The Golden Years*. Marries Mary Grace Slattery on August 5. She works as a waitress and as an editor to support them while Miller writes.
1941	Completes two radio scripts: *The Pussycat and the Expert Plumber Who Was a Man* and *William Ireland's Confession*. Works in box factory, as scriptwriter in bond drives, and as ship fitter's helper at the Brooklyn Navy Yard.
1942	Writes *The Four Freedoms*, a radio play.
1943	Completes *The Half-Bridge*. Becomes interested in Marxism and attends a study course. *That They May Win*, a one-act play in support of the war effort, produced by a Brooklyn community theater group.
1944	Jane Miller is born on September 7. *The Man Who Had All the Luck*, his first Broadway play about the rivalry between two brothers for the affection of the father, closes after six performances and is published in *Cross-Section: A Collection of New American Writing*. Earlier in the year, Miller had been gathering background information for the filming of Ernie Pyle's *Story of GI Joe* (1945) and turned his research into a wartime journal called *Situation Normal*, featuring interviews of American servicemen.
1945	*Focus* is published, a novel about anti-Semitism, the title referring to the metamorphosis the hero undergoes when a new pair of glasses makes him look Jewish; *Grandpa and the Statue*, a radio play, and *That They May Win* are published. In an article in *New Masses*, Miller attacks Ezra Pound for supporting fascism.
1946	"The Plaster Masks," a short story, is published.
1947	Robert Miller is born on May 31. *All My Sons* opens on Broadway; auctions off manuscript to support Progressive Citizens of America. "It Takes a Thief" is published in

Collier's; *The Story of Gus* is included in *Radio's Best Plays*, and his adaptation of Ferenc Molnar's *The Guardsman* appears in *Theater Guild on the Air*; an essay, "Subsidized Theater," is published in the *New York Times*.

1949   *Death of a Salesman* opens on Broadway; wins New York Drama Critics Award and the Pulitzer Prize. "Tragedy and the Common Man" and "Arthur Miller on 'The Nature of Tragedy'" are published.

1950   Meets Marilyn Monroe. *Death of a Salesman* closes after 742 performances; Miller's version of Ibsen's *An Enemy of the People* runs for thirty-six performances.

1951   *An Enemy of the People* is published; a short story, "Monte Saint Angelo," appears in *Harper's*; writes screenplay, *The Hook*.

1953   *The Crucible* opens on Broadway.

1955   One-act versions of *A View from the Bridge* and *A Memory of Two Mondays* are produced on Broadway. Contracted to write film script for New York City Youth Board; dropped from project after *New York Herald Tribune* publishes article attacking his leftist political connections.

1956   Miller is divorced from Mary Grace Slattery and marries Marilyn Monroe. He is subpoenaed to appear before the House Un-American Activities Committee ("HUAC") and is cited for contempt of Congress when he refuses to name the other attendees at a meeting of communist writers in 1947. A two-act version of *A View from the Bridge* opens in London and runs for 220 performances.

1957   Due to his refusal to answer the committee's questions, Miller is put on trial for contempt of Congress. "The Misfits," a short story, is published in *Esquire*. Miller also publishes *Collected Plays*.

1958   *The Misfits* is filmed and is Marilyn Monroe's last film. Miller's contempt conviction is reversed on a technicality by the U.S. Court of Appeals.

1959   "I Don't Need You Any More," a short story, is published in *Esquire*.

1960   "Please Don't Kill Anything," a short story, is published in *Noble Savage*.

1961   Marilyn Monroe applies for Mexican divorce. Miller's mother dies in March. "Please Don't Kill Anything" is published in *Redbook*; "The Prophecy" is published in *Esquire*; Italian operatic version of *A View from the Bridge* is produced in Rome; the New York City Opera Company performs Robert Ward's version of *The Crucible*.

1962   In February, Miller marries Ingeborg Morath, a photographer. On August 4, Marilyn Monroe commits suicide from an overdose of sleeping pills. Miller does not attend her funeral. "Glimpse at a Jockey" is published in *Noble Savage*.

1963   Miller begins *After the Fall*, the central theme of which is how its protagonist, Quentin, is struggling with three crises in his life--the Nazi death camps, the suicide of his wife, and his interrogation by the House Committee on Un-American activities. Miller publishes a children's story, *Jane's Blanket*.

1964   *After the Fall* is performed by the Lincoln Center Repertory Theater where most of the interest is focused on the ways in which the character of Maggie were similar to that of Marilyn Monroe. *Incident at Vichy* opens at Lincoln Center. Miller attends Nazi trials at Frankfurt, Germany, as special commentator for the *New York Herald-Tribune*.

1965   *Incident at Vichy* is published. Miller is elected president of International PEN.

1966   *Death of a Salesman* is produced for television. "The Recognitions" is published in *Esquire*; "Search for a Future" is published in the *Saturday Evening Post*.

1967   Collection of short stories, *I Don't Need You Anymore*, is published; *The Crucible* is produced for television; *Una sguardo dal ponte* is performed at the Philadelphia Lyric Opera.

1968   *The Price* opens on Broadway; the millionth copy of *Death of a Salesman* is sold. Miller attends Democratic National Convention as delegate for Eugene McCarthy. Petitions Soviet government to lift ban on works of Aleksandr Solzhenitsyn.

1969   *The Price* closes after 425 performances. Miller refuses to allow publication of his works in Greece in protest of oppression of writers. *The Reason Why*, an antiwar allegory, is filmed. With Inge Morath, Miller publishes *In Russia*.

1970   Miller receives Creative Arts Award Medal from Brandeis University. Two one-act plays, *Fame* and *The Reason Why*, run for twenty performances at New York's New Theater Workshop. Soviet Union, in response to *In Russia*, bans all Miller's works.

| 1971 | *The Price* and *A Memory of Two Mondays* are produced for television. Miller's version of *An Enemy of the People* opens at Lincoln Center for a brief run; he is elected to the American Academy of Arts and Letters. *The Portable Arthur Miller*, a collection of writings, is published. |

1971 — *The Price* and *A Memory of Two Mondays* are produced for television. Miller's version of *An Enemy of the People* opens at Lincoln Center for a brief run; he is elected to the American Academy of Arts and Letters. *The Portable Arthur Miller*, a collection of writings, is published.

1972 — An all-black production of *Death of a Salesman* opens in Baltimore. *The Crucible* is revived at Lincoln Center; *The Creation of the World and Other Business* opens to poor reviews and closes after twenty performances.

1973 — *The Creation of the World and Other Business* is published. Miller is appointed adjunct professor-in-residence at the University of Michigan for the academic year.

1974 — *After the Fall* is produced for television.

1975 — *Death of a Salesman* is produced in New York at Circle in the Square. Miller denounces the United Nations' policies towards Israel; protests treatment of writers in Iran; appears on panel before Senate to support freedom of writers throughout the world.

1976 — *The Crucible* is produced at Stratford, Connecticut; *The Archbishop's Ceiling* is produced in New Haven. "Ham Sandwich" and *The Poosidin's Resignation* appear in the *Boston University Quarterly*. Miller participates in symposium on Jewish culture and Jewish writers.

1977 — *In the Country*, with photographs by Inge Morath, is published; *The Archbishop's Ceiling* opens for a limited run at the Kennedy Center, Washington D.C., and receives poor reviews. Miller joins in letter to Czech head of state to protest oppression of Czech writers.

1978 — *Fame* is produced for television; *The Theater Essays of Arthur Miller* is published. Miller participates in protest over arrests of Soviet dissidents. Miller and Inge visit the People's Republic of China.

1979 — *The Price* is revived on Broadway to critical and financial success. Miller writes the screenplay for Fania Fenelon's *Playing for Time* and is criticized for his support of Vanessa Redgrave for the leading role. A film, *Arthur Miller on Home Ground*, is shown in New York; *Chinese Encounters*, with Inge Morath, is published.

1980 — Presents "Theater in Modern China" with Cao Yu, China's most prominent dramatist, at Columbia University. *The*

American Clock opens to critical praise. Signs letter with other American Jews protesting Israel's expansion on the West Bank; supports Polish solidarity movement. *Playing for Time* is shown on television to critical acclaim. *The American Clock* opens on Broadway for twelve performances.

1981   *Collected Plays*, *Volume Two* and *Playing for Time* are published. Miller narrates concert version of *Up from Paradise* at the Whitney Museum, New York.

1982   *Elegy for a Lady* and *Some Kind of Love Story* produced in New Haven; *The American Clock* is published.

1983   *A View from the Bridge* revived on Broadway; *Death of a Salesman* produced in Beijing, China; *Up from Paradise* is revived off-Broadway. Miller receives Bobst Medal Award and a $2,500 stipend from New York University.

1984   Publishes *"Salesman" in Beijing*, with photographs by Inge Morath, and revised version of *The Archbishop's Ceiling*. *Death of a Salesman* is revived on Broadway. He and Inge are awarded honorary doctorates from the University of Hartford.

1985   *The Price* is revived on Broadway. Miller announces that he is writing his autobiography. Travels to Istanbul with Harold Pinter in support of Turkish writers. *Death of a Salesman* is shown on television.

1986   *The Crucible* is revived at Trinity Repertory Company in New York, *All My Sons* in New Haven. *The American Clock* and *The Archbishop's Ceiling* are revived in London. *Danger: Memory!*, *I Don't Remember Anything*, and *Clara* are published.

1987   *All My Sons* is revived on television; *Danger: Memory!* opens at Lincoln Center; *All My Sons* is revived on Broadway and wins Tony award; Miller's autobiography, *Timebends: A Life*, is published.

2005   Miller dies at his home in Roxbury, Connecticut, on February 10.

Contributors

HAROLD BLOOM is Sterling Professor of the Humanities at Yale University. He is the author of thirty books, including *Shelley's Mythmaking* (1959), *The Visionary Company* (1961), *Blake's Apocalypse* (1963), *Yeats* (1970), *A Map of Misreading* (1975), *Kabbalah and Criticism* (1975), *Agon: Toward a Theory of Revisionism* (1982), *The American Religion* (1992), *The Western Canon* (1994), and *Omens of Millennium: The Gnosis of Angels, Dreams and Resurrection* (1996). *The Anxiety of Influence* (1973) sets forth Professor Bloom's provocative theory of the literary relationships between the great writers and their predecessors. His most recent books include *Shakespeare: The Invention of the Human* (1998), a 1998 National Book Award finalist, *How to Read and Why* (2000), *Genius: A Mosaic of One Hundred Exemplary Creative Minds* (2002), *Hamlet: Poem Unlimited* (2003), *Where Shall Wisdom by Found?* (2004), and *Jesus and Yahweh: The Names Divine* (2005). In 1999 Professor Bloom received the prestigious American Academy of Arts and Letters Gold Medal for Criticism. He has also received the International Prize of Catalonia, the Alfonso Reyes Prize of Mexico, and the Hans Christian Andersen Bicentennial Prize of Denmark.

EDWARD MURRAY is the author of *Varieties of Dramatic Structure: A Study of Theory and Practice* (1990), *The Cinematic Imagination: Writers and the Motion Pictures* (1972), and *Nine American Film Critics: A Study of Theory and Practice* (1975).

E. MILLER BUDICK is professor of American studies at the Hebrew University of Jerusalem. She is the author of *Engendering Romance: Women*

Writers and the Hawthorne Tradition 1850–1990, Nineteenth-Century American Romance: Genre and the Construction of Democratic Culture, Aharon Appelfeld's Fiction: Acknowledging the Holocaust, and *Blacks and Jews in Literary Conversation.*

EDMUND S. MORGAN is Sterling Professor of History Emeritus at Yale. He is the author of *The Genuine Article: A Historian Looks at Early America* (2004), *Inventing the People: The Rise of Popular Sovereignty in England and America* (1988), and *The Puritan Dilemma: The Story of John Winthrop* (1958).

WENDY SCHISSEL has taught at St. Peter's College in Muenster, Saskatchewan, and was appointed copresident of the college, an affiliate college of the University of Saskatchewan. She is the author of *Home/bodies: Geographies of Self, Place, and Space* (2006).

THOMAS P. ADLER is professor of English at Purdue University and the author of *"A Streetcar Named Desire": The Moth and the Lantern* (1990) and *American Drama, 1940–1960: A Critical History* (1994). He has written widely on modern British and American playwrights, including Pinter, O'Neill, Albee, Williams, and Hellman.

ARTHUR MILLER (1915–2005) was a prominent American playwright and essayist. His best-known plays include *The Crucible, A View from the Bridge, All My Sons,* and *Death of a Salesman,* which continue to be studied and performed worldwide. His autobiography, *Timebends: A Life,* was published in 1987.

TERRY OTTEN is professor emeritus of English at Wittenberg University. He is the author of *The Crime of Innocence in the Fiction of Toni Morrison* (1989), *After Innocence: Visions of the Fall in Modern Literature* (1982), and *The Deserted Stage: The Search for Dramatic Form in Nineteenth-Century England* (1972).

STUART MARLOW has been a documentary filmmaker and a lecturer in literature and professor at the Universität Essen. He is currently professor of drama at Stuttgart University of the Media.

STEPHEN A. MARINO teaches at St. Francis College, Brooklyn, New York. He is the author of "Arthur Miller's 'Weight of Truth'" (1995) and the editor of *The Salesman has a Birthday": Essays Celebrating the Fiftieth Anniversary of Arthur Miller's Death of a Salesman* (2000).

CHRISTOPHER BIGSBY has been professor of American studies at the University of East Anglia. He is the author of *Modern American Drama, 1945– 1990* (1992), *Contemporary American Playwrights* (1999), and *Remembering and Imagining the Holocaust: The Chain of Memory* (2006), and editor of *The Cambridge Companion to Modern American Culture* (2006).

Bibliography

Bergeron, David M. "Arthur Miller's *The Crucible* and Nathaniel Hawthorne: Some Parallels." *English Journal* 59, vol. 58, no. 1 (1969): 47–55.

Bergman, Herbert. "'The Interior of a Heart': *The Crucible* and *The Scarlet Letter.*" *University College Quarterly,* vol. 15, no. 4 (1970): 27–32.

Bloom, Harold, ed. *Modern Critical Interpretations: The Crucible.* Philadelphia: Chelsea House Publishers, 1999.

Bonnet, Jean-Marie. "Society vs. the Individual in Arthur Miller's *The Crucible.*" *English Studies* 63 (February 1982): 32–36.

Calarco, Joseph. "Production as Criticism: Miller's *The Crucible.*" *Educational Theory Journal* 29 (1977): 354–361.

Carson, Neil. *Arthur Miller.* New York: Grove Press (1982): 60–76.

Caruso, Cristina C. "One Finds What One Seeks: Arthur Miller's *The Crucible* as a Regeneration of the American Myth of Violence." *Journal of American Drama and Theatre,* vol. 7, no. 3 (Fall 1995): 30–42.

Cohn, Ruby. "Manipulating Miller." *Arthur Miller's America: Theater & Culture in a Time of Change,* Enoch Brater, ed. Ann Arbor: University of Michigan Press (2005): 191–201.

Ditsky, John. "Stone, Fire, and Light: Approaches to *The Crucible.*" *North Dakota Quarterly,* vol. 46, no. 2 (1978): 65–72.

Douglas, James W. "Miller's *The Crucible:* Which Witch is Which?" Renascence 15 (1963): 145–151.

Ferres, John H., ed. *Twentieth-Century Interpretations of* "The Crucible." Englewood Cliffs, NJ: Prentice-Hall, 1974.

Foulkes, Peter A. "Arthur Miller's The Crucible: Contexts of Understanding and Misunderstanding." *Theater and Drama in Amerika: Aspekte und Interpretationen.* Berlin: Schmidt (1978): 295–309.

Levin, David. "Salem Witchcraft in Recent Fiction and Drama." *New England Quarterly* (December 1955): 537–542.

Martin, Robert A. *Arthur Miller's The Crucible: Background and Sources.* Boston: G.K. Hall and Company, 1979.

McGill, William J., Jr. "*The Crucible* in History: Arthur Miller's John Proctor." *New England Quarterly*, vol. 54, no. 2 (June 1981): 258–264.

Meserve, Walter J. "*The Crucible*: 'This Fool and I.'" *Arthur Miller: New Perspectives*, Robert A. Martin, ed. Englewood Cliffs, NJ (1982): 127–138.

Morgan, Marie. "The Crucible." *New England Quarterly*, vol. 70, no. 1 (March 1997).

O'Neal, Michael J. "History, Myth, and Name Magic in Arthur Miller's *The Crucible*." *CLIO*, vol. 12, no. 2 (Winter 1983): 111–122.

Pearson, Michelle. "John Proctor and the Crucible of Individuation in Arthur Miller's *The Crucible*." *Studies in American Drama, 1945 to Present*, vol. 6, no. 1 (1991): 15–27.

Popkin, Henry. "Arthur Miller's The Crucible." *College English* 26 (November 1964): 139–146.

———. "Arthur Miller: The Strange Encounter." *Sewanee Review* 68 (Winter 1960): 34–60.

Strout, Cushing. "Analogical History: *The Crucible*." *The Veracious Imagination: Essays on American History, Literature, and Biography*, Cushing Strout, ed. Middletown, CT: Wesleyan University Press (1981).

Walker, Philip. "Arthur Miller's *The Crucible*: Tragedy or Allegory?" *Western Speech* 20 (1956): 222–224.

Warshow, Robert. "The Liberal Conscience in The Crucible." *Commentary* 15 (1953): 265–271.

Weales, Gerald, ed. *The Crucible: Text and Criticism.* New York: Viking, 1971.

Acknowledgments

Edward Murray, "*The Crucible*" from *Arthur Miller, Dramatist*: pp. 52–75. Copyright © 1967 by Frederick Ungar Publishing. Reprinted by permission of the Continuum International Publishing Group.

E. Miller Budick, "History and Other Spectres in Arthur Miller's *The Crucible*," from *Modern Drama*, vol. 28, December 1985: pp. 535–552. © 1985 University of Toronto. Published for the Graduate Centre for the Study of Drama by the University of Toronto Press Incorporated. Reprinted by permission of University of Toronto Press Incorporated (www.utpjournals.com)

Edmund S. Morgan, "Arthur Miller's *The Crucible* and the Salem Witch Trials: A Historian's View," from *The Golden & The Brazen World: Papers in Literature and History, 1650–1800*, edited by John M. Wallace: pp. 171–186. Copyright © 1985 by the Regents of the University of California. Reprinted with permission.

Wendy Schissel, "Re(dis)covering the Witches in Arthur Miller's *The Crucible*: A Feminist Reading," from *Modern Drama*, vol. XXXVII, no. 3, Fall 1994: pp. 461–473. (c) 1994 University of Toronto. Published for the Graduate Centre for the Study of Drama by the University of Toronto Press Incorporated. Reprinted by permission of University of Toronto Press Incorporated (www.utpjournals.com)

Thomas P. Adler, "Conscience and Community in *An Enemy of the People* and *The Crucible*," from *The Cambridge Companion to Arthur Miller*, edited by Christopher Bigsby: pp. 86–100. © Cambridge University Press 1997. Reprinted with the permission of Cambridge University Press.

Arthur Miller, "The Crucible in History." © 2000 by Arthur Miller, permission of the Wylie Agency.

Terry Otten, reprinted from *The Temptation of Innocence in the Dramas of Arthur Miller* by permission of the University of Missouri Press. Copyright © 2002 by the Curators of the University of Missouri.

Stuart Marlow, "Interrogating *The Crucible*: Revisiting the Biographical, Historical and Political Sources of Arthur Miller's Play," from *Staging a Cultural Paradigm: The Political and the Personal in American Drama*, edited by Barbara Ozieblo & Miriam Lopez-Rodriguez: pp. 79–100. © P.I.E.-Peter Lang, S.A., Brussels, 2002. Reprinted with permission.

Stephen A. Marino, "Poetry and Politics in *the Crucible*," from *A Language Study of Arthur Miller's Plays: The Poetic in the Colloquial*: pp. 55–80. Copyright 2002 The Edwin Mellen Press, Lewiston, NY. Reprinted with permission.

Christopher Bigsby, "'The Crucible,'" from *Arthur Miller: A Critical Study*: pp. 147–171. © Christopher Bigsby 2005. New York: Cambridge University Press. Reprinted with the permission of Cambridge University Press.

Every effort has been made to contact the owners of copyrighted material and secure copyright permission. Articles appearing in this volume generally appear much as they did in their original publication with few or no editorial changes. In some cases, foreign language text has been removed from the original essay. Those interested in locating the original source will find the information cited above.

Index